· SERMONS ON ·

MEN OF THE OLD TESTAMENT

Books of Sermons by Charles Spurgeon
from Hendrickson Publishers

Sermons on the Lord's Supper

Sermons on the Passion of Christ

Sermons on Women of the Old Testament

Sermons on Men of the Old Testament

Sermons about Christmas

Sermons on the Prayers of Christ

Sermons on Cries from the Cross

Sermons on the Resurrection

Sermons on the Love of Christ

Sermons on the Holy Spirit

Sermons on Prayer

Sermons on Great Prayers of the Bible

Sermons on the Second Coming of Christ

Sermons on Heaven and Hell

Sermons on Women of the New Testament

Sermons on Men of the New Testament

· SERMONS ON ·
MEN OF THE OLD TESTAMENT

C. H. Spurgeon

HENDRICKSON PUBLISHERS

Sermons on Men of the Old Testament

P. O. Box 3473
Peabody, Massachusetts 01961-3473

ISBN 978-1-61970-268-4

Originally published by Hendrickson Publishers in *Sermons on Men of the Bible.*

Printed in the United States of America

Cover photo of Charles Haddon (C. H.) Spurgeon by Herbert Rose Barraud is used by permission of the University of Minnesota Libraries, Special Collections and Rare Books.

Contents

In memory of Patricia Klein (1949–2014), our colleague and friend, who spent her life caring for words and who edited this series. She is truly missed.

Preface

Charles Haddon Spurgeon
1834–1892

Ask most people today who Charles Haddon Spurgeon was, and you might be surprised at the answers. Most know he was a preacher, others remember that he was Baptist, and others go so far as to remember that he lived in England during the nineteenth century. All of this is true, yet Charles Haddon Spurgeon was so much more.

Born into a family of Congregationalists in 1834, Spurgeon's father and grandfather were both Independent preachers. These designations seem benign today, but in the mid-nineteenth century, they describe a family committed to a Nonconformist path—meaning they did not conform to the established Church of England. Spurgeon grew up in a rural village, a village virtually cut off from the Industrial Revolution rolling over most of England.

Spurgeon became a Christian at a Primitive Methodist meeting in 1850 at age sixteen. He soon became a Baptist (to the sorrow of his mother) and almost immediately began to preach. Considered a preaching prodigy—"a boy wonder of the fens"—Spurgeon attracted huge audiences and garnered a reputation that reached throughout the countryside and into London. As a result of his great success, Spurgeon was invited to preach at the New Park Street Chapel in London in 1854, when he was just nineteen. When he first preached at the church, they were unable to fill even two hundred seats. Within the year, Spurgeon filled the twelve-hundred-seat church to overflowing. He soon began preaching in larger and larger venues, outgrowing each, until finally in 1861 the Metropolitan Tabernacle was completed, which seated six thousand persons. This would be Spurgeon's home base for the rest of his career, until his death in 1892 at age fifty-seven.

Spurgeon married Susannah Thompson in 1856 and soon they had twin sons, Charles and Thomas, who would later follow him in his work. Spurgeon opened Pastors' College, a training school for preachers, which trained over nine hundred preachers during his lifetime. He also opened orphanages for underprivileged boys and girls, providing education to each of the orphans. And with Susannah, he developed a program to publish and distribute Christian literature. He is said to have preached to over ten million people in his forty years of ministry. His sermons sold over twenty-five thousand copies each week and were translated into twenty languages. He was utterly committed to spreading the gospel through preaching and through the written word.

During Spurgeon's lifetime, the Industrial Revolution transformed England from a rural, agricultural society to an urban, industrial society, with all the attendant difficulties and horrors of a society in major transition. The people displaced by these sweeping changes—factory workers and shopkeepers—became Spurgeon's congregation. From a small village himself and transplanted to a large and inhospitable city, he was a common man and understood innately the spiritual needs of the common people. He was a communicator who made the gospel so relevant, who spoke so brilliantly to people's deepest needs, that listeners welcomed his message.

Keep in mind that Spurgeon preached in the days before microphones or speakers; in other words, he preached without benefit of amplifier systems. Once he preached to a crowd of over twenty-three thousand people without mechanical amplification of any sort. He himself was the electrifying presence on the platform: he did not stand and simply read a stilted sermon. Spurgeon used an outline, developing his themes extemporaneously, and speaking "in common language to common people." His sermons were filled with stories and poetry, drama and emotion. He was larger than life, always in motion, striding back and forth across the stage. He gestured broadly, acted out stories, used humor, and painted word pictures. For Spurgeon, preaching was about communicating the truth of God, and he would use any gift at his disposal to accomplish this.

Spurgeon's preaching was anchored in his spiritual life, a life rich in prayer and the study of Scripture. He was not tempted by fashion, be it theological, social, or political. Scripture was the cornerstone of Spurgeon's life and his preaching. He was an expositional preacher mostly, exploring a passage of Scripture for its meaning both within the text as well as in the lives of each member of his congregation. To Spurgeon, Scripture was alive and specifically relevant to people's lives, whatever their social status, economic situation, or time in which they lived.

One has a sense that Spurgeon embraced God's revelation completely: God's revelation through Jesus Christ, through Scripture, and through his own prayer and study. For him, revelation was not a finished act: God still reveals himself, if one made oneself available. Some recognize Spurgeon for the mystic he was, one who was willing and eager to explore the mysteries of God, able to live with those bits of truth that do not conform to a particular system of theology, perfectly comfortable with saying, "This I know, and this I don't know—yet will I trust."

Each of the sermons in this collection was preached at a different time in Spurgeon's career and each has distinct characteristics. These sermons are not a series, as they were not created or intended to be sequential, nor have they been homogenized or edited to sound as though they are all of a kind. Instead, they reflect the preacher himself, allowing the voice of this remarkable man to ring clearly as he guides the reader into a particular account, a particular event—to experience, with Spurgeon, God's particular revelation.

As you read, *listen*. These words were meant to be heard, not merely read. Listen carefully and you will hear the cadences of this remarkable preaching, the echoes of God's timeless truth traveling across the years. And above all, enjoy Spurgeon's enthusiasm, his fire, his devotion, his zeal to recognize and respond to God's timeless invitation to engage the Creator himself.

Adam: How God Comes to Man

Published on Thursday, September 8, 1904; delivered on Thursday evening, July 13, 1876, at the Metropolitan Tabernacle, Newington. No. 2900.

> *And they heard the voice of the* Lord *God walking in the garden in the cool of the day: and Adam and his wife hid themselves from the presence of the* Lord *God amongst the trees of the garden. And the* Lord *God called unto Adam, and said unto him, "Where art thou?"*—Genesis 3:8–9

"How will God come to us now that we have rebelled against him?" That is a question which must have greatly perplexed our first parents, and they may have said to one another, "Perhaps God will not come to us at all, and then we shall be orphans indeed. If spared to live on, we must continue to live without God and without hope in the world." It would have been the worst thing that could have happened to our race if God had left this planet to take its own course, and had said, concerning the people upon it, "I will leave them to their own way, for they are given over to idols."

But if he came to our first parents, in what way would he come? Surely Adam and Eve must have feared that he would be accompanied by the angels of vengeance, to destroy them straightaway, or, at any rate, to bind them in chains and fetters forever. So they questioned among themselves, "Will he come; and if he does, will his coming involve the total destruction of the human race?" Their hearts must have been sorely perplexed within them while they were waiting to see what God would do to them as a punishment for the great sin they had committed.

I believe they thought that he would come to them. They knew so much of his graciousness, from their past experience, that they felt sure that he would come; yet they also understood so much of his holy anger against sin that they must have been afraid of his coming; so they went and hid themselves among the trees of the garden, although every tree must have upbraided them for their disobedience, for every one of the trees would seem to say, "Why come you here? You have eaten of the fruit of the tree whereof you were forbidden to partake. You have broken your Maker's command, and his sentence of death has already gone out against you. When he comes, he will certainly come to deal with you in judgment according to his faithful word; and when he does, what will become of you?" Every leaf, as it rustled, must have startled and alarmed them. The breath of the evening breeze, as it passed through the garden, must have filled them with fear and dread as to the doom awaiting them.

Now "in the cool of the day" or, as the Hebrew has it, "in the wind of the evening," when the evening breeze was blowing through the garden, God came. It is difficult for us even to imagine how he revealed himself to our first parents. I suppose he condescended to take upon himself some visible form. It was "the voice of the LORD God" they heard in the garden, and you know that it is the Word of God who has been pleased to make himself visible to us in human flesh. He may have assumed some form in which they could see him; otherwise, as a pure Spirit, God could not have been recognized either by their ears or their eyes.

They heard his voice speaking as he walked in the garden in the cool of the day; and when he called unto Adam, albeit that there was righteous anger in the tone of his voice, yet his words were very calm and dignified, and, as far as they should be, even tender; for, while you may read the words thus, "Adam, where art thou?" you may also read them thus, "Where art thou, poor Adam, where art thou?" You may put a tone of pity into the words, and yet not misread them. So the Lord comes thus in gentleness in the cool of the day, and calls them to account; patiently listens to their wicked excuses, and then pronounces upon them a sentence, which, heavy though it be toward the serpent, and heavy though it be toward all who are not saved by the woman's wondrous seed, yet has much mercy mingled with it in the promise that the seed of the woman shall bruise the head of the serpent—a promise which must have shone in their sad and sinful souls as some bright particular star shines in the darkness of the night. I learn, from this incident, that God will come to sinful men, sooner or later, and we may also learn, from the way in which he came to our first parents, how he is likely to come to us. His coming will be different to different men; but we gather, from this incident, that God will certainly come to guilty men, even if he waits till the cool of the day; and we also understand a little about the way in which he will ultimately come to all men.

Remember this, sinner, however far you may get away from God, you will have to come close to him one of these days. You may go and pluck the fruit that he forbids you to touch, and then you may go and hide yourself among the thick boughs of the trees in the garden, and think that you have concealed yourself; but you will have to come face to face with your Maker at some time or other. It may not be today or tomorrow; it may not be until "the cool of the day" of time; no, it may not be till time itself shall be no more; but, at last, you will have to confront your Maker. Like the comet, that flies far off from the sun, wandering into space for an altogether inconceivable distance, and yet has to come back again, however long the time its circuit takes, so you will have to come back to God, either willingly, repentingly, believingly, or else unwillingly, and in chains, to receive your sentence of doom from the lips of the Almighty, whom you have provoked to anger by your sin. But God and you have to meet, as surely as you are now living here; at some time or other, each one of you must hear the voice of the Lord God saying to you, as he said to Adam, "Where art thou?"

Now, from this meeting between God and fallen man, I learn a few lessons, which I will pass on to you as the Holy Spirit shall enable me.

I. The first is this. When God did meet with fallen man, it was not until the cool of the day. This suggests to me *God's great patience with the guilty.*

Whether Adam and Eve sinned in the early morning, or in the middle of the day, or toward evening, we do not know. It is not necessary that we should know this; but it is probable that the Lord God allowed an interval to intervene between the sin and the sentence. He was not in a hurry to come, because he could not come except in anger, to bring their sins home to them. You know how quick the tempers of some men are. If they are provoked, it is a word and a blow with them, for they have no patience. It is our littleness that makes us impatient. God is so great that he can endure far more than we can; and though our first parents' sin greatly provoked him—and it is his glory that he is so holy that he cannot look upon iniquity without indignation—yet he seemed to say to himself, "I must go and call these two creatures of mine to account for their sin; yet judgment is my strange work, it is mercy in which I delight. This morning, I drew back the curtains that had shielded them during the night, and poured the sunlight in upon them, not a second beyond the appointed time, and I was glad to do it; and, all day long, I have been showering mercies upon them, and the refreshing night dews are already beginning to fall upon them. I will not go down to them till the latest possible moment. I will put it off till the cool of the day." God will do nothing in the heat of passion; everything shall be deliberate and calm, majestic and divine.

The fact that God did not come to question his sinful creatures till the cool of the day ought to teach us the greatness of his patience, and it should also teach us to be ourselves patient with others. How wondrously patient God has been with some of you who are here! You have lived many years and enjoyed his mercies, yet you have scarcely thought about him. Certainly you have not yielded your hearts to him; but he has not come to deal with you in judgment yet. He has waited twenty years for you young people; thirty years, forty years, for you middle-aged folk; fifty years, sixty years, for you who are getting past that period; seventy years, perhaps, or even eighty years he has been known to tarry, for "he delighteth in mercy," but he does not delight in judgment. Seventy years form a long life-day, yet many persons spend all that time in perpetrating fresh sin. Called to repentance over and over again, they only become the more impenitent through resisting the call of mercy. Favored with blessings as many as the sands of the seashore, they only prove themselves the more ungrateful by failing to appreciate all those blessings. It is wonderful that God is willing to wait till the cool of such a long, long day of life as seventy or eighty years make up.

How patient, then, we ought to be with one another! Yet are you, parents, always patient with your children, your young children who may not have willingly or consciously offended you? What patience you ought always to exercise toward them! And have you a like patience toward a friend or a brother who may use rough speech, and provoke you? Yet such your patience ought to be. Never should we take our brother by the throat, and say to him, "Pay me what you owe," so long as we find God deliberately waiting till the cool of the day before he comes to those who have offended him, and even then uttering no more words of anger than should be uttered, and mingling even those words with mercy that has no bound.

II. The second thing that I gather from the Lord's coming to Adam and Eve in the cool of the day is *his divine care for the guilty.*

Though he did not come till the cool of the day, thus manifesting his patience, he did come then, thus manifesting his care for those who had sinned against him. He might have left them all night long—all night long without their God, all night long without him after they had done just what he had forbidden them to do; all night long—a sleepless night, a fearful night, a night that would have been haunted with a thousand fears; all night long with this great battle trembling in the balance, with the great question of their punishment unsolved, and an indefinable dread of the future hanging over them. Many of you know that the trial of being kept in suspense is almost worse than any other trouble in the world. If a man knew that he had to be beheaded, it would be easier for him to die at once than to have to kneel with his neck on the block, and the gleaming axe uplifted above him, and not knowing when it might fall. Suspense is worse than death; we seem to feel a thousand deaths while we are kept in suspense of one. So God would not leave Adam and Eve in suspense through the whole night after they had sinned against him, but he came to them in the cool of the day.

There was this further reason why he came to them, notwithstanding the fact that they had disobeyed him, and that he would have to punish them; he remembered that they were still his creatures. He seemed to be saying within himself, "What shall I do unto them? I must not utterly destroy them, but how can I save them? I must carry out my threatening, for my word is true; yet I must also see how I can spare them, for I am gracious, and my glory is to be increased by the display of my grace toward them." The Lord looked upon them as the appointed progenitors of his elect, and regarded Adam and Eve themselves also, let us hope, as his elect, whom he loved notwithstanding their sin, so he seemed to say, "I will not leave them all night without the promise which will brighten their gloom." It was only one promise; and, perhaps, it was not clearly understood by them; still, it was a promise of God, even though it was spoken to the serpent, "I will put enmity between thee and the woman, and between thy seed and her seed; it shall bruise thy head, and thou shalt bruise his heel." So not one night were God's poor fallen creatures left without at least one star to gleam in the darkness for them, and thus he showed his care for them. And still, dear friends, though God is slow to anger, yet is he always ready to pardon, and very tender and compassionate even when he has to pass sentence upon the guilty. "He will not always chide; neither will he keep his anger forever." You can see his care and consideration even for the most unworthy of us, because he has not cut us off in our sins. We are—

Not in torment, not in hell.

We can see the marks of his goodness in the very garments on our backs and the food of which we partake by his bounty. Many of his gifts come, not merely to those who do not deserve them, but to those who deserve to be filled with the gall and wormwood of almighty wrath forever.

III. Now, third, I want to show you that, *when the Lord did come, he afforded us a pattern of how the Spirit of God comes to arouse the consciences of men.*

I have already said that, sooner or later, God will come to confront each one of us. I pray that, if he has never come to you, dear friend, in the way of awakening your conscience, and making you feel yourself a sinner, he may come to you very speedily. And when he does come, to arouse and awaken you, it is somewhat in this way.

First, *he comes seasonably*: "in the cool of the day." Adam's work was done, and Eve had no more to do until the next day. At that hour, they had been accustomed, in happier times, to sit down and rest. Now God comes to them, and the Spirit of God, when he comes to arouse men, generally visits them when they have a little time for quiet thought. You dropped in, and heard a sermon; the most of it slipped from your memory, but there were some few words that struck you so that you could not get rid of them. Perhaps, though, you thought no more about the message to which you had listened. Something else came in and took off your attention. But, a little while after, you had to watch all night by the bedside of a sick friend; and then God came to you, and brought to your remembrance the words that you had forgotten. Or it may be that some texts of Scripture, which you learned when you were a child, began to speak to you throughout the watches of the night. Or perhaps you were going along a lone country road, or, it may be, that you were out at sea on a dark night, and the billows rolled heavily so that you could not sleep, and you even feared that you would be swallowed up by the raging sea. Then, then came the voice of the Lord God speaking personally to you. When other voices were silenced, there was an opportunity for his voice to be heard.

Not only did the Lord come to Adam and Eve seasonably, but *he spoke to Adam personally*, and said, "Where art *thou*?" One of the great mistakes in connection with all preaching is that so many hearers will persist in lending other people their ears. They hear a faithful gospel sermon, and then say, "That message would fit Neighbor So-and-So admirably. What a pity Mrs. So-and-So did not hear it! That would have been the very word for her." Yes; but when God comes to you, as he came to Adam and Eve—and if you are not converted, I pray that he may—the sermon he will deliver to you will be every word of it for yourself. He will say, "Adam," or, "John," or, "Mary," or whatever your name be, "where art *thou*?" The question will be addressed to yourself alone; it will have no relation to any of your neighbors, but to yourself alone. The question may take some such form as this: "Where are you? What have you been doing? What is your condition now? Will you now repent, or will you still go on in your sins?" Have not you, young man, had some such experience as this? You went to the theater; but when you came home, you said that you had not enjoyed it, and that you wished you had not gone. You went to bed, but you could not sleep. It seemed as if God had come to wrestle with you, and to reason with you about your past life, bringing up one thing after another in which you have sinned against him. At all events, this is the way he deals with many; and if he deals thus with you, be thankful for it, and yield yourself up to him, and do not struggle against him. I am always glad when men cannot be happy in the world; for, as long as they can be, they will be. It is always a great mercy when they begin to be sick of the dainties of Egypt, for then we may lead them, by God's guidance, to seek after the milk and honey of the land of Canaan; but not till then. It is a great blessing when the Lord puts before you, personally, a true view of your own condition in his sight, and makes you look at it so earnestly, concentrating your whole thought upon it, so that you cannot even begin to think about others because you are compelled to examine your own selves, to see what your real condition is in relation to God.

When the Lord thus comes to men, and speaks personally with them, *he makes them realize their lost condition*. Do you not see that this is implied in the question, "Where art thou?" Adam was lost—lost to God, lost to holiness, lost to happiness. God himself says, "Where art thou?" That was to let Adam know this: "I have lost you, Adam; at one time, I could speak with you as with a friend, but I cannot do so any longer. You were my obedient child once, but you are not so now; I have lost you. Where art thou?" May God the Holy Spirit convince every unconverted person here that he or she is lost, not only lost to themselves and to heaven and to holiness and to happiness, but lost to God. It was God's lost ones of whom Christ so often spoke. He was himself the good Shepherd, who called together his friends and neighbors, saying unto them, "Rejoice with me; for I have found my sheep which was lost"; and he represents his Father saying of his son when he has come back to him, "This my son was dead"—dead to me—"and is alive again; he was lost"—lost to me—"and is found." The value of a soul to God, and God's sense of loss in the case of each individual soul, is something worth thinking over, and worth calculating, if it can be calculated. God makes man realize that he is lost by his own moanings and pleadings, even as he said to Adam, "Where art thou?"

You will observe, too, that the Lord not only came to Adam, and questioned him personally, but *he also made Adam answer him*; and if the Lord has, in this way, laid hold of any of you, talking with you in the cool of the day, and questioning you about your lost condition, he will make you confess your sin, and bring you to acknowledge that it was really your own. He will not leave you as Adam wanted to be left, namely, laying the blame for the disobedience upon Eve; and he will not leave you as Eve tried to be left, namely, passing the blame on to the devil. Before the Lord has done with you, he will bring you to this point, that you shall feel and confess and acknowledge that you are really guilty of your own sin, and that you must be punished for it. When he brings you down to that point, and you have nothing at all to say for yourself, then he will pardon you.

I recollect well when the Lord brought me to my knees in this way and emptied out all my self-righteousness and self-trust, until I felt that the hottest place in hell was my due desert, and that, if he saved everybody else, but did not save me, yet still he would be just and righteous, for I had no right to be saved. Then, when I was obliged to feel that it must be all of grace, or else there could be no salvation for me, then he spoke tenderly and kindly unto me; but, at the first, there did not seem to be any tenderness or pity to my soul. There was the Lord coming to me, laying bare my sin, revealing to me my lost condition, and making me shiver and tremble, while I feared that the next thing he would say to me would be, "Depart from me, accursed one, into everlasting fire in hell"; instead of which, he said to me, in tones of wondrous love and graciousness, "I have put thee among my children"; "I have loved thee with an everlasting love, therefore with lovingkindness have I drawn thee." Blessed be the name of the Lord, forever and ever, for such amazing treatment as this meted out to the guilty and the lost.

IV. Now, fourth, and very solemnly, I want to show you that *this coming of the Lord to Adam and Eve is also prophetical of the way in which he will come as a judging Spirit to those who reject him as an arousing Spirit.*

I have already reminded you unconverted ones that, as surely as you live, you will have to come to close terms with God, like the rest of us. Sooner or later, you will have to know him, and to know that he knows you. There will be no way of escaping from an interview which will be most serious and most terrible for you. It will happen "in the cool of the day." I do not know when that may be. On my way to this service, I was called to see a young lady, to whom "the cool of the day" has come at five and twenty, or thirty years of age. Consumption has made her life-day a comparatively short one; but, blessed be God, his grace has made it a very happy one; and she is not afraid, "in the cool of the day," to hear the voice of the Lord God calling her home. It is well that she is not afraid, but you, who have not believed in Jesus, will have to hear that same divine voice in the cool of your life's day. You may be spared to grow old; the strength of youth and of manhood will have gone, and you will begin to lean on your staff, and to feel that you have not the vigor you used to have, and that you cannot do such a hard day's work as you used to do, and you must not attempt to run up the hills as you once did. That will be "the cool of the day" to you, and then the Lord God will come in to you, and say, "Set thine house in order, for thou shalt die, and not live."

Sometimes that cool of the day comes to a man just when he would have liked it to be the heat of the day. He is making money, and his children are multiplying around him, so he wants to stop in this world a little longer. But that cannot be; he must go up to his bed, and he must lie there for so many days and nights, and then he must hear the voice of the Lord God as he begins to question him, and say, "Where art thou in relation to me? Have you loved me with all your heart and mind and soul and strength? Have you served me? Are you reconciled to me through the death of my Son?" Such questions as these will come to us as surely as God made us, and we shall have to give an account of the deeds done in the body, whether they have been good or whether they have been evil. I pray you to think of these things, and not to say, "Ah! that will not happen just yet." That is more than any of us can tell; and let me remind you that life is very short even at the longest. I am especially appealing to those who are of my own age. Do not you, dear friends, find that, when you are between forty and fifty years of age, the weeks seem to be much shorter than they used to be when you were young? I therefore gather that, when our friends are seventy or eighty years of age, time must seem far shorter to them than it ever was before. I think that one reason why Jacob, when he was a hundred and thirty years old, said to Pharaoh, "Few and evil have the days of the years of my life been," was simply this: that he was really such an old man, though not so old as his ancestors, that time seemed even shorter to him than it did to younger men. If that was so, then I suppose that the longer a man lives, the shorter would time appear to be. But, short or long, your share of it will soon be over, and you will be called upon to gather up your feet in the bed, and meet your fathers' God.

When that solemn and decisive hour comes, your interview with God will have to be a personal one. Sponsors will be of no use to anyone upon a dying bed. It will be of no avail, then, to call upon Christian friends to take a share of your burden. They will not be able to give you of their oil, for they have not enough grace for themselves and you. If you live and die without accepting the aid of the one Mediator between God and man, all these questions will have to be settled between your soul and God without anyone else coming between yourself and your Maker; and all this may happen at any moment. This personal talk between God and your soul, at the end of your life, may be ordained to take place this very night; and I am sent, as a forerunner, just to give you this warning, so that you may not meet your God altogether by surprise, but may, at any rate, be invited and exhorted to be prepared for that great interview.

Whenever that interview takes place, God will deal with you in solemn earnestness, personally bringing home your sin to you. You will be unable to deny it, for there will be One present, at that interview, who has seen it all, and the inquiries which he will make about the state of your soul will be very searching ones. He will not merely ask about one sin, but about all your sins. He will not only ask about your public life, but also about your private life; nor yet merely inquire about your doings, but about your sayings, and your willings and your thinkings and about your whole position in relation to himself, even as he asked Adam, "Where art thou?"

In imagination—I pray that it may be only in imagination—I see some of you die unsaved; and I see you as you pass into the next world unpardoned, and your soul realizes, for the first time, what was the experience of the rich man, of whom our Savior said, "In hell he lifted up his eyes"—as though he had been asleep before, and had only just awakened to his true condition. "He lifted up his eyes" and gazed all around, but he could see nothing except that which caused him dismay and horror; there was no trace of joy or hope, no trace of ease or peace. Then, through the awful gloom, there came the sound of such questions as these, "Where are you, sinner? You were in a house of prayer a few weeks ago, and the preacher urged you to seek the Lord; but you procrastinated. Where are you now? You said that there was no such place as hell; but what do you say about it now? Where are you? You despised heaven and refused Christ; where are you now?" What horror will seize the disembodied spirit as it rejects that it has brought itself into the condition of which it was warned, and from which it was invited to escape, but which it willfully chose for itself, thus committing eternal suicide! The Lord in mercy preserve all of you from doing that! But if you will do it, then shall come forth from the lips of the justly offended God the irrevocable sentence, "Depart from me, ye cursed."

One of the most dreadful things in connection with this meeting of God with Adam was that Adam had to answer the Lord's questions. The Lord said to him, "Hast thou eaten of the tree, whereof I commanded thee that thou shouldest not eat?" In our courts of law, we do not require men to answer questions which would incriminate them, but God does; and, at the last great day, the ungodly will be condemned on their own confession of guilt. While they are in this world, they put on a brazen face, and declare that they have done no wrong to anybody, not even to God; they pay their way, and they are as good as their neighbors, and better than the most of them; but all their brag and bravado will be gone at the day of judgment, and they will either stand speechless before God—and by their speechlessness acknowledge their guiltiness in his sight; or if they do speak, their vain excuses and apologies will but convict themselves. They will, out of their own mouths, condemn themselves, like that wicked and slothful servant, who was cast into the outer darkness where there was weeping and gnashing of teeth. God grant that we may never know, from sad personal experience, what that expression means!

V. Now, last, this meeting of God with Adam should lead us, who believe in Christ, to *expect to meet him on the most loving terms.*

For if, even when he came to question guilty Adam, and to pass sentence upon him, he did it so gently, and mingled with the thunder of his wrath the soft shower of his grace, when he gave the promise that the seed of the woman should bruise the serpent's head, may we not expect him to meet us, by-and-by, on the most loving terms, if we are in that woman's seed, and have been saved by Jesus Christ his Son?

He will come in the evening, brother and sister, when the day's work is done; so do not fret about the burden and heat of the day. The longest and hottest day will come to an end; you will not live here forever. You will not always have to wear your fingers to the bone in trying to earn a scanty livelihood. You will not always have to look around upon your children, and wonder where the bread will be found with which to feed them. No; the days on earth cannot last forever; and, with many of you, the sun has already climbed the hill, and begun to go down the other side, and "the cool of the day" will soon come. I can look upon a good many of you who have already reached that period. You have retired from active service, you have shaken off a good deal of business care, and now you are waiting for your Master to come to you. Rest assured that he will not forget you, for he has promised to come to you. You will hear his voice, before long, telling you that he is walking in the garden, and coming to you. Good old Rowland Hill, when he found himself getting very feeble, said, "I hope they have not forgotten poor old Rowley up there." But he knew that he was not forgotten, nor will you be, beloved.

You will hear your Lord's voice before long; and the mercy is, that you will know it when you do hear it. Have you not often heard it before now? Many a time, in this house, you have heard his voice, and you have been glad. In the cool of many an evening, you have sat still, and communed with God. I like to see an old Christian woman, with her big Bible open, sitting by the hour together, and tracing with her finger the precious words of the Lord; eating them, digesting them, living on them, and finding them sweeter to her soul than honey or the droppings of the honeycomb to her taste. Well, then, as you have heard your Lord's voice, and know its tones so well, as you have been so long accustomed to hear it, you will not be astonished when you hear it in those last moments of your life's day. You will not run to hide yourself, as

Adam and Eve did. You are covered with the robe of Christ's righteousness, so you have no nakedness to fear; and you may respond, "Did you ask, my Lord, 'Where art thou?' I answer, 'Here am I, for you did call me.' Didst you ask where I am? I am hidden in your Son; I am 'accepted in the Beloved.' Did you say, 'Where art thou?' Here I stand, ready and waiting to be taken up by him, according to his promise that, where he is, there I shall be also, that I may behold his glory." Why, surely, beloved, as this is the case, you may even long for the evening to come when you shall hear his voice, and shall go up and away from this land of shadows and chilly night dews, into that blessed place where the glory burns on forever and ever, and the Lamb is the light thereof, and the days of your mourning shall be ended forever.

God grant that you may all have a part and a lot in that glory, for his dear Son's sake! Amen.

Enoch: Walking with God

Delivered on Lord's Day morning, July 30, 1876, at the Metropolitan Tabernacle, Newington. No. 1307.

> *And Enoch lived sixty and five years, and begat Methuselah: and Enoch walked with God after he begat Methuselah three hundred years, and begat sons and daughters: and all the days of Enoch were three hundred sixty and five years: and Enoch walked with God: and he was not; for God took him.* —GENESIS 5:21–24

> *By faith Enoch was translated that he should not see death; and was not found, because God had translated him: for before his translation he had this testimony, that he pleased God. But without faith it is impossible to please him: for he that cometh to God must believe that he is, and that he is a rewarder of them that diligently seek him.*—HEBREWS 11:5–6

> *And Enoch also, the seventh from Adam, prophesied of these, saying, "Behold, the Lord cometh with ten thousands of his saints, to execute judgment upon all, and to convince all that are ungodly among them of all their ungodly deeds which they have ungodly committed, and of all their hard speeches which ungodly sinners have spoken against him."*—JUDE 14–15

The three passages of Scripture which I have read are all the authentic information we have concerning Enoch, and it would be idle to supplement it with the fictions of ancient commentators. Enoch is called the seventh from Adam, to distinguish him from the other Enoch of the line of Cain, who was the third from Adam. In the first patriarchs God was pleased to manifest to men portions of the truth in reference to true religion. These men of the olden times were not only themselves taught of God, but they were also teachers of their age, and types in whom great truths were exhibited. Abel taught the need of approaching the Lord with sacrifice, the need of atonement by blood: he laid the lamb upon the altar, and sealed his testimony with his own blood. Atonement is so precious a truth that to die for its defense is a worthy deed, and from the very first it is a doctrine which has secured its martyrs, who being dead yet speak.

Then Seth and Enos taught men the necessity of a distinct avowal of their faith in the Lord, and the need of assembling for his worship, for we read concerning the days of Enos and Seth, "Then began men to call upon the name of the LORD." Those who worshiped through the atoning sacrifice separated themselves from the rest of men, assembled a church in the name of the Lord, and worshiped, calling upon the name of Jehovah. The heart must first believe in the great sacrifice with Abel, and then the mouth must confess the same with Seth. Then came Enoch, whose life went beyond the reception and confession of the atonement, for he set before men the great truth of communion with God; he displayed in his life the relation of the believer to the most High, and showed how near the living God condescends to be to his own children. May our progress in knowledge be similar to the growth of the patriarchal teaching. Brethren, you do know as Abel did the sacrificial lamb, your confidence is in the precious blood, and so by faith you bring to God the most acceptable of all offerings. Having advanced so far the most of us have proceeded a step further, and we have called upon the name, and are the avowed followers of Jesus. We have given ourselves up to the Lord in the solemn burial of baptism, when we were baptized into the name of the Father, and of the Son, and of the Holy Ghost, because we reckoned ourselves dead in Christ to all the world, and risen with him into newness of life. Henceforth the divine name is named on us, and we are no more our own. And now we gather together in our church capacity, we assemble around the table of fellowship, we unite in our meetings for prayer and worship, and the center for us all is the name of the Lord. We are separated from the world, and set apart to be a people who declare his name. Thus far, well; we have seen the sacrifice of Jesus as the way with Abel; and we have avowed the truth with Seth; now let us take the next step and know the life with Enoch. Let us endeavor to walk with God as Enoch did.

Perhaps a meditation upon the holy patriarch's life may help us to imitate it; while considering what he was, and under what circumstances he came to be so, he may by the Holy Spirit be helped to reach the point to which he attained. This is the desire of every godly man, all the saints desire communion with the Father, and with his Son Jesus Christ. The constant cry of our soul is to our Lord, "Abide with me." I buried yesterday one of the excellent of the earth, who loved and feared and served his God far better than most of us; he was an eminently devout brother, and one of the last wishes of his heart he had committed to writing in a letter to a friend, when he little thought of dying. It was this "I have longed to realize the life of Enoch, and to walk with God"—

Oh, for a closer walk with God!

He did but write what you and I also feel. If such be your desires, and such I feel sure they are, so surely as you are the Lord's people, then I hope a consideration of the life of Enoch may help you toward the realization of your wish.

First, then, *what does Enoch's walking with God imply*? It is a short description of a man's life, but there is a mint of meaning in it; second, *what circumstances were connected with his remarkable life*? for these are highly instructive: and third, *what was the close of it*? It was as remarkable as the life itself.

I. First, then, *what is meant by Enoch's walking with God?*

Paul helps us to our first observation upon this by his note in the Hebrews. His walk with God was a testimony that *Enoch was well pleasing to God*. "Before his translation he had this testimony, that he pleased God." This is evidently the apostle's interpretation of his walking with God, and it is a most correct one, for the Lord will not walk with a man in whom he has no pleasure. Can two walk together, except they be agreed? If men walk contrary to God, he will not walk *with* them, but contrary to them. Walking together implies amity, friendship, intimacy, love, and these cannot exist between God and the soul unless the man is acceptable unto the Lord. Doubtless Enoch, like Elijah, was a man of like passions with ourselves. He had fallen with the rest of mankind in the sin of Adam; there was sin about him as there is sin about us by nature, and he had gone astray in act and deed as all we, like sheep, have done: and therefore he needed pardon and cleansing, even as we do. Then to be pleasing with God, it was needful that he should be forgiven and justified, even as we are; for no man can be pleasing to God till sin is pardoned and righteousness is imputed. To this end there must be faith, for there can be no justification except by faith, and as we have said already, there is no pleasing God except our persons are justified. Right well, then, does the apostle say, "Without faith it is impossible to please God," and by faith Enoch was made pleasing to God, even as we are at this day. This is worthy of earnest notice, brethren, because this way of faith is open to us. If Enoch had been pleasing to God by virtue of some extraordinary gifts and talents, or by reason of marvelous achievements and miraculous works, we might have been in despair; but if he was pleasing to God through faith, that same faith which saved the dying thief, that same faith which has been worked in you and in me, then the wicket gate at the head of the way in which men walk with God is open to us also.

If we have faith we may enter into fellowship with the Lord. How this ought to endear faith to us! The highest grades of spiritual life depend upon the lower ones, and rise out of them. If you want to walk with God as a man of God, you must begin by believing in the Lord Jesus Christ, simply, as a babe in grace. The highest saintship must commence by the confession of our sinnership, and our laying hold upon Christ crucified. Not otherwise does the strongest believer live than the weakest believer; and if you are to grow to be among the strongest of the Lord's warriors, it must be by faith which lays hold upon divine strength. Beginning in the Spirit you are not to be made perfect in the flesh; you are not to proceed a certain distance by faith in Christ, and then to commence living by your own works; your walk is to continue as it began. "As ye have received Christ Jesus the Lord, so walk ye in him."

Enoch was always pleasing to God, but it was because he always believed, and lived in the power of his faith. This is worth knowing and remembering, for we may yet be tempted to strive for some imaginary higher style of religious life by looking to our feelings instead of looking alone to the Lord. We must not remove our eye from looking alone to Jesus himself even to admire his image within ourselves; for if we do so we shall go backward rather than forward. No, beloved, by faith Enoch became pleasing to God, and by faith he walked with God: let us follow in his track.

Next, when we read that Enoch walked with God we are to understand that *he realized the divine presence*. You cannot consciously walk with a person whose existence is not known to you. When we walk with a man, we know that he is there; we hear his footfall if we cannot see his face; we have some very clear perception that there is such a person at our side. Now if we look to the Hebrews again, Paul tells us, "He that cometh to God must believe that he is, and that he is the rewarder of them that diligently seek him." Enoch's faith, then, was a realizing faith. He did not believe things as a matter of creed, and then put them up on the shelf out of the way, as too many do: he was not merely orthodox in head, but the truth had entered into his heart, and what he believed was true to him, practically true, true as a matter of fact in his daily life. He walked with God: it was not that he thought of God merely, that he speculated about God, that he argued about God, that he read about God, that he talked about God, but he walked with God, which is the practical and experimental part of true godliness. In his daily life he realized that God was with him, and he regarded him as a living friend, in whom he confided and by whom he was loved. O beloved, do you not see that if you are to reach to the highest style of Christian life, you must do it through the realization of those very things which by faith you have received? Grasp them, let them be to you substance and evidence. Make them sure, look upon them, handle them, taste them in your inmost soul, and so know them beyond all question. You must see him who is invisible, and possess that which cannot be as yet enjoyed. Believe not only that God is, but that he is the rewarder of them that diligently seek him, for this according to Paul is the Enoch faith. God realized as existing, observing, judging, and rewarding human deeds: a real God, really with us—this we must know, or there is no walking with God.

Then, as we read that Enoch walked with God, we have no doubt it signifies that *he had very familiar intercourse* with the most High. I scarcely know an intercourse that is more free, pleasant, and cordial than that which arises out of constant walking with a friend. If I wished to find a man's most familiar friend, it would surely be one with whom he daily walked. If you were to say, "I sometimes go into his house and sit a little while with him," it would not amount to so much as when you can say, "I have from day to day walked the fields and climbed the hills with him." In walking, friends become communicative: one tells his trouble, and the other strives to console him under it, and then imparts to him his own secret in return. When persons are constantly in the habit of walking together from choice, you may be quite sure there are many communications between them with which no stranger may intermeddle. If I wanted to know a man through and through, I should want to walk with him for a time, for walking communion brings out parts of the man which even in domestic life may be concealed. Walking for a continuance implies and engenders close fellowship and great familiarity between friends. But will God in very deed thus walk with men? Yes, he did so with Enoch, and he has done so with many of his people since. He tells us his secret, the secret of the Lord, which he reveals only to them that fear him, and we tell to him alike our joys in praise, our sorrows in prayer, and our sins in confession. The heart unloads itself of all its cares into the heart of him that careth for us; and the Lord pours forth his floods of goodness as he imparts to the beloved ones a sense of his own everlasting love to them. This is the very flower and sweetness of Christian experience, its lily and its rose, its calamus and myrrh. If you would taste the cream of Christian life, it is found in having a realizing faith, and entering into intimate intercourse with the heavenly Father. So Enoch walked with God.

Next it is implied in the term *walked* that *his intercourse with God was continuous*. As an old divine has well remarked, he did not take a turn or two with God and then leave his company, but he walked with God for hundreds of years. It is implied in the text that this was the tenor of his life throughout the whole of its 365 years. Enoch walked with God after Methuselah had been born, three hundred years, and doubtless he had walked with him before. What a splendid walk! A walk of three hundred years! One might desire a change of company if he walked with anybody else, but to walk with God for three centuries was so sweet that the patriarch kept on with his walk until he walked beyond time and space, and walked into paradise, where he is still marching on in the same divine society. He had heaven on earth, and it was therefore not so wonderful that he glided away from earth to heaven so easily. He did not commune with God by fits and starts, but he abode in the conscious love of God. He did not now and then climb to the heights of elevated piety and then descend into the marshy valley of lukewarmness, but he continued in the calm, happy, equable enjoyment of fellowship with God from day to day. Night with its sleep did not suspend it; day with its cares did not endanger it. It was not a run, a rush, a leap, a spurt, but a steady flow.. On, on, through three happy centuries and more did Enoch continue to walk with God.

It is implied also in this phrase that *his life was progressive*: for if a man walks either by himself or with anybody else, he makes progress, he goes forward. Enoch walked with God. At the end of two hundred years he was not where he began; he was in the same company, but he had gone forward in the right way. At the end of the third hundred years Enoch enjoyed more, understood more, loved more, had received more, and could give out more, for he had gone forward in all respects. A man who walks with God will necessarily grow in grace, and in the knowledge of God and in likeness to Christ. You cannot suppose a perpetual walk with God year after year, without the favored person being strengthened, sanctified, instructed, and rendered more able to glorify God. So I gather that Enoch's life was a life of spiritual progress; he went from strength to strength, and made headway in the gracious pilgrimage. May God grant us to be pressing onward ourselves.

Suffer a few more observations upon Enoch's walk. In Kitto's *Daily Bible Readings*, there is an exceedingly pleasing piece, illustrating what it must be to walk with God by the figure of a father's taking his little son by the hand and walking forth with him upon the breezy hills. He says, "As that child walks with thee, so do thou walk with God. That child loves thee now. The world—the cold and cruel world—has not yet come between his heart and thine. His love now is the purest and most beautiful he will ever feel, or thou wilt ever receive. Cherish it well, and as that child walks *lovingly* with thee, so do thou walk *lovingly* with God." It is a delight to such children to be with their father. The roughness of the way or of the weather is nothing to them: it is joy enough to go for a walk with father. There is a warm, tender, affectionate grip of the hand and a beaming smile of the eye as they look up to father while he conducts them over hill and dale. Such a walk is *humble* too, for the child looks upon its father as the greatest and wisest man that ever lived. He considers him to be the incarnation of everything that is strong and wise, and all that his father says or does he admires. As he walks along he feels for his father the utmost affection, but his reverence is equally strong: he is very near his father, but yet he is only a child, and looks up to his father as his king. Moreover such a walk is one of *perfect confidence*. The boy is not afraid of missing his way; he trusts implicitly his father's guidance. His father's arm will screen him from all danger, and therefore he does not so much as give it a thought—why should he? If care is needed as to the road, it is his father's business to see to it, and the child, therefore, never dreams of anxiety; why should he? If any difficult place is to be passed, the father will have to lift the boy over it, or help him through it—the child meanwhile is merry as a bird—why should he not be? Thus should the believer walk with God, resting on eternal tenderness and rejoicing in undoubted love. A believer should be unconscious of dread either as to the present or to the future. Beloved friend in Christ, your Father may be trusted, he will supply all your need.

Thou art as much his care as if beside
No man or angel lived in heaven or earth.

What an *instructive* walk a child has with a wise, communicative parent! How many of his little puzzles are explained to him, how everything about him is illuminated by the father's wisdom. The boy every step he takes becomes the wiser for such companionship. O happy children of God, who have been taught of their Father while they have walked with him! Enoch must have been a man of profound knowledge and great wisdom as to divine things. He must have dived into the deep things of God beyond most men.

His life must also have been a *holy* life, because he walked with God, and God never walks out of the way of holiness. If we walk with God, we must walk according to truth, justice, and love. The Lord has no company with the unjust and rebellious, and therefore we know that he who walked with God must have been an upright and holy man.

Enoch's life must, moreover, have been a *happy* one. Who could be unhappy with such a companion? With God himself to be with us the way can never be dreary. "Yea, though I walk through the valley of the shadow of death, I will fear no evil; for thou art with me." Granted that God is your companion, and your road must be a way of pleasantness and a path of peace.

Did Enoch walk with God, then his pilgrimage must have been safe. What a guard is the great Jehovah! He is Sun and Shield; he giveth grace and glory. He that dwelleth in the secret place of the most High, shall abide under the shadow of the Almighty. Nothing can harm the man who is walking with the Lord God at his right hand.

And oh, what an *honorable* thing it is to walk with the Eternal! Many a man would give thousands to walk with a king. Numbers of people are such worshipers of dignities that if a king did but smile at them they would be intoxicated with delight. What, then, is the honor of walking with the King of kings! What a patent of nobility it is to be permitted to walk with the blessed and only Potentate all one's life long! Who is he that is thus favored to be the King's companion, to walk alone with him, and to become his familiar friend? Jehovah rules earth and heaven, and hell, and is Lord of all who shall walk with him! If it were only for the honor of it, O Christians, how you ought to pant to walk with God. Enoch found it safe, happy, holy, honorable, and I know not how much more that is excellent, but certainly this was a golden life: where shall we find anything to equal it?

II. Second, let us consider *what circumstances were connected with Enoch's walking with God.*

The first remark is that *the details of his life are very few*. We do not know much about Enoch, and this is to his advantage. Happy is the nation which has no history, for a nation which has a history has been vexed with wars and revolutions, and bloodshed; but a nation that is always happy, peaceful, and prosperous has no chronicle to attract the lover of sensations. Happy is Enoch that we cannot write a long biography of him; the few words, "Enoch walked with God," suffice to depict his whole career, until "he was not, for God took him." If you go and look at a farmer's field, and you can say of it when you come back, "I saw yellow flowers covering it till it seemed a cloth of gold, and then I spied out here and there white flowers like silver buttons set on the golden vesture, and blue cornflowers also looked up with their lovely eyes and begemmed the whole," you will think that it is a very pretty field if you are a child; but the farmer shakes his head, for he knows that it is in bad condition and overrun with weeds; but if you come back and simply say, "It is as fine a piece of wheat as ever grew, and that is all," then your description, though brief, is very satisfactory. Many of those dazzling events and striking incidents and sensational adventures which go to make up an interesting biography may attract attention, but they do not minister to the real excellence of the life. No life can surpass that of a man who quietly continues to serve God in the place where providence has placed him. I believe that in the judgment of angels and all pure-minded beings that woman's life is most to be admired which consists simply of this: "She did what she could"; and that man's life shall be the most noteworthy of whom it can be said: "He followed the Lord fully." Enoch's life has no adventures; is it not adventure enough for a man to walk with God? What ambition can crave a nobler existence than abiding in fellowship with the Eternal?

But some will say, "Well, but Enoch must have been very peculiarly situated: he was no doubt placed in very advantageous circumstances for piety." Now, observe that this was not so, for first, *he was a public man*. He is called the "seventh from Adam." He was a notable man, and looked up to as one of the fathers of his age. A patriarch in those days must have been a man of mark, loaded with responsibility as well as with honor. The ancient custom was that the head of the family was prophet, priest, and king in his household, and abroad if he was a man of station and substance he was counselor, magistrate, and ruler. Enoch was a great man in his day, one of the most important of the period; hence we may be sure he had his trials, and bore the brunt of opposition from the powerful ungodly party which opposed the ways of godliness. He is mentioned among a noble list of men. Some have unwisely thought, "I could walk with God if I had a little cottage, if I lived in a quiet village, but, you see, I am a public man; I occupy a position of trust, and I have to mix with my fellowmen. I do not see how I am to walk with God." Ah, my dear friend, but Enoch did; though he was undoubtedly a man distinguished in his time, and full of public cares, yet he lost not the thread of sacred converse with heaven, but held on in his holy course through a life of centuries.

Note again that *Enoch was a family man*. "Enoch walked with God and begat sons and daughters." Some have said, "Ah, you cannot live as you like if you have a lot of children about you. Do not tell me about keeping up your hours of prayer and quiet reading of the Scriptures if you have a large family of little ones; you will be disturbed, and there will be many domestic incidents which will be sure to try your temper and upset your equanimity. Get away into the woods, and find a hermit's cell; there with your brown jug of water and your loaf of bread, you may be able to walk with God, but with a wife, not always amiable, and a troop of children who are never quiet, neither by day nor night, how can a man be expected to walk with God?" The wife on the other hand exclaims, "I believe that had I remained a single woman I might have walked with God. When I was a young woman I was full of devotion, but now with my husband, who is not always in the best of tempers, and with my children, who seem to have an unlimited number of wants, and never to have them satisfied, how is it possible that I can walk with God?" We turn to Enoch again, and we are confident that it can be done. "Enoch walked with God after he begat Methuselah three hundred years, and begat sons and daughters, and all the days of Enoch were three hundred and sixty-five years." Thus, you see, he was a public man, and he was a family man, and yet he walked with God for more than three hundred years. There is no need to be a hermit, or to renounce the married life, in order to live near to God.

In addition to this, *Enoch lived in a very evil age*. He was prominent at a time when sin was beginning to cover the earth, not very long before the earth was corrupt and God saw fit to sweep the whole population from off its surface on account of sin. Enoch lived in a day of mockers and despisers. You know that from his prophecy, as recorded by Jude. He prophesied, saying, "The Lord cometh with ten thousands of his saints, to execute judgment upon all, and to convince all that are ungodly among them of all their ungodly deeds which they have ungodly committed, and of all their hard speeches which ungodly sinners have spoken against him." He lived when few loved God and when those who professed to do so were being drawn aside by the blandishments of the daughters of men. Church and state were proposing an alliance, fashion and pleasure ruled the hour, and unhallowed compromise was the order of the day. He lived toward the close of those primitive times wherein long lives had produced great sinners, and great sinners had invented great provocations of God. Do not complain, therefore, of your times and of your neighbors and other surroundings, for amid them all you may still walk with God.

Enoch walked with God, and in consequence thereof *he bore his witness for God*. "Enoch the seventh from Adam prophesied." He could not be silent; the fire burned within his soul, and could not be restrained. When he had delivered his testimony it is clear that he encountered opposition. I am certain that he did so from the context in Jude, because the passage in Jude has to do with murmurers and "complainers, walking after their own lusts; and their mouth speaketh great swelling words," and Enoch is brought in as having had to do with such persons. His sermon shows that he was a man who stood firm amid a torrent of blasphemy and rebuke, carrying on the great controversy for the truth of God against the wicked lives and licentious tongues of the scoffers of his age; for he says, "Behold, the Lord cometh with myriads of his saints, to execute judgment upon all, and to convince all that are ungodly among them of all their ungodly deeds which they have ungodly committed." It is clear that they spoke against Enoch, they rejected his testimony, they grieved his spirit, and he mourned that in this they were speaking against God; for he speaks "of all their hard speeches which ungodly sinners have spoken against him." He saw their ungodly lives and bore witness against them. It is remarkable that his great subject should have been the second advent, and it is still more noteworthy that the two other men whom one would select as living nearest to

God, namely, Daniel and John, were both men who spoke much concerning the coming of the Lord and the great judgment day. I need not quote the words of Daniel, who tells us of the judgment which is to be set, and of the Ancient of Days who shall come upon his throne; nor need I repeat the constant witness of John concerning the Lord's second coming; I will only mention his fervent exclamation, "Even so, come quickly, Lord Jesus."

Thus you see that Enoch was a preacher of the word of God, and therefore he had a care over and above that which falls to the lot of most of you: and yet with that and all the rest put together he could please God until his life's end, if I may speak of an end to a life which ran into an endless state of joy: he continued as long as he was here to walk in faith, to walk in a manner in which God was pleased, and so his communion with the Lord was never broken.

III. This brings us to conclude with the third head: *what was the close of Enoch's walk?*

We would first remark that *he finished his work early*. Enoch walked with God, and that was such a good, sure, progressive walk that he traveled faster, and reached his house sooner, than those of us who walk with God sometimes and with the world at other times. Three hundred and sixty-five years would have been a long life to us, but it was a short life for that period when several patriarchs attained to nearly a thousand years of age. Enoch's life as compared to the usual life of the period was like a life of thirty or thirty-five years in these short-lived ages; in fact, the best parallel to it is the life of our Lord. As with the extended ages of men of his period, Enoch's life was of about the same length as that of the Lord Jesus in comparison with such lives as ours. He passed away comparatively a young man, as our dear brother and elder Verdon, just departed, has done: and we do not wonder that he did. They say, "whom the gods love die young": and both Enoch and Verdon were men greatly beloved. Perhaps these holy men ended their career so soon because they had done their lifework so diligently that they finished in good time. Some workmen if they have a job to do in your house are about it all day long, or rather all the week long, and make no end of chips and confusion. No wonder that some people live a long while, for they had need to do so to do anything at all! But this man did his work so well, and kept so close to God that his day's work was done at noon, and the Lord said, "Come home, Enoch, there is no need for you to be out of heaven any longer; you have borne your testimony, you have lived your life; through all the ages men will look upon you as a model man, and therefore you may come home." God never keeps his wheat out in the fields longer than is necessary; when it is ripe he reaps it at once: when his people are ready to go home, he will take them home. Do not regret the death of a good man while he is young; on the contrary, bless God that still there is some early ripening wheat in the world, and that some of his saints are sanctified so speedily.

But what did happen to Enoch? I am afraid I have said he died, or that I shall say so, it is so natural to speak of men as dying, but he alone and one other of all the human race are all that have entered the heavenly Canaan without fording the river of death. We are told concerning him that "he was not." Those gentlemen who believe that the word to *die* signifies to be annihilated, would have been still more confirmed in their views if the words in my text, "he was not," had been applied to all departed men, for if any expression might signify annihilation on their mode of translation, this is the one. "He was not" does not, however, mean that he was annihilated, and neither does the far feebler term of *dying* signify anything of the kind. "He was not"; that is to say, he was not *here*, that is all. He was gone from earth, but he was *there*, there where God had translated him. He was, he is with God, and that without having tasted death. Do not grudge him his avoidance of death. It was a favor, but not by any means so great as some would think, for those who do not die must undergo a change, and Enoch was changed. "We shall not all sleep," says the apostle, "but we shall all be changed." The flesh and blood of Enoch could not inherit the kingdom of God: in a moment he underwent a transformation which you and I will have to undergo in the day of the resurrection; and so, though he was not on earth, he was translated or transplanted from the gardens of earth to the paradise above. Now if there is any man in the world that shall never die, it is he who walks with God. If there is any man to whom death will be as nothing, it is the man who has looked to the second advent of Christ and gloried in it; if there is any man who, though he pass through the iron gates of death shall never feel the terror of the grim foe, it is the man whose life below has been perpetual communion with God. Go not about by any other way to escape the pangs of death, but walk with God, and you will be able to say, "O death, where is thy sting? O grave, where is thy victory?"

It is said of him that *"God took him."* A very remarkable expression. Perhaps he did it in some visible manner. I should not wonder. Perhaps the whole of the patriarchs saw him depart even as the apostles were present when our Lord was taken up. However that may be, there was some special rapture, some distinct taking up of this choice one to the throne of the most High. "He was not, for God took him."

Note that *he was missed*. This is one thing which I could not overlook. *He was missed*, for the apostle says he "was not found." Now if a man is not found, it shows that somebody looked after him. When Elijah went to heaven, you remember fifty men of the sons of the prophets went and searched for him. I do not wonder that they did; they would not meet with an Elijah every day, and when he was gone away, body and all, they might well look for him. Enoch was not found, but they looked after him. A good man is missed. A true child of God in a church like this, working and serving his Master, is only one among five thousand; but if he has walked with God his decease is lamented. The dear brother whom we have just buried we shall miss; his brother elders will miss him; the many who have been converted to God and helped by his means will miss him, and assuredly I shall miss him. I look toward the spot where he used to sit—I trust that someone else will sit there who will be half as useful as he was; it will be almost more than I can expect. We do not want so to live and die that nobody will care whether we are on earth or not. Enoch was missed when he was gone, and so will they be who walk with God.

Last of all, *Enoch's departure was a testimony*. What did he say by the fact that "he was not, for God took him," but this: there is a future state. Men had begun to doubt it, but when they said, "Where is Enoch?" and those who had witnessed his departure said, "God took him," it was to them an evidence that there was a God, and that there was another world. And when they said, "But where is his body?" there was another lesson. Two men had died before him, I mean two whose deaths are recorded in Scripture: Abel was killed, and his witness was that the seed of the serpent hates the woman's seed; Adam, too, had died about fifty years before Enoch's translation, whose witness was that, however late the penalty may come, yet the soul that sins it shall die. Now comes Enoch, and his testimony is that the body is capable of immortality. He could not bear testimony to resurrection, for he did not die: for that we have testimony in Christ, who is the firstfruits from among the dead; but the testimony of Enoch went a good way toward it, for it bore evidence that the body was capable of being immortal, and of living in a heavenly condition. "He was not, for God took him."

His departure also was a testimony to mankind that there is a reward for the righteous, that God does not sit with stony eyes regardless of the sins of the wicked, or of the virtues of his saints, but that he sees and is pleased with his people who walk with him, and that he can give them even now present rewards by delivering them from the pangs of death, and therefore he will certainly give rewards to all his people in some way or other. Thus you see, living and dying—no, not dying, again I do mistake—living and being translated,

Enoch was still a witness to his generation, and I do pray that all of us, whether we live or whether we sleep, may be witnesses for God. Oh, that we could live as my good brother Verdon, whom we have lately buried, lived, whose soul was on fire with love to Christ. He had a very passion for souls. I scarcely think there is one among us who did as much as he, for though he had to earn his daily bread, his evenings were spent with us in the service of the Lord, or in preaching the gospel, and then all night long he frequently paced the weary streets, looking after the fallen, that he might bring them in, and often went to his morning's work unrested, except by the rest which he found in the service of Christ. He would sometimes meet a brother with eyes full of joy, and say, "Five souls won for Christ last night." At other times after a sermon here he was a great soul hunter and would fetch inquirers downstairs into the prayer meeting, and when he had squeezed my hand he would say in his Swiss tones, which I cannot imitate, "Jesus saved some more last night: more souls were brought to Jesus." For him to live was to win souls. He was the youngest in our eldership, but the gray-heads do him honor. As we stood weeping about his tomb, there was not one among us but what felt that we had lost a true brother and a valiant fellow soldier. The Lord raise up others among you to do what Elder Verdon did! The Lord quicken the older brethren to be more active than they are, and make the young ones more devoted. Our ranks are broken, who shall fill up the gap? We are getting fewer and fewer as the Lord takes one and another home of the best instructed and of the bravest hearted; but recruits are daily coming in. May others come forward; yes, Lord, bring them forward by thy Holy Spirit to be leaders in the front rank, that as the vanguard melts into the church triumphant, the rear may continually find additions. Translated to the skies are some; may others be translated out of darkness into marvelous light, for Christ's sake. Amen.

Abraham: Prompt Obedience to the Call of God

Delivered on Lord's Day morning, June 27, 1875, at the Metropolitan Tabernacle, Newington. No. 1242.

By faith Abraham, when he was called to go out into a place which he should after receive for an inheritance, obeyed; and he went out, not knowing whither he went.— HEBREWS 11:8

One is struck with the practical character of this verse. Abraham was called, and he obeyed. There is no hint of hesitation, parleying, or delay; when he was called to go out, he went out. Would to God that such conduct were usual, yes, universal; for with many of our fellowmen, and I fear with some now present, the call alone is not enough to produce obedience. "Many are called, but few are chosen." The Lord's complaint is, "I called and ye refused." Such calls come again and again to many, but they turn a deaf ear to them; they are hearers only, and not doers of the word; and, worse still, some are of the same generation as that which Zechariah spoke of when he said, "They pulled away the shoulder, and stopped their ears that they should not hear."

Even among the most attentive hearers how many there are to whom the word comes with small practical result in actual obedience. Here we are in midsummer again, and yet Felix has not found his convenient season. It was about midwinter when he said he should find one, but the chosen day has not arrived. The mother of Sisera thought him long in coming, but what shall we say of this laggard season? We can see that the procrastinator halts, but it were hard to guess how long he will do so. Like the countryman who waited to cross the river when all the water had gone by, he waits till all difficulties are removed, and he is not one whit nearer that imaginary period than he was years ago. Meanwhile, the delayer's case waxes worse and worse, and, if there were difficulties before, they are now far more numerous and severe. The man who waits until he shall find it more easy to bear the yoke of obedience, is like the woodman who found his bundle of wood too heavy for his idle shoulder, and, placing it upon the ground, gathered more wood and added to the bundle, then tried it, but finding it still an unpleasant load, repeated the experiment of heaping on more, in the vain hope that by-and-by it might be of a shape more suitable for his shoulder. How foolish to go on adding sin to sin, increasing the hardness of the heart, increasing the distance between the soul and Christ, and all the while fondly dreaming of some enchanted hour in which it will be more easy to yield to the divine call and part with sin. Is it always going to be so? There are a few weeks and then cometh harvest; will another harvest leave you where you are, and will you again have to say, "The harvest is passed, the summer is ended, and we are not saved"? Shall God's longsuffering mercy only afford you opportunities for multiplying transgressions? Will you always resist his Spirit? Always put him off with promises to be redeemed tomorrow? Forever and forever shall the tenderness and mercy of God be thus despised? Our prayer is that God of his grace may give you to imitate the example of Abraham, who, when he was called, obeyed at once.

The sad point about the refusals to obey the call of the gospel is that men are losing a golden opportunity, an opportunity for being numbered among the choice spirits of the world, among those who shall be blessed among men and women. Abraham had an opportunity, and he had grace to grasp it, and at this day there is not on the beadroll of our race a nobler name than that of "the father of the faithful." He obtained a supreme grandeur of rank among the truly great and good: far higher is he in the esteem of the right minded than the conqueror blood-red from battle, or the emperor robed in purple. He was an imperial man, head and shoulders above his fellows. His heart was in heaven, the light of God bathed his forehead, and his soul was filled with divine influences, so that he saw the day of the Lord Jesus and was glad. He was blessed of the Lord that made heaven and earth, and was made a blessing to all nations. Some of you will never gain such honor; you will live and die ignoble, because you trifle with supreme calls, and yet, did you believe in God, did you but live by faith, there would be before you also a course of immortal honor, which would lead you to eternal glory. Instead thereof, however, choosing the way of unbelief and neglect and delay, you will, I fear, one day awake to shame and to everlasting contempt, and know, to your eternal confusion, how bright a crown you have lost. I am in hopes that there are some among you who would not be losers of the crown of life; who desire, in fact, above all things, to obtain the prize of the high calling of God in Christ Jesus, and to them I shall speak, and while I speak, may the Holy Spirit cause every word to fall with power.

To help them, we shall consider, first, *what was Abraham's special experience which led to his being what he became*? and, second, *what was there peculiar in Abraham's conduct*? and then, third, *what was the result of that conduct*?

I. *What was Abraham's special experience*, which led to his becoming so remarkable a saint?

The secret lies in three things: he had a call, he obeyed it, and he obeyed it because he had faith.

First, then, *he had a call*. How that call came we are not told; whether it reached him through a dream, or by an audible voice from heaven, or by some unmentioned prophet, we cannot tell. Most probably he heard a voice from heaven speaking audibly to him and saying, "Get thee out from thy kindred and from thy father's house." We, too, have had many calls, but perhaps we have said, "If I heard a voice speaking from the sky I would obey it," but the form in which your call has come has been better than that, for Peter in his second epistle tells us that he himself heard a voice out of the excellent glory when he was with our Lord in the holy mount, but he adds, "We have also a more sure word of prophecy," as if the testimony which is written, the light that shines in a dark place, which beams forth from the Word of God, was more sure than even the voice which he heard from heaven. I will show you that it is so; for, if I should hear a voice, how am I to know that it is divine? Might it not, even if it were divine, be suggested to me for many reasons that I was mistaken, that it was most unlikely that God should speak to a man at all, and more unlikely still that he should speak to me? Might not a hundred difficulties and doubts be suggested to lead me to question whether God had spoken to me at all? But the most of you believe the Bible to be inspired by the Spirit of God, and to be the voice of God. Now in this Book you have the call—"Come ye out from among them, be ye separate, touch not the unclean thing; and I will be a Father unto you, and ye shall be my sons and daughters." Do not say that you would accept that call if it were spoken with a voice rather than written; you know that it is not so in daily life. If a man receives a written letter from his father or a friend, does he attach less importance to it than he would have done to a spoken communication? By no means. I reckon that many of you in business are quite content to get written orders for goods, and when you get them you do not require a purchaser to ask you in person, you would just as soon that he should not; in fact, you commonly say that you like to have it in black and white. Is it not so? Well, then, you have your wish, here is the call in black and white; and I do but speak according to common sense when I say that if the Lord's call to you be written in the Bible, and it certainly is, you do not speak truth when you say, "I would listen to it if it were spoken, but I cannot listen to it because it is written." The call as given by the Book of inspiration ought to have over your minds a masterly power, and if your hearts were right before God the word spoken in the Scriptures by the Holy Ghost would be at once obeyed.

Moreover, my undecided hearers, you have had other calls besides those from the Book. There have been calls through the living ministry, when the minister has spoken as pointedly to you as if he were a prophet, and you have known that the Lord spoke by him, for he has depicted your circumstances, described your condition, and the word has come to you, and you have with astonishment owned that it found you out. The message has also been spoken to you by a mother's tender love and by a father's earnest advice. You have had the call, too, in the form of sickness and sore trouble. In the silence of the night, when you could not sleep, your conscience has demanded to be heard, the inward strivings of the Holy Ghost have been with you, and loud have been the knocks at your door. Who among us has not known the like? But, alas, the Lord has called and has been refused, he has stretched out his hands and has not been regarded. Is it not so with many of you? You have not been like Samuel, who said, "Here am I, for thou didst call me," but like the adder which shuts her ear to the voice of the charmer. This is not to be done without incurring great guilt and involving the offender in heavy punishment.

Abraham had a call. So have we, but here was the difference: *Abraham obeyed*. Well does Paul say, "They have not all obeyed the gospel": for to many the call comes as a common call, and the common call falls on a sealed ear, but to Abraham and to those who by grace have become the children of faithful Abraham, to whom are the blessings of grace, and with whom God has entered into league and covenant, to touch it comes as a special call, a call attended with a sacred power which subdues their wills and secures their obedience. Abraham was prepared for instant obedience to any command from God; his journey was appointed, and he went. He was bidden to leave his country, and he left it; to leave his friends, and he left them all. Gathering together such substance as he had, he exiled himself that he might be a sojourner with his God, and took a journey in an age when traveling was infinitely more laborious than now. He knew not the road that he had to take, nor the place to which his journey would conduct him: it was enough for him that the Lord had given him the summons. Like a good soldier, he obeyed his marching orders, asking no questions. Toward God a blind obedience is the truest wisdom, and Abraham felt so, and therefore followed the path that God marked out for him from day to day, feeling that sufficient for the day would be the guidance thereof. Thus Abraham obeyed! Alas, there are some here present, some, too, to whom we have preached now for years, who have not obeyed. Oh, sirs, some of you do not require more knowledge; you need far more to put in practice what you know. Would you wonder if I should grow weary of telling some of you the way of salvation any longer? Do you not yourselves weary of persuading those who will not yield? So far as I have reason to fear that my task is hopeless it becomes a heavy one. Again and again and again have I explained the demands of the gospel and described the blessings of it, and yet I see its demands neglected and its blessings refused. Ah sirs, there will be an end to this before long, one way or the other. Which shall it be? O that you were wise and would yield obedience to the truth! The gospel has about it a divine authority, and is not to be trifled with. Notwithstanding that grace is its main characteristic, it has all the authority of a command. Do we not read of those who "stumbled at the word, being disobedient"? Surely there must be a command and a duty, or else there could not be disobedience. It is awful work when through disobedience to the command of the gospel it becomes a savor of death unto death instead of life unto life, and instead of a cornerstone it becomes a stone of stumbling and a rock of offense. Remember, upon whomsoever it shall fall it will grind him to powder. Christ himself has said it, and so it must be. May he of his infinite mercy give us the willing and the obedient mind that we may not pervert the gospel to our own destruction.

But I reminded you that the main point concerning Abraham was this, *he obeyed the call because he believed God*. Faith was the secret reason of his conflict. We read of certain persons that "the word preached did not profit them, not being mixed with faith in them that heard it," and again we read that "some when they had heard did provoke." But in Abraham's case there was neither unbelief nor provocation. He believed God with a childlike faith. His faith, I suppose, lay in the following items: when the Lord spoke he believed that it was the living God who addressed him. Believing that God spoke, he judged him worthy of his earnest heed; and he felt that it was imperative upon him to do as he was bidden. This settled, he desired nothing more to influence his course: he felt that the will of God must be right, and that his highest wisdom was to yield to it. Though he did not know where he was to go, he was certain that his God knew, and though he could hardly comprehend the reward promised to him, he was sure that the bounteous God never mocked his servants with deceitful gifts. He did not know the land of Canaan, but he was sure if it was a country chosen by God as a peculiar gift to his called servant, it must be no ordinary land. He left all such matters with his heavenly Friend, being fully persuaded that what he had promised he was able also to perform.

What a mighty sway faith has over a man, and how greatly it strengthens him. Faith was to the patriarch his authority for starting upon his strange journey, an authority which enabled him to defy alike the worldly wisdom which advises, and the worldly folly which scoffs. Perhaps they said to him, "Why will you leave your kinsfolk, Abraham?" but he replied, "God bids me." That was for him a sufficient warrant; he wanted no further argument. This also became to him the guide of his steps. If any said, "But, strange old man, how can you journey when you know not the way?" He replied, "I go where the Lord bids me." Faith found in God, chart, compass, and polestar, all in one. The word of the Lord also became the nourishment for his journey. If any said, "How will you be supplied, Abraham, in those wild lands, where will you find your daily bread?" he replied, "God bids me go: it is not possible that he should desert me. He can spread a table in the wilderness, or make me live upon the word which comes out of his mouth, if bread should fail." Probably these suggestions of trial may never have occurred to Abraham, but if they did, his faith swept them aside from his path as so many cobwebs. Perhaps some even dared to say, "But where go you? There is no such country, it is an enthusiast's dream, a land which flows with milk and honey. Where will you find it? O gray-beard, you are in your dotage, seventy years and five have bewildered you." But he replied, "I shall find it, for the Lord has given it to me and leads me to it." He believed God, and took firm hold, and therefore he endured as seeing him that is invisible.

See, then, dear friends, what we must have if we are to be numbered with the seed of Abraham—we must have faith in God and a consequent obedience to his commands. Have we obtained these gifts of the Spirit? I hope that many of us have the living faith which walks by love, and if so we shall rejoice in the will of the Lord, let it be what it may; if we know anything to be right we shall delight to do it, but as for doubtful or sinful deeds we renounce them. For us henceforth our leader is the Lord alone. But is it so with all of you? Let the personal question go around and cause great searching of heart, for I fear that in many instances precious faith is absent. Many have heard, but they have not believed; the sound of the gospel has entered into their ears, but its inner sense and sacred power have not been felt in their hearts. Remember that "without faith it is impossible to please God," so that you are displeasing to the Lord. How long shall it be so? How long shall unbelief lodge within you and grieve the Holy Spirit? May the Lord convince you, yes, at this moment, may he lead you to decision, and enable you henceforth to live by faith. It may be now or never with you. God grant it may be now!

II. This brings me to the second part of our subject: *what was there peculiar in Abraham's conduct?*

For whatever there was essential in his conduct there must be the same in us, if we are to be true children of the father of the faithful. The points of peculiarity in Abraham's case seem to me to have been five.

The first was this, *that he was willing to be separated from his kindred*. It is a hard task to a man of loving soul to put long leagues of distance between himself and those he loves, and to become a banished man. Yet in order to have salvation, brethren, we must be separated from this untoward generation. Not that we have to take our journey into a far country, or to forsake our kindred—perhaps it would be an easier task to walk with God if we could do so—but our calling is to be separate from sinners, and yet to live among them: to be a stranger and a pilgrim in their cities and homes. We must be separate in character from those with whom we may be called to grind at the same mill or sleep in the same bed; and this I warrant you is by no means an easier task than that which fell to the patriarch's lot. If believers could form a secluded settlement where no tempters could intrude, they would perhaps find the separated life far more easy, though I am not very sure about it, for all experiments in that direction have broken down.

There is, however, for us no "garden walled around," no "island of saints," no utopia; we sojourn among those whose ungodly lives cause us frequent grief, and the Lord Jesus meant it to be so, for he said, "Behold I send you forth as sheep among wolves." Come, now, my hearer, are you willing to be one of the separated? I mean this—dare you begin to think for yourself? You have let your grandmother's religion come to you with the old armchair and the antique china, as heirlooms of the family, and you go to a certain place of worship because your family have always attended there. You have a sort of hereditary religion in the same way as you have a display of family plate; pretty battered it is, no doubt, and rather light in weight by this time, but still you cling to it. Now, young man, dare you think for yourself? Or do you put out your thinking to be done for you, like your washing? I believe it to be one of the essentials of a Christian man, that he should have the courage to use his own mental faculties, and search the Bible for himself; for God has not committed our religious life to the guidance of the brain in our neighbor's head, but he has bestowed on each of us a conscience, and an understanding which he expects us to use. Do your own thinking, my friend, on such a business as this. Now if the grace of God helps you rightly to think for yourself, you will judge very differently from your ungodly friends; your views and theirs will differ, your motives will differ, the objects of your pursuit will differ. There are some things which are quite customary with them which you will not endure. You will soon become a speckled bird among them. The Jews in all time have been very different from all other nations, and although other races have become permanently united, the Jewish people have always been a family by themselves. Though now residing in the midst of all nations, it is still true "the people shall dwell alone, they shall not be reckoned among the nations." In all the cities of Europe there are remains of the "Jews' quarter," and we in London had our "Old Jewry," the Jews being evermore a peculiar people. We Christians are to be equally distinct, not in meats, and drinks, and garments, and holy days, but as to spirituality of mind and holiness of life. We are to be strangers and foreigners in the land wherein we sojourn. For we are not resident traders in this Vanity Fair; we pass through it because it lies in our way home, but we are ill at ease in it. In no tent of all the fair can we rest.

O traders in this hubbub of trifles, we have small esteem for your great bargains and tempting cheats; we are not buyers in the Roman row nor in the French row; we would give all that we have to leave your polluted streets, and be no more annoyed by Beelzebub, the lord of the fair. Our journey is toward the celestial city, and when the sons of earth cry to us, "What do you buy?" we answer, "We buy the truth." O young man, can you take up in the warehouse the position of being a Christian though there is no other believer in the house? Come, good woman, dare you serve the Lord, though husband and children ridicule you? Man of business, dare you do the right thing in business and play the Christian, though around you the various methods of trading render it hard for you to be unflinchingly honest? This singularity is demanded of every believer in Jesus. You cannot be blessed with Abraham unless like him you come out and stand forth as true men.

Dare to be a Daniel
Dare to stand alone;
Dare to have a purpose true,
Dare to make it known.

May God grant to us grace to be Daniels, even if the lions' den should threaten us.

A second peculiarity of Abraham's conduct is seen in the fact that *he was ready for all the losses and risks that might be involved in obedience to the call of God.* He was to leave his native country, as we have already said: to some of us that would be a hard task, and I doubt not it was such to him. The smoke out of my own chimney is better than the fire on another man's hearth. There is no place like home wherever we may wander. The home feeling was probably as strong in Abraham as in us, but he was never to have a home on earth any more, except that he was to realize what Moses afterward sang, "Lord, thou hast been our dwelling place in all generations." For him there was no rooftree [ridge-pole] and paternal estate, he owned no portion of the land in which he sojourned, and his sole alcove was a frail tent, which he removed from day to day as his flocks required fresh pasturage. He could say to his God, "I am a stranger and a sojourner with thee." He had to leave those whom he loved, for, though they accompanied him part of the way, they would not go farther; if he followed the Lord fully he must go alone. The patriarch knew nothing of half measures; he went through with his obedience, and left all his kindred to go to Canaan, to which he had been summoned. Those who wished to stop at Haran might stop there. Canaan was his destination, and he could not stop short of it.

No doubt he had many risks to encounter on his journey and when be entered the country. The Canaanite was still in the land, and the Canaanites were a fierce and cruel set of heathen who would have utterly destroyed the wanderer if the Lord had not put a spell upon them, and said, "Touch not mine anointed, and do my prophets no harm." It was a country swarming with little tribes, who were at war continually. Abraham himself was, for Lot's sake, to gird on his sword, and go forth to fight, peace-lover as he was. Of all discomforts and dangers, loss of property, and parting with friends, Abraham made small account. God commanded, and Abraham went.

Now, brethren, can you and I do the same? O you who desire to be saved, I say, can you do this? Have you counted the cost and determined to pay it? You must not expect that you will wear silver slippers and walk on green rolled turf all the way to heaven: the road was rough which your Lord traversed, and if you walk with him yours will be rough too. Can you bear for Jesus' sake all earthly loss? Can you bear the scoff, the cold shoulder, the cutting jest, the innuendo, the sarcasm, the sneer? Could you go further and bear loss of property and suffering in purse? Do not say that it may not occur, for many believers lose all by having to leave the ill pursuits by which they once earned their bread. You must in your intention give all up for Jesus, and in act you must give up all to Jesus. If he be yours, you must henceforth have all things in common with him; you must be joint heirs together, his yours and yours his; you may be well content to make joint stock, when you have so little and he has so much. Oh, can you stand to it, and give up all for him? Well, if you cannot, do not pretend to do it. Yet, except ye take up your cross, ye cannot be his disciples. Except you can give up everything for him, do not pretend to follow him. Listen to this. If you think heaven worth nothing, and Christ worth nothing, if you consider worldly gain to be everything, and comfort everything, and honor everything, if you could not die a martyr's death for Christ, your love to him is not worth much, and the Abraham spirit is not in you. May God enable us to take our places in the battle in the front of the foe, where the fight is most furious. May grace make us sing—

Jesus, I my cross have taken,
All to leave and follow thee,
Destitute, despised, forsaken,
Thou, from hence, my all shalt be.

If that be said in truth, it is well, my brother; you bid fair to be in all things a partaker with faithful Abraham: you also shall find much blessing in the separated life.

Third, one great peculiarity in Abraham was that *he waived the present for the future.* He went out to go into a place which he should after receive for an inheritance. He left the inheritance he then had to receive one which was yet to come. This is not the way of the world. The proverb says, "A bird in the hand is worth two in the bush," and especially in such a bush as Abraham saw before him. It did not seem very likely he would ever obtain that land; but still he let his bird in the hand go and took to the bird in the bush, being fully persuaded that he should have it in God's good time. Mr. Bunyan sets this forth in his picture of two children, Passion and Patience. Passion would have all his good things now, and he sat among his toys and joys, and laughed and rejoiced. Patience had to bear to see his brother Passion full of mirth, and to hear his scoffing; but then, as Master Bunyan beautifully says, Patience came in last for his portion, and it lasted forever, for there is nothing after the last. So, then, if we are to have our heaven last it will last, and no cloud shall mar it, no calamity bring it to an end. He is the wise man who lets go the shadow to grasp the substance, even though he should have to wait twenty, thirty, or forty years for it. He is blessed who leaves earth's wind and rubble and feeds on more substantial meat. God grant us grace to live more for the future than we have been accustomed to do.

O you ungodly ones, you do not care about the future, for you have never realized death and judgment. You are afraid to look over the edge of this narrow life. As to death, nothing frightens you so much. As for hell, if you are warned to escape from it, instead of thanking the preacher for being honest enough to warn you of it, you straightaway call him a "hell-fire" preacher, or give him some other ugly name. Alas, you little know how pained he is to speak to you on so terrible a subject! You little dream how true a lover of your soul he is, or he would not warn you of the wrath to come. Do you want to have flatterers about you? Such are to be had in plenty if you desire them. As for heaven, you seem to have no regard for it; at any rate you are not making your title to it sure or clear by caring about divine things. If you would have the birthright you must let the present mess of pottage go. The eternal future must come far before the fleeting trifles of today; you must let the things which are seen sink, and bid the "things not seen as yet" rise in all their matchless grandeur and reality before your eyes. You must give up chasing butterflies and shadows and pursue things eternal. My soul immortal pines only for immortal joys. I leave my present lot to be appointed of the Lord as he wills, so long as he will shed his love abroad in my heart. We must be prepared for eternity, and for that purpose we should concentrate our faculties upon divine truth and personal religion, that we may be ready to meet our God. This, then, was the third excellence in Abraham's walk, that he waived present comfort for the sake of the future blessing.

Fourth, and this is the main point, *Abraham committed himself to God by faith.*

From that day forward Abraham had nothing but his God for a portion, nothing but his God for a protector. No squadron of soldiers accompanied the good man's march; his safeguard lay in him who had said, "Fear not, Abraham, I am thy shield and thy exceeding great reward." He had to trust the Lord for his daily bread and daily guidance, for he was to march on and not know half a mile before him. He was ignorant when to stop and when to journey on, except as the Lord God guided him hour by hour. I must not say that Abraham became a poor pensioner upon the daily provision of God, but I will use a better term and describe him as "a gentleman commoner upon the royal bounty of his heavenly King." His lot was to have nothing but to be heir of heaven and earth. Can you thus walk by faith? Has the grace of God brought you who have been hesitating to resolve henceforth to believe God and trust him? If you do you are saved, for faith is the deciding matter. To realize the existence of God and to trust in him, especially to trust in his mercy, through Jesus Christ, is the essential matter. As for the life and walk of faith, they are the most singular things in the world. I seem myself to have been climbing a series of mysterious staircases, light as air and yet as solid as granite. I cannot see a single step before me, and often there seems to the eye to be nothing whatsoever to form a foothold for the next step. I look down and wonder how I came where I am, but still I climb on, and he who has brought me so far supplies me with confidence for that which lies before me. High into things invisible the ethereal ladder has borne me, and onward and forward to glory its rounds will yet conduct me. What I have seen has often failed me, but what I have not seen, and yet have believed, has always held me stably. Have not you found it so, all you children of God? Let us pray that the Lord may lead others to tread the same mystic ascent by beginning today the life of faith.

The last specialty in Abraham's procedure was *what he did was done at once*. There were no "ifs" and "ands" debatings, considerings, and delays. He needed no forcing and driving—

> *God drew him and he followed on,*
> *Charmed to confess the voice divine.*

At once, I say, he went. Promptness is one of the brightest excellencies in faith's actings. Delay spoils all. Someone asked Alexander to what he owed his conquests, and he said, "I have conquered because I never delayed." While the enemy were preparing, he had begun the battle, and they were routed before they knew where they were. After that fashion faith overcomes temptation. She runs in the way of obedience, or rather she mounts on the wings of eagles, and so speeds on her way. With regard to the things of God our first thoughts are best: considerations of difficulty entangle us. Whenever you feel a prompting to do a good thing, do not ask anybody whether you should do it or not; no one ever repents of doing good. Ask your friends afterward rather than beforehand, for it is ill consulting with flesh and blood when duty is plain. If the Lord has given you substance, and you are prompted to be generous to the cause of God, do not count every sixpence over, and calculate what others would give; count it after you have given it, if it must be counted at all, but it would be better still not to let your left hand know what your right hand does. It cannot be wrong to do the right thing at once; no, in matters of duty, every moment of delay is a sin. Thus we have Abraham before us; may the Holy Spirit make us like him.

Now this morning, who will listen to the call of God? Who, like Abraham, will quit the world, with all its folly, and resolve henceforth to be upon the Lord's side? O Spirit of the living God, constrain many a hidden Abraham to come forth!

III. We have to close with two or three words about what was *the result of Abraham's action.*

The question of many will be, *did it pay?* That is the inquiry of most people, and within proper bounds it is not a wrong question. Did it answer Abraham's purpose? Our reply is, it did so gloriously. True, it brought him into a world of trouble, and no wonder: such a noble course as his was not likely to be an easy one. What grand life ever was easy? Who wants to be a child and do easy things? Yet we read in Abraham's life, after a whole host of troubles, "And Abraham was old and well stricken in years, and the Lord had blessed Abraham in all things." That is a splendid conclusion—God had blessed Abraham in all things. Whatever happened, he had always been under the divine smile, and all things had worked for his good. He was parted from his friends, but then he had the sweet society of his God, and was treated as the friend of the most High, and allowed to intercede for others, and clothed with great power on their behalf. I almost envy Abraham. I should do so altogether if I did not know that all the saints are permitted to enjoy the same privileges. What a glorious degree Abraham took when he was called "the friend of God"; was not his loss of earthly friendships abundantly made up to him? What honor, also, the patriarch had among his contemporaries; he was a great man, and held in high esteem. How splendidly he bore himself; no king ever behaved more royally. That pettifogging king of Sodom wanted to make a bargain with him, but the grand old man replied, "I will not take from a thread even to a shoe-latchet, lest thou shouldest say, I have made Abraham rich." Those sons of Heth also were willing to make him a present of a piece of land around the cave of Machpelah; but he did not want a present from Canaanites, and so he said, "No, I will pay you every penny. I will weigh out the price to you, whatever you may demand." In noble independence no man could excel the father of the faithful; his contemporaries look small before him, and no man seems to be his equal, save Melchizedek. His image passes across the page of history rather like that of a spirit from the supernal realms than that of a mere man; he is so thorough, so childlike, and therefore so heroic. He lived in God, and on God, and with God. Such a sublime life recompensed a thousandfold all the sacrifice he was led to make.

Was not his life a happy one? One might wisely say, "Let my life be like that of Abraham." As to temporal things, the Lord enriched him, and in spirituals he was richer still. He was wealthier in heart than in substance, though great ever, in that respect. And now Abraham is the father of the faithful, patriarch of the whole family of believers, and to him alone of all mortal men God said, "In thee shall all the families of the earth be blessed." This very day, through his matchless seed, to whom be glory forever and ever, even Jesus Christ of the seed of Abraham, all tribes of men are blessed. His life was both for time and for eternity, a great success; both for temporals and for spirituals the path of faith was the best that he could have followed.

And now may we all be led to imitate his example. If we never have done so, may we this morning be led to give God his due by trusting him, to give the blood of Christ its due by relying upon it, to give the Spirit of God his due by yielding ourselves to him. Will you do so, or not? I pause for your reply. The call is given again, will you obey it or not? Nobody here will actually declare that he will not, but many will reply that *they hope they shall*. Alas! my sermon is a failure to those who so speak: if that be your answer, I am foiled again. When Napoleon was attacking the Egyptians he had powerful artillery, but he could not reach the enemy, for they were ensconced in a mud fort, and it made Napoleon very angry, because, if they had been behind granite walls, he could have battered them down, but their earthworks could not be blown to pieces; every ball stuck in the mud, and made the wall stronger. Your hopes and delays are just such a mud wall. I had a good deal sooner people would say, "There, now, we do not believe in God nor in his Christ," and speak out straightforwardly, than go on forever behind this mud wall of "we will by-and-by," and "we hope it will be so one day." The fact is, you do not mean to obey the Lord at all. You are deceiving yourselves if you think so. If God be God tomorrow he is God today; if Christ be worth having next week he is worth having today. If there is anything in religion at all, it demands a present surrender to its claims and a present obedience to its laws; but if you judge it to be a lie, say so, and we shall know where you are. If Baal be God, serve him; but if God be God, I charge you by Jesus Christ, fly to him as he is revealed and come forth from the sin of the world and be separate, and walk by faith in God. To this end may the Spirit of God enable you. Amen and amen.

Jacob: Worshiping on His Staff

Delivered at the Metropolitan Tabernacle, Newington. Published in 1878. No. 1401

By faith Jacob, when he was a dying, blessed both the sons of Joseph; and worshiped, leaning upon the top of his staff.— HEBREWS 11:21

"When he was dying." Death is a thorough test of faith. Beneath the touch of the skeleton finger shams dissolve into thin air, and only truth remains; unless indeed a strong delusion has been given, and then the spectacle of a presumptuous sinner passing away in his iniquities is one which might make angels weep. It is hard, very hard, to maintain a lie in the presence of the last solemnities; the end of life is usually the close of self-deception. There is a mimic faith, a false assurance, which lasts under all ordinary heats of trial, but this evaporates when the fires of death surround it. Certain men are at peace and quiet in their conscience, they stifle convictions, they refuse to allow such a thing as self-examination, they count an honest self-suspicion to be a temptation of the devil, and boast of their unbroken tranquility of mind, and go on from day to day with perfect confidence; but we would not be of their order. Their eyes are closed, their ears are dull of hearing, and their heart has waxed gross. A siren song forever enchants them with delight, but also entices them to destruction. Terrible will be their awakening when they lie dying: as a dream their false peace will vanish, and real terrors will come upon them.

That expression, "when he was a dying," reminds me of many deathbeds; but I shall not speak of them now, for I desire each one of you to rehearse the scene of his own departure, for soon of every one a tale will be told commencing—"when he was a dying." I want each one to project his mind a little forward to the time when he must gather up his feet in the bed, pronounce his last farewell, and yield up the ghost. Before your actual departure, probably, there may be allotted to you, unless you are carried away with a sudden stroke, a little time in which it shall be said, "He was a dying." Perhaps it is a desirable thing to occupy some weeks in departure, till the mind seems to have passed through the gate and to be already in the glory, while yet the body lingers here; but as we have had no experience, we are scarcely able to form a judgment.

The text tells us that the patriarch's faith was firm while he was a dying, so that he poured forth no murmurs, but plentiful benedictions, as he blessed both the sons of Joseph. May your faith and mine also be such that whenever we shall be dying, our faith will perform some illustrious exploit that the grace of God may be admired in us. Paul does not say anything about Jacob's life but selects the death scene. There were many instances of faith in Jacob's life story, but you recollect that in the epistle to the Hebrews, Paul is walking through the histories and plucking a flower here and a flower there, and he complains that time fails him even in doing that, so fertile is the garden of faith. I do not doubt, however, that he gathered the best out of each biography; and, perhaps, the finest thing in Jacob's life was the close of it. He was more royal between the curtains of his bed than at the door of his tent: greater in the hour of his weakness than in the day of his power.

The old man of 147 might have been willing to depart through infirmities of age, but yet he had much to keep him below, and make him wish to live as long as possible. After a very troublous life he had enjoyed seventeen years of remarkable comfort, so much so that, had it been ourselves, we should probably have begun to strike our roots into the soil of Goshen, and dread the bare thought of removal; yet there sits the venerable patriarch, with his hand on his staff, ready to go, seeking no delay, but rather waiting for the salvation of God. After all his tossings to and fro, when he had been so long a pilgrim, it must have been a pleasant thing for him to have settled down in a fat land with his sons, and his grandsons, and great-grandsons all around him, all comfortably provided for, with Joseph at the head of the whole country—prime minister of Egypt—reflecting honor upon his old father, and taking care that none of the family wanted anything. The last course of Jacob's feast of life was by far the sweetest, and the old man might have been loathe to retire from so dainty a table. The children of Israel were a sort of foreign aristocracy in the land, and against them would not a dog dare to move its tongue, lest the renowned Joseph should put forth his hand. That seventeen years must have been bright, and full of rest to the old man. But sense has not killed his faith, luxury has not destroyed his spirituality; his heart is still in the tents where he had dwelled as a sojourner with God. You can see that he has not even with one single rootlet of his soul taken hold upon Egypt. His first anxiety is to take care that not even his bones shall lie in Goshen, but that his body shall be taken out of the country as a protest to his family that they are not Egyptians, and cannot be made into subjects of Pharaoh, and that Canaan is their possession to which they must come. By his dying charge to bury him in Machpelah, he practically teaches his descendants that they must set loose by all the good land which they possessed in Goshen, for their inheritance did not lie on the banks of the Nile, but on the other side of the desert in Canaan, and they must be on tiptoe to journey there. The blessing which he gave to the sons of Joseph was but an utterance of his firm faith in the covenant which gave the land to him and to his seed. It was suggested by that faith of his which let go the present and grasped the future, renounced the temporal and seized the eternal, refusing the treasures of Egypt and clinging to the covenant of God.

I. First, then, *his blessing.*

He blessed the two sons of Joseph. Will you have patience with me while I try to show that his blessing the sons of Joseph was an act of faith? Because, first, *only by faith could the old man really give a blessing to anyone.* Look at him. He is too feeble to leave his bed. When he sits up supported by pillows, at what is called the bed's head, he calls for his trusty staff that he may lean upon it while he raises himself up a little, to be in a position to stretch out his hands and to use his voice. He has no strength, and his eyes are dim, so that he cannot see which is Ephraim and which is Manasseh. He is failing in most of his faculties: every way you can see that he is a worn-out old man, who can do nothing for the children whom he loves. If he is able to bestow a blessing, it cannot be by the power of nature; and yet he can and does bless them, and therefore we feel sure that there must be an inner man within that feeble old Jacob; there must be a spiritual Israel hidden away in him, an Israel who by prevailing with God as a prince has obtained a blessing, and is able to dispense it to others. And so there is; and at half a glance we see it. He rises to the dignity of a king, a prophet, and a priest when he begins to pronounce a blessing upon his two grandchildren. He believed that God spoke by him; and he believed that God would justify every word that he was uttering. He believed in the God that hears prayer; his benediction was a prayer; and as he pronounced blessings upon his grandsons he felt that every word he was speaking was a petition which the Lord was answering. They were blessed, and they should be blessed, and he discerned it by faith. Thus, we see, he was manifesting his faith in offering believing prayer and in uttering a confident benediction.

Whether we live or whether we die, let us have faith in God: whenever we preach or teach the gospel, let us have faith; for without faith we shall labor in vain. Whenever you distribute religious books or visit the sick, do so in faith, for faith is the lifeblood of all our service. If only by faith can a dying Jacob bless his descendants, so only by faith can we bless the sons of men. Have faith in God, and the instruction which you give shall really edify, the prayers you offer shall bring down showers of mercy, and your endeavors for your sons and daughters shall be prospered. God will bless what is done in faith; but if we believe not, our work will not be established. Faith is the backbone and marrow of the Christian's power to do good: we are weak as water till we enter into union with God by faith, and then we are omnipotent. We can do nothing for our fellowmen by way of promoting their spiritual and eternal interests if we walk according to the sight of our eyes; but when we get into the power of God, and grasp his promise by a daring confidence, then it is that we obtain the power to bless.

You will notice, also, that *not only the power to bless came to him by faith, but the blessings which he allotted to his grandsons were his upon the same tenure.* His legacies were all blessings which he possessed by faith only. He gave to Ephraim and Manasseh a portion each: but where and what? Did he fetch out a bag from an iron safe and say, "Here, young men, I give you the same portion of ready money as I give my sons"? No, there does not seem to have been a solitary shekel in the case. Did he call for the map of the family estates and say, "I give over to you, my boys, my freehold lands in such a parish, and my copyhold farms under such a manor"? No, no, he gave them no portion in Goshen, but each had a lot in Canaan.

Did that belong to him? Yes, in one sense, but not in another. God had promised it to him, but he had not yet a foot of land in it. The Canaanites were swarming in the land; they were dwelling in cities walled up to heaven and held the country by the right of possession, which is nine points of the law. But the good old man talks about Canaan as if it was all his own, and he foresees the tribes growing into nations as much as if they were already in actual possession of the country. He had, as a matter of fact, neither house nor ground in Palestine, and yet he counts it all his own, since a faithful God had promised it to his fathers. God had said to Abraham, "Lift up now thine eyes and behold to the east and to the west, to the north and to the south. All this will I give thee." And Jacob realizes that gift of God as being a charter and title deed of possession, and he acts upon it while he says, "This is for Ephraim: this is for Manasseh," though the sneering infidel standing by would have said, "Hear how the old man dotes and maunders, giving away what he has not got!" Faith is the substance of things hoped for, and she deals seriously and in a business manner with that which she makes real to herself: blind reason may ridicule, but faith is justified of all her children.

Beloved, in this manner believers bless the sons of men, namely, by faith. We pray for them, and we tell them of good things yet to come, not to be seen of the eye, or to be perceived by the senses, but inconceivably good things laid up by God for them that love him, which shall be the portion of our children and our friends if they believe in the living God. By faith we believe in things not seen as yet. We confess that, like Abraham, Isaac, and Jacob, we are strangers here, and we are journeying toward a place of which God has spoken to us: "A city which hath foundations, whose builder and maker is God." We have learned to talk about the crown which the Lord has laid up for us, and not for us only but for all them that love his appearing; and we delight to tell others how to win this crown. We point them to the narrow gate and to the narrow way, neither of which they can see, and to the end of that narrow road, even to the hilltops crowned with the celestial city where the pilgrims of the Lord shall dwell forever, and enjoy an eternal reward. Faith is wanted to enable us to point men to the invisible and eternal, and if we cannot do this how can we bless them? We must believe for those we love and have hope for them; thus shall we have power with God for them and shall bless them. O you worldly fathers, you may give your sons what heritage you can, and divide among your daughters what wealth you please, but as for us, our longing is to see our children and our children's children dowried with the riches which come from above. If they win a share in the land on the other side of Jordan, as yet unseen, and have a portion now in Christ Jesus, we shall be glad—infinitely more glad than if they were the richest among mankind. Our legacies to our sons are the blessings of grace, and our dowries to our daughters are the promises of the Lord.

It is well worthy of our notice that *the venerable patriarch Jacob in his benediction particularly mentioned the covenant.* His faith, like the faith of most of God's people, made the covenant its pavilion of delightful abode, its tower of defense, and its armory for war. No sweeter word was on his tongue than the covenant, and no richer consolation sustained his heart. He said to Joseph, "God almighty appeared unto me at Luz in the land of Canaan, and blessed me, and said unto me, 'Behold I will make thee fruitful, and multiply thee.'" His confidence rested in the promise of the Lord, and in the divine fidelity: that was the fountain truth from which he drew the inspiration which led him to bless his grandchildren. And, also, you notice, how he dwells upon the name of his father Abraham, and of his father Isaac, with whom the covenant had aforetime been established: the memories of covenant love are precious, and every confirmatory token is treasured up and dwelled upon. Dying men do not talk nonsense. They get to something solid, and the everlasting covenant made with their fathers, and confirmed in their own persons, has been one of the grand things about which dying saints have been wont to deliver their souls. Recollect how David said, "Although my house be not so with God, yet hath he made with me an everlasting covenant, ordered in all things and sure."

While we are sitting here, we can talk about the matter coolly, but when the death dew lies cold upon the brow, and the pulse is failing, and the throat is gradually choking up, it will be blessed to fix the eye upon the faithful Promiser and to feel a calm within the soul which even death pangs cannot disturb, because we can then exclaim, "I know whom I have believed, and I am persuaded that he is able to keep that which I have committed to him until that day."

I want to call your attention to one point which I think extraordinarily illustrates the faith of Jacob. In distributing to these two grandchildren his blessings as to the future, he takes them right away from Joseph, and says, "As Simeon and Reuben shall they be mine." Do you know who those two young gentlemen were? Think a while, and you will see that they were very different in rank, station, parentage, and prospects from any of the sons of Jacob. Jacob's sons had been brought up as laboring men, without knowledge of polite society or learned arts. They were countrymen, mere Bedouins, wandering shepherds, and nothing else; but these two young gentlemen were descended from a princess, and had, no doubt, been liberally educated. Pharaoh had given to Joseph a daughter of Potipherah, priest of On, and the priests of Egypt were the highest class of all—the nobility of the land. Joseph himself was prime minister, and these were partakers of his lofty rank. The sons of Reuben and Simeon were nobodies in the polite circles of Egypt—very good, decent people, farmers and graziers, but not at all of the high class of the Right Honorable Lord Manasseh and the Honorable Ephraim. Indeed, every shepherd was an abomination to the Egyptians, and therefore inadmissible to Egypt's nobility; but Manasseh and Ephraim were of a superior caste, and gentlemen of position and fortune. But *Jacob showed his faith by ignoring worldly advantages for his grandsons.* He says to Joseph, "They are not to be yours. I do not know them as Egyptians, I forget all about their mother's rank and family. The boys have attractive prospects before them; they can be made priests of the idol temple, and rise to high dignities among the Egyptians; but all that glitter we reject for them, and in token thereof I adopt them as my own sons; they are mine; as Simeon and Reuben they shall be mine. For all the gold of Egypt you would not have one of them serve an idol, for I know that you are true to your father's God and your father's faith." And so he takes the boys right away, you see, from all their brilliant opportunities, and bestows upon them that which, to the carnal mind, appears to be an estate in dreamland, a chateau in Spain, something intangible and unmarketable. This was a deed of faith, and blessed are they who can imitate it, choosing rather the reproach of Christ for their sons than all the treasures of Egypt. The joy of it is that these lads accepted the exchange, and let the golden possessions of Egypt go like Moses after them. May our heirs and successors be of like mind, and may the Lord say of them, "Out of Egypt have I called my son"; and again, "When Ephraim was a child then I loved him, and called my son out of Egypt."

We are not done yet, for we notice that Jacob *showed his faith by blessing Joseph's sons in God's order.* He placed Ephraim before Manasseh. It was not according to the rule of nature, but he felt the impulse upon him, and his faith would not resist the divine guidance: blind as he was he would not yield to the dictation of his son, but crossed his hands to obey the divine monition. Faith resolves to do the right thing in the right way. Some persons' faith leads them to do the right thing the wrong way upward, but matured faith follows the order which God prescribes. If God will have Ephraim first, faith does not quarrel with his decree. We may wish to see a favorite child blessed more than another, but nature must forgo her choice, for the Lord must do what seems him good. Faith prefers grace to talent, and piety to cleverness; she lays her right hand where God lays it, and not where beauty of person or quickness of intellect would suggest. Our best child is that which God calls best; faith corrects reason and accepts the divine verdict.

Notice that *he manifested his faith by his distinct reference to redemption.* He alone who has faith will pray for the redemption of his children, especially when they exhibit no signs of being in bondage, but are hopeful and amiable. The good old man prayed, "The angel which redeemed me from all evil, bless the lads." Let your faith bring down upon your children a share in redemption's blessings, for they need to be redeemed even as others. If they are washed in the blood of Jesus, if they are reconciled to God by the blood of his Son, if they have access to God by the blood of atonement, you may die well satisfied; for what is to harm them when once the angel that redeemed you has also redeemed them? From sin, from Satan, from death, from hell, from self—"from all evil" does our Redeemer set us free; and this is the greatest of all benedictions which we can pronounce upon our dearest children.

Jacob showed his faith by his assurance that God would be present with his seed. How cheering is the old man's dying expression, made not only to his boys, but concerning all his family. He said, "Now I die, but God will be with you." It is very different from the complaints of certain good old ministers when they are dying. They seem to say, "When I die, the light of Israel will be quenched. I shall die, and the people will desert the truth. When I am gone the standard-bearer will have fallen, and the watchman on the walls will be dead." Many in dying are afraid for the chariot of Israel and the horsemen thereof; and, sometimes, we who are in good health talk very much in the same fashion as though we were wonderfully essential to the progress of God's cause. I have known some of our church members speak in that manner, and inquire: "What should we do if Mr. So-and-So were dead? If our pastor were gone, what would the church do?" I will tell you what you will do without us: I will put the case as though I were myself to die: "Now I die, but God will be with you." Whoever passes away, the Lord will abide with his people, and the church will be secure. The grand old cause does not depend on one or two of us. God forbid! The truth was mighty in the land before the best man living was born, and the truth will not be buried with him, but in its own immortal youth will still be powerful; yes, and fresh advocates will arise more full of life and vigor than we are, and greater victories will be won. It is grand to say with Jacob, "Now I die, but God will be with you." Such language honors God and bespeaks a mind greatly trustful and completely delivered from the self-conceit which dreams itself important, if not necessary, to the cause of God.

II. We are told, next, that the old man "worshiped"—*worshiped by faith.*

Very briefly let me tell you what worship I think he rendered.

First, while he was dying he offered the worship of *gratitude.* How pleasing is the incident recorded in the tenth and eleventh verses, "Now the eyes of Israel were dim for age, so that he could not see. And Joseph brought his two sons near unto him; and he kissed them and embraced them. And Israel said unto Joseph, 'I had not thought to see thy face: and, lo, God hath showed me also thy seed.'" Ah, yes, we shall often have to say, "O Lord, I had not thought that thou wouldst do as much as this, but thou hast gone far beyond what I asked or even thought." I hope that this will be among our dying speeches and confessions, that the half was never told us, that our good Lord kept the best wine till the last, and that the end of the feast on earth, being but the beginning of the feast eternal in heaven, was the crown of all. Let us declare concerning our Lord that we found him better and better and better and better, even till we entered into his rest. He has been at first better than our fears, then better than our hopes, and finally better than our desires.

Did he not also offer the worship of *testimony,* when he acknowledged God's goodness to him all his life? He says, "The God that fed me all my life long," thus owning that he had been always dependent but always supplied. He had been a shepherd, and he uses a word here which means "the God that shepherdized me—who was a Shepherd to me all my life long." It was a testimony to the care and tenderness of Jehovah. Yes, and I hope we also shall finish life by magnifying the goodness of the Lord. Be this our witness, "He fed me all my life long. I was in straits sometimes, and I wondered where the next bit of bread would come from; but if he did not send a raven, or if he did not find a widow woman to provide for me, yet somehow or other he did feed me all my life long. He worked in his own wise way, so that I never lacked, for the Lord was my Shepherd all my life long."

Notice, too, how reverently he worships the covenant Messenger with the adoration of *reverent love.* He speaks of "the Angel who redeemed me from all evil." He thinks of the Angel that wrestled with him, and the Angel that appeared to him when he fell asleep at Bethel. This is the Angel, not an ordinary angel, but the true archangel—Jesus Christ—the Messenger of the covenant whom we delight in. It is he that has delivered us from all evil by his redeeming blood, for no other being could have accomplished a redemption so complete. Do you remember when he came to you personally, and wrestled with you and tore away your self-righteousness, and made you limp upon your thigh? This it may be was your first introduction to him. You saw him by night, and thought him at the first to be rather your enemy than your friend. Do you recollect when he took your strength away from you, and then at last saved you, because in utter weakness, you were about to fall to the ground, you laid hold of him and said, "I will not let thee go except thou bless me," and so you won a blessing from him? You had thought beforehand that you had strength in yourself, but now you learned that you were weakness itself, and that only as you became consciously weak would you become actually strong. You learned to look out of self to him, and do you not bless him for having taught you such a lesson? Will you not when you come to die bless him for what he did for you then, and all your life long? O my brethren, we owe all things to the redeeming Angel of the covenant. The evils which he has warded off from us are terrible beyond conception, and the blessings he has brought us are rich beyond imagination.

Thus you have had a picture of the old man blessing by faith, and worshiping by faith: faith was the mainspring of the two actions, their essence, their spirit, and their crown.

III. The last matter for us to speak upon is *his attitude.*

He "worshiped leaning upon the top of his staff." The Romanists have made fine mischief out of this text, for they have read it, "He worshiped the top of his staff," and their notion has been, I suppose, that there was a pretty little god carved on the top—an image of a saint or a cross, or some other symbol, and that he held up that emblem, and so worshiped the top of his staff. We know that he did no such thing, for there is no trace in Abraham, Isaac, or Jacob of anything like the worship of images; though teraph worship lingered in their families, it was not with their consent. They were not perfect men, but they were perfectly clear from idolatry, and never worshiped an image. No, no, no; they worshiped God alone. He worshiped on the top of his staff—leaning on it, supporting himself upon it. In Genesis you read that he "bowed himself upon the bed's head." It is a very curious thing that the word for *bed* and the word for *staff* in the Hebrew are so exceedingly like each other that unless the little points had been used, which I suppose were not used at all in the olden time, it would be difficult to tell whether the word is "bed" or "staff." I do not, however, think either Moses or Paul can be wrong. Jacob strengthened himself and sat upon the bed, and he leaned upon his staff too. It is very easy to realize a position in which both descriptions would be equally true. He could sit upon the bed, and lean on the top of his staff at the same time.

But why did he lean on his staff? What was that for? I think besides the natural need which he had of it, because of his being old, he did it emblematically. Do you not remember his saying, "With my staff I cross this Jordan"? I believe he kept that staff throughout life as a memorial. It was a favorite staff of his which he took with him on his first journey, and he leaned upon it as he took his last remove. "With my staff I crossed this Jordan," he had said before, and now with that staff in hand he crosses the spiritual Jordan. That staff was his life companion, the witness with himself of the goodness of the Lord, even as some of us may have an old Bible or a knife or a chair which are connected with memorable events of our lives.

But what did that staff indicate? Let us hear what Jacob said at another time. When he stood before Pharaoh he exclaimed, "Few and evil have been the days of my pilgrimage." What made him use that word *pilgrimage*? Why, because upon his mind there was always the idea of his being a pilgrim. He had been literally so during the early part of his life, wandering hither and thither; and now, though he has been seventeen years in Goshen, he keeps the old staff, and he leans on it to show that he had always been a pilgrim and a sojourner like his fathers, and that he was so still. While he leans on that staff he talks to Joseph, and he says, "Do not let my bones lie here. I have come hither in the providence of God, but I do not belong here. This staff indicates that I am only a sojourner here, and want to be gone. I am in Egypt, but I am not of it. Take my bones away. Do not let them lie here, for if they do, my sons and daughters will mingle with the Egyptians, and that must not be, for we are a distinct nation. God has chosen us for himself, and we must keep separate. To make my children see this, lo, here I die with my pilgrim staff in my hand."

Now, Christian brother, I want you to live in the same spirit, feeling that this is not your rest nor your native country. There is nothing here that is worthy of you. Your home is yonder, on the other side of the desert, where God has mapped out your portion. Christ has gone to prepare your place, and it would ill become you to have no desires for it. The longer you live, the more let this thought grow upon you: "Give me my staff. I must be gone. Poor world, thou art no rest for me; I am not of thy children, I am an alien and a stranger. My citizenship is in heaven, I take my share in Egypt's politics and Egypt's labor, yes, and in Egypt's griefs, but I am no Egyptian; I am a stranger bound for another land." Worship on the top of your staff, and sing—

A scrip on my back, and a staff in my hand,
I march on in haste through an enemy's land;
There is nothing on earth which can tempt me to stay,
My staff is the emblem of "up and away."

Singular enough is it that each descendant of Jacob came to worship on the top of his staff at last, for on the paschal supper night, when the blood was sprinkled on the lintel and the side posts, they each one ate the lamb with their loins girt and with a staff in his hand. The supper was a festival of worship, and they ate it each one leaning on his staff, as those that were in haste to leave home for a pilgrimage through the wilderness.

My dear hearers, this advice does not apply to all of you, for you are not all Jacobs, nor do you belong to the believing seed. I cannot bid you take your staff, for if you were to take your staff and start off, where would you go? You have no portion in the next world, no promised land, no Canaan flowing with milk and honey. Whither will you go? You must be banished from the presence of the Lord, and from the glory of his power. Alas for you! You cannot worship, for you know not God; you cannot bless others, for you have not been blessed yourselves. May the Lord bring you to his dear Son Jesus Christ, and lead you to put your trust in him, and then I shall hope that being saved you will by faith imitate Jacob, and both bless men, worship God, and wait with your staff in your hand, ready to journey to the eternal rest.

Joseph: A Miniature Portrait

Delivered on Lord's Day morning, July 24, 1881, at the Metropolitan Tabernacle, Newington. No. 1610.

The LORD was with Joseph.—GENESIS 39:2

Scripture frequently sums up a man's life in a single sentence. Here is the biography of Joseph sketched by inspiration—"God was with him," so Stephen testified in his famous speech recorded in Acts 7:9. Here is the life story of Abraham: "Abraham believed God." Of Moses we read, "The man Moses was very meek." Take a New Testament life, such as that of John the Baptist, and you have it in a line: "John did no miracle: but all things that he spoke concerning Jesus were true." The mere name of John—"that disciple whom Jesus loved"—would serve for all an epitaph of him: it pictures both the man and his history. Holy Scripture excels in this kind of full-length miniature painting. As Michaelangelo is said to have drawn a portrait with a single stroke of his crayon, so the Spirit of God sketches a man to the life in a single sentence. "The LORD was with Joseph."

Observe, however, that the portraits of Scripture give us not only the outer, but the inner life of the man. Man looks at the outward appearance, but the Lord looks upon the heart; and so the scriptural descriptions of men are not of their visible life alone, but of their spiritual life. Here we have Joseph as God saw him, the real Joseph. Externally it did not always appear that God was with him, for he did not always seem to be a prosperous man; but when you come to look into the inmost soul of this servant of God, you see his true likeness—he lived in communion with the Most High, and God blessed him: "The LORD was with Joseph, and he was a prosperous man." Dear friends, how would you like to have your inner biography sketched? How would your soul appear if set out in detail before all the world as to its desires, affections, and thoughts? Many lives have looked well on paper, but beneath their surface the biographer never dared to dive, or, perhaps, could not have dived had he been anxious to do so. It is often thought wise in writing a man's life to suppress certain matters: this may be prudent if the design be to guard a reputation, but it is scarcely truthful. The Spirit of God does not suppress the faults even of those whom we most admire, but writes them fully, like the Spirit of truth, as he is. The man who above others was "a man after God's own heart" was yet in some points exceedingly faulty, and he committed one foul deed which will remain through all time as a blemish upon his character. There was in David so firm and undeviating an attachment to the Lord God, and so sincere a desire to do right, and so deep a repentance when he had erred, that the Lord still regarded him as after his own heart, although he smote him heavily for his transgressions. David was a truly sincere man despite the faults into which he fell, and it is the heart of David which is sketched. So here, the Spirit is not looking so much at Joseph as a favorite child or an Egyptian prime minister, as at the innermost and truest Joseph, and therefore he thus describes him: "The LORD was with Joseph."

This striking likeness of Joseph strongly reminds us of our Master and Lord, that greater Joseph, who is Lord over all the world for the sake of Israel. Peter, in his sermon to the household of Cornelius, said of our Lord that he "went about doing good, and healing all that were oppressed of the devil; for God was with him." Exactly what had been said of Joseph. It is wonderful that the same words should describe both Jesus and Joseph, the perfect Savior and the imperfect patriarch. When you and I are perfected in grace, we shall wear the image of Christ, and that which will describe Christ will also describe us. Those who live with Jesus will be transformed by his fellowship till they become like him. To my mind, it is very beautiful to see the resemblance between the firstborn and the rest of the family, between the great typical man, the Second Adam, and all those men who are quickened into his life, and are one with him.

This having the Lord with us is the inheritance of all the saints; for what is the apostolic benediction in the epistles but a desire that the triune God may be with us? To the church in Rome Paul says, "Now the God of peace be with you all." To the church in Corinth he writes, "The grace of the Lord Jesus Christ, and the love of God, and the communion of the Holy Ghost, be with you all. Amen." To the Thessalonians he says, "The Lord be with you all." Did not our glorious Lord say, "Lo, I am with you always, even unto the end of the world"? How better could I salute you this morning than in the words of Boaz to the reapers, "The LORD be with you"? What kinder answer could you give me than "The LORD bless thee"? High up upon the mountains which form the back wall of Mentone I happened one day to meet a Quaker, in the usual costume, a warm-hearted lover of all who love Jesus. He saluted me, and we found great unity of spirit. On parting, I said, "Friend, the Lord be with thee"; and he answered, "And with thy spirit," adding, "It is the first bit of the liturgy that I have ever used." Truly, the more often we can use it with our hearts the better, for none can object to it. Thus do I say to all of you this day, "The Lord be with you," and I know that you are responding, "And with thy spirit." May you find that your desire is granted, by the Holy Spirit's being with my Spirit that I may speak words which shall refresh your hearts.

Now let us think of Joseph and see what we can learn from him. "The LORD was with Joseph": let us consider, first, the fact; second, the evidence of that fact; and third, the result of that fact.

I. First, we will run over Joseph's life, and note *the fact*: "The LORD was with Joseph."

God was gracious to Joseph as *a child*. His father loved him because he was the son of his old age, and also because of the gracious qualities which he saw in him. Before he was seventeen years of age, God had spoken with him in dreams and visions of the night, of which we read that "his brethren envied him; but his father observed the saying." Dear young people, it may be that God will not appear to you in dreams, but he has other ways of speaking to his young Samuels. You remember he said, "Samuel, Samuel," and the beloved child answered, "Speak, LORD, for thy servant heareth." May you answer in the same manner to the call of God by his word. It was the happy privilege of some of us before we had left boyhood and girlhood to have received gracious communications from God: he led us to repentance, he led us to faith in Christ, and he revealed his love in our hearts before we had left the schoolroom and the playground. They begin well who begin early with Christ: he will be with us to the end if we are with him at the beginning. If Joseph had not been a godly boy, he might never have been a gracious man: grace made him to differ from his brothers in youth, and he remained their superior all his days. If we are gracious while we are yet children, we may be sure that the Lord will be gracious to us even should we live to old age, and see our children's children. Early piety is likely to be eminent piety. Happy are those who have Christ with them in the morning, for they shall walk with him all day, and sweetly rest with him at eventide.

"The LORD was with Joseph" when Joseph was at home, and he did not desert him when he was sent away from his dear father and his beloved home and was sold for *a slave*. Bitter is the lot of a slave in any country, and it was worst of all in those early days. We are told by Stephen that the patriarchs, moved with envy, sold Joseph into Egypt, but the Lord was with him; even when he was being sold the Lord was with Joseph. It must have been a very dreadful journey for him across the desert, urged onward by those rough Ishmaelites, probably traveling in a gang, as slaves do to this day in the center of

Africa. May God put an end to the abominable system! This delicate child of an indulgent father, who had been clothed with a princely garment of many colors, must now wear the garb of a slave, and march in the hot sun across the burning sand; but never was captive more submissive under cruel treatment; he endured as seeing him who is invisible; his heart was sustained by a deep confidence in the God of his father Jacob, for "Jehovah was with him." I think I see him in the slave market exposed for sale. We have heard with what trembling anxiety the slave peers into the faces of those who are about to buy. Will he get a good master? Will one purchase him who will treat him like a man, or one who will use him worse than a brute? "The LORD was with Joseph" as he stood there to be sold, and he fell into good hands. When he was taken away to his master's house, and the various duties of his service were allotted to him, the Lord was with Joseph.

The house of the Egyptian had never been so pure, so honest, so honored before. Beneath Joseph's charge it was secretly the temple of his devotions, and manifestly the abode of comfort and confidence. That Hebrew slave had a glory of character about him which all perceived, and especially his master, for we read, "His master saw that the LORD was with him, and that the LORD made all that he did to prosper in his hand. And Joseph found grace in his sight, and he served him: and he made him overseer over his house, and all that he had he put into his hand. And it came to pass from the time that he had made him overseer in his house, and over all that he had, that the LORD blessed the Egyptian's house for Joseph's sake; and the blessing of the LORD was upon all that he had in the house and in the field." Joseph's diligence, integrity, and gentleness won upon his master, as well they might. O that all of you who are Christian servants would imitate Joseph in this, and so behave yourselves that all around you may see that the Lord is with you.

Then came a crisis in his history, the time of testing. We see Joseph *tried by a temptation* in which, alas, so many perish. He was attacked in a point at which youth is peculiarly vulnerable. His comely person made him the object of unholy solicitations from one upon whose goodwill his comfort greatly depended, and had it not been that the Lord was with him he must have fallen. The mass of mankind would scarcely have blamed him had he sinned: they would have cast the crime upon the tempter, and excused the frailty of youth. I say not so; God forbid I should; for in acts of uncleanness neither of the transgressors may be excused; but God was with Joseph, and he did not slide when set in slippery places. Thus he escaped that deep pit into which the abhorred of the Lord do fall. He was rescued from the snare of the strange woman, of whom Solomon has said, "She hath cast down many wounded;

yes, many strong men have been slain by her. Her house is the way to hell, going down to the chambers of death." Slavery itself was a small calamity compared with that which would have happened to young Joseph had he been enslaved by wicked passions. Happily, the Lord was with him, and enabled him to overcome the tempter with the question, "How can I do this great wickedness, and sin against God?" He fled. That flight was the truest display of courage. It is the only way of victory in sins of the flesh. The apostle says, "Flee youthful lusts which war against the soul." When Telemachus was in the isle of Calypso his mentor cried, "Fly, Telemachus, fly; there remains no hope of a victory but by flight." Wisely Joseph left his garment and fled, for God was with him.

The scene shifts again, and he who had been first a favored child at home, and then a slave, and then a tempted one, now becomes *a prisoner.* The prisons of Egypt were, doubtless, as horrible as all such places were in the olden times, and here is Joseph in the noisome dungeon. He evidently felt his imprisonment very much, for we are told in the Psalms that "the iron entered into his soul." He felt it a cruel thing, to be under such a slander, and to suffer for his innocence. A young man so pure, so chaste, must have felt it to be sharper than a whip of scorpions to be accused as he was; yet as he sat down in the gloom of his cell, the Lord was with him. The degradation of a prison had not deprived him of his divine companion. Blessed be the name of the Lord, he does not forsake his people when they are in disgrace: no, he is more pleasant with them when they are falsely accused than at any other time, and he cheers them in their low estate. God was with him, and very soon the kindly manners, the gentleness, the activity, the truthfulness, the industry of Joseph had won upon the keeper of the prison, so that Joseph rose again to the top, and was the overseer of the prison. Like a cork, which you may push down, but it is sure to come up again, so was Joseph: he must swim, he could not drown, the Lord was with him. The Lord's presence made him a king and a priest wherever he went, and men tacitly owned his influence. In the little kingdom of the prison Joseph reigned, for "God was with him."

He will rise higher than that, however, when opportunity arises for a display of *prophetic power.* Two of those under his charge appeared to be despondent one morning, and with his usual gentleness he asked, "Wherefore look ye so sadly today?" He was always kindly and sympathetic, and so they told him their dreams, and he interpreted them as the events actually fell out. But why did he interpret dreams? It was because God was with him. He tells them there and then that "interpretations belong unto God." It was not that he had knowledge of an occult art, or was clever at guessing, but the Spirit of God rested upon him, and so he understood the secrets veiled beneath the dreams.

This led to further steps, for after having been tried from seventeen to thirty, after having served thirteen years' apprenticeship to sorrow he came to stand *before Pharaoh,* and God is with him there. You can see that he is inwardly upheld, for the Hebrew youth stands boldly forth and talks of God in an idolatrous court. Pharaoh believed in multitudes of gods: he worshiped the crocodile, the ibis, the bull, and all manner of things, even down to leeks and onions, so that one said of the Egyptians, "Happy people, whose gods grow in their own gardens"; but Joseph was not ashamed to speak of his God as the only living and true God. He said, "What God is about to do he showeth unto Pharaoh." Calmly, and in a dignified manner, he unravels the dream, and explains it all to Pharaoh, disclaiming, however, all credit for wisdom. He says, "It is not in me: God shall give Pharaoh an answer of peace." God was with him indeed.

Joseph was made *ruler* over all Egypt, and God was with him. Well did the king say, "Can we find such a man as this is in whom the Spirit of God is?" His policy in storing up corn in the plenteous years succeeded admirably, for God was evidently working by him to preserve the human race from extinction by famine. His whole system, if looked at as executed in the interest of Pharaoh, his master, was beyond measure sensible and successful. He was not the servant of the Egyptians: Pharaoh had promoted him, and Pharaoh he enriched, and at the same time saved a nation from hunger.

God was with him in bringing down his father and the family into Egypt, and locating them in Goshen, and with him till he himself came to die, when he "took an oath of the children of Israel, saying God will surely visit you, and ye shall carry up my bones from hence." The Lord was with him, and kept him faithful to the covenant, and the covenanted race, even to the close of a long life of 110 years. He died faithful to the close to the God of his fathers, for he would not be numbered with Egypt, with all its learning and all its wealth; he chose to be accounted an Israelite and to share with the chosen race, whatever their fortunes might be. He, like the rest of the patriarchs, died in faith, looking for the promised inheritance, and for its sake renouncing the riches and glories of the world, for the Lord was with him.

II. We shall next review *the evidence of the fact* that God was with him.

What is the evidence that the Lord was with Joseph? The first evidence of it is this: *he was always under the influence of the divine presence,* and lived in the enjoyment of it. I shall not need to quote the instances—all of them, at any rate—for everywhere, whenever Joseph's heart speaks, he lets you know that he is conscious that God is with him. Take him under temptation especially. Oh, what a mercy it was for him that he was a God-fearing man! "How can I do this great wickedness, and sin against Potiphar?" No. Yet he would have sinned against Potiphar, who had been a kindly master to him. Does he say, "How shall I do this great wickedness, and sin against this woman?" for it would have been a sin against her. No; but just as David said, "Against thee, thee only, have I sinned, and done this evil in thy sight," making the main point and consideration to be sin against God, so did Joseph, as he fled from the seducer, argue thus, "How can I do this great wickedness, and sin against God?" Oh, if you and I always felt that God was near, looking steadily upon us, we should not dare to sin. The presence of a superior often checks a man from doing what else he might have ventured on, and the presence of God, if it were realized, would be a perpetual barrier against temptation, and would keep us steadfast in holiness. When Joseph afterward at any time spoke of God, when God helped him not only to stand against temptation but to do any service, you will notice how he always ascribes it to God. He will not interpret Pharaoh's dream without first telling him, "It is not in me: God hath showed Pharaoh what he is about to do." He was as conscious of the presence of God when he stood before the great monarch as when he refused that sinful woman. It was the same in his domestic life.

Let me read out of his family register. "And unto Joseph were born two sons before the years of famine came, which Asenath the daughter of Potipherah priest of On bare unto him. And Joseph called the name of the firstborn Manasseh: For God, said he, hath made me forget all my toil, and all my father's house. And the name of the second called he Ephraim: For God hath caused me to be fruitful in the land of my affliction." When his aged father said to him, "Who are these?" he replied very beautifully, "They are my sons, whom God hath given me in this place." I am afraid that we do not habitually talk in this fashion, but Joseph did. Without the slightest affectation he spoke out of his heart, under a sense of the divine presence and working. How like he is in this to our divine Lord! I cannot help speaking of it. If there is any good thing more marked about our Lord Jesus than another it is his sense of the divine presence. You see it when he is a child: "Knew ye not that I must be about my Father's business?" You hear it in the words, "I am not alone, because the Father is with me"; and again, "I know that thou hearest me always."

You perceive it forcibly in the last moment of his earthly life, when the sharpest pang that tortures him is that which makes him cry, "My God, my God, why hast thou forsaken me?" The presence of God was everything to

Christ as it was to Joseph. Now, if you and I set the Lord always before us, if our soul dwells in God, depend upon it, God is with us. There is no mistake about it. If you are under the influence of that text, "Thou God seest me," you may be sure that his presence will go with you, and he will give you rest. No man ever perceived God to be present and therefore walked before him in holiness, and afterward discovered that he had been under a delusion. Grace in the life proves that the God of grace is with us.

The next evidence is this: God was certainly with Joseph because *he was pure in heart.* "Blessed are the pure in heart, for they shall see God"; no other can do so. God will not manifest himself to those whose hearts are unclean. He that hath clean hands and a pure heart, he shall dwell on high. Our Lord Jesus said, "If a man love me, he will keep my words: and my Father will love him, and we will come unto him, and make our abode with him." When the heart is shocked at sin, and enamored of holiness, then it can enter into communion with God, and not till then. "Can two walk together unless they be agreed?" When I hear some professors admit that they have little communion with God, can I wonder at it? How can God have fellowship with us unless we walk obediently in his ways? What fellowship hath light with darkness? Or "what concord hath Christ with Belial?" The intense purity of Joseph was a proof that the thrice holy God was ever with him. He will keep the feet of his saints. When they are tempted he will deliver them from evil, for his presence sheds an atmosphere of holiness around the heart in which he dwells.

The next evidence in Joseph's case was *the diligence with which he exercised himself wherever he was.* God was with Joseph, and therefore the man of God hardly cared as to the outward circumstances of his position, but began at once to work that which is good. He was in the pit: yes, but the Lord was with Joseph, and the pit was not horrible to him: he pleaded with his brothers, and although they would not hear, he did his duty in warning them of their crime. He was carried captive of the Ishmaelites; but in the caravan he was safe, for God was with him. When he came to be a slave in Potiphar's house, the Lord was with him, and he was a prosperous man; the change of scene was not a change of his dearest company. He did not strike an attitude and make a display of his grand intentions, but he went to work where he was, and performed ordinary duties with great heartiness, for the Lord was with him. Many would have said, "I have been unrighteously sold for a slave. I ought not to be here, and I am not bound to perform any duties to Potiphar: rightfully I am a free man, as free as Potiphar, and I shall not work for him for nothing." No, the Lord was with him, and therefore he applied himself to that which lay next to hand, and went to work with a will. No doubt he performed menial service in the house at first, and then, by degrees, he rose to be the manager of the establishment. The truly godly man is ready for anything: he does not vie for place, but accepts the state in which he is found, and does good in it, for the Lord's sake.

The Lord was with Joseph nonetheless when he was cast into the prison. He knew God was with him in prison, and therefore he did not sit down sullenly in his sorrow, but he bestirred himself to make the best of his afflicted condition. Since the Lord was with him there, he was comforted; it would be infinitely better to be there with God than on the throne of Pharaoh without God. He did not mourn and moan, and spend his time in writing petitions to Potiphar, or making appeals to Potiphar. He set himself to be of service to his fellow prisoners and the warders, and very soon he was to the front again, for "The LORD was with him." When he came to be exalted, and Pharaoh made him to be ruler over Egypt, notice what he did. He did not strut about, or take his case at court; he did not stop to enjoy his honors in peace, and leave others to do the business, but he set to his work personally and at once. Read Genesis 41:45: "And Joseph went out over all the land of Egypt." Then read the next verse: "And Joseph went out from the presence of Pharaoh, and went throughout all the land of Egypt." No sooner did he get the office than he gave himself to the execution of it, personally inspecting the whole country. Many are so worn out by their toils in getting a place that they have no strength left for performing its duties. When they get a new situation, their first consideration is how they shall spend the profits of it. Place hunters seldom try to make themselves fit for the situation, but crave the position whether they are fit for it or not. Many when they get an office are exceedingly skillful in showing how not to do it; they get into the circumlocution office, and pass on everything to the next clerk, and, he to the next, so that nothing is done with them: procrastination is the very hinge of business, and punctuality the thief of time. They do as little as they can for the money, upon the theory that if you are too energetic your labors will be too cheap. Joseph, however, was not of that sort, for no sooner was he made commissioner-general of Egypt, than he was up to his eyes in the task of building storehouses, and gathering up grain to fill them. By his wonderful economic policy he supplied the people in the time of famine, and in the process the power of Pharaoh was greatly strengthened. The Lord was with him, therefore he did not think of the honor to which he had been promoted, but of the responsibility which had been laid upon him, and he gave himself wholly to his great work. That is what you and I must do if we are to give practical proof that God is with us.

But notice again, God was with Joseph, and *that made him tender and sympathetic.* Some men who are prompt enough in business are rough, coarse, hard; but not so Joseph. His tenderness distinguishes him; he is full of loving consideration. When he had prisoners in his charge, he did not treat them roughly, but with much consideration. He watched their countenances, inquired into their troubles, and was willing to do all in his power for them. This was one secret of his success in life; he was everybody's friend. He who is willing to be the servant of all, the same shall be the chief of all. God was with Joseph, and taught him compassion, for God himself is very pitiful, and full of sympathy for the suffering.

Perhaps you will object to this, that Joseph seemed for a while to afflict and tantalize his brothers. By no means. He was seeking their good. The love he bore to them was wise and prudent. God, who is far more loving than Joseph, frequently afflicts us to bring us to repentance and to heal us of many evils. Joseph wished to bring his brethren into a right state of heart, and he succeeded in it, though the process was more painful to him than to them. At last he could not restrain himself, but burst into weeping before them all, for there was a big loving heart under the Egyptian garb of Joseph. He loved with all his soul, and so will every man who has God with him, for "God is love." If you do not love, God is not with you. If you go through the world selfish and morose, bitter, suspicious, bigoted, hard, the devil is with you, God is not; for where God is he expands the spirit, he causes us to love all mankind with the love of benevolence, and he makes us take a sweet complacency in the chosen brotherhood of Israel, so that we specially delight to do good to all those who are of the household of faith. This was a mark that God was with him.

Another mark of God's presence with Joseph is *his great wisdom.* He did everything as it ought to be done. You can scarcely alter anything in Joseph's life to improve it, and I think if I admire his wisdom in one thing more than another it is in his wonderful silence. It is easy to talk, comparatively, easy to talk well, but to be quiet is the difficulty. He never said a word, that I can learn, about Potiphar's wife. It seemed necessary to his own defense, but he would not accuse the woman; he let judgment go by default, and left her to her own conscience and her husband's cooler consideration. This showed great power; it is hard for a man to compress his lips, saying nothing when his character is at stake. So eloquent was Joseph in his silence that there is not a word of complaint throughout the whole record of his life. We cannot say that of all the Bible saints, for many of them complained bitterly, indeed we have whole books of lamentations. We do not condemn those who did complain, but we greatly admire those who, like sheep before the shearers, were dumb. The iron entered into his soul, but he does not tell us so; we look to the Psalms for that information; he bore in calm resignation all the great Father's will. When his brothers stood before him, the cruel men who sold him, he did not upbraid them, but he comforted them, saying, "Now therefore be not grieved, nor angry with yourselves, that ye sold me hither: for God did send me before you to preserve life." Making sweet excuse for them, he said, "And God sent me before you to preserve you a posterity in the earth, and to save yourselves by a great deliverance. So now it was not you that sent me hither, but God."

How different from the spirit of those people who pry about, seeking to discover faults, and when an imperfection is marked, they cry, "Look! Do you see that? I told you so. These good men are no better than they should be." Yes, it may be true that there are spots in the sun, but there are greater spots in your eyes or you would see more of the light. Those who see faults so readily have plenty of their own. Like the man who stole the goods and ran away, they try to turn the scent by calling, "thief, thief," after others. May God make us blind to the faults of his people, sooner than allow us to have a lynx eye for their flaws and an inventive faculty to ascribe ill motives to them. I wish we were as wisely silent as Joseph was. We may often repent of speech, but I think very seldom of silence. You may complain and be justified in the complaint, but you will have far more glory if you do not complain. For what was there, after all, for Joseph to complain of, since the Lord was with him? He was in prison: that is something to complain of. Yes, but if the Lord was with him the prison was no longer dreary. I would gladly go to prison any day if the Lord would be with me. Who would not? But Joseph was away from his beloved father, and the trotting of those little feet that be loved so much to hear—the feet of little brother Benjamin. I am sure Joseph always missed his mother's only other son, his only full brother. It was a great grief to him to be away from home, but still he was quiet, calm, and happy. God is with him if Benjamin is not; if father Jacob is away, God is present; thus he finds no cause for bitter lament, but much reason for accepting his lot and doing his best in each condition.

"God was with him," and this is the last evidence I give of it, that *he was kept faithful to the covenant,* faithful to Israel and to Israel's God right through. Pharaoh gave him in marriage the daughter of a priest; and the priests were the highest class throughout Egypt, and Joseph was thus promoted to be of the nobility by marriage, as well as to be at the head of all the nobility by office. They cried before him, "Bow the knee," and everyone honored him throughout all the land of Egypt. Yet he would not be an Egyptian: he was an Israelite still, and his good old father, when he came down into Egypt, found him one of the family in heart and soul. His father's blessing was greatly prized by him, and he obtained it for himself and for his sons. I notice with much pain that many professors who prosper in this world have not God with them, for they turn into Egyptians: they do not now care for the simple worship of God's people, but they sigh for something more showy and more respectable. They want society, and so they seek out a fashionable church, and swallow their principles. They lay it all upon their children, for who can expect young ladies and gentlemen to attend an ordinary meetinghouse, where such low people go? For the sake of the young people they are bound to mix with society, and so they leave their principles, their people, and their God. They become Egyptians; indeed, some of them would become devil worshipers to gain rank and status. Off they go to Egypt, shoals of them, I have seen it, and shall see it again. If some of you get rich I dare say you will do the same; it seems to be the way of men. As soon as a professor prospers in the world he is ashamed of the truth he once loved. Such apostates will find it heavy work to die. Verily, I say unto you, instead of their being ashamed of us, we have good reason to be ashamed of them, for it is to their disgrace that they cannot be content to associate with God's chosen because they happen to be poor and perhaps illiterate.

Joseph stuck to his people and to their God: though he must live in Egypt, he will not be an Egyptian; he will not even leave his dead body to lie in an Egyptian pyramid. The Egyptians built a very costly tomb for Joseph: it stands to this day, but his body is not there. "I charge you," says he, "take my bones with you; for I do not belong to Egypt, my place is in the land of promise." "He gave commandment concerning his bones." Let others do as they will; as for me, my lot is cast with those who follow the Lord fully. Yes, my Lord, where you dwell, I will dwell; your people shall be my people, and your God my God, and may my children be your children to the last generation. If the Lord is with you, that is what you will say, but if he is not with you, and you prosper in the world, and increase in riches, you will turn your back on Christ and his people, and we shall have to say, as Paul did, "Demas hath forsaken me, having loved this present world."

III. Third, let us observe, *the result of God's being with Joseph.*

The result was that "he was a prosperous man"; but notice that, although the Lord was with Joseph, *it did not screen him from hatred.* The Lord was with him, but his brethren hated him. Yes, and if the Lord loves a man, the world will spite him. We know that we are God's children, because the adversaries of God are our adversaries. Furthermore, "The LORD was with Joseph," but it did not screen him from *temptation* of the worst kind: it did not prevent his mistress casting her wicked eyes upon him. The best of men may be tempted to the worst of crimes. The presence of God did not screen him from *slander*: the base woman accused him of outrageous wickedness, and God permitted Potiphar to believe her. You and I would have said, "If the Lord be with us, how can this evil happen to us?" Ah, but the Lord was with him, and yet he was a slandered man. No, the divine presence did not screen him from *pain*: he sat in prison wearing fetters till the iron entered into his soul, and yet the Lord was with him. That presence did not save him from *disappointment*. He said to the butler, "Think of me when it is well with thee"; but the butler altogether forgot him. Everything may seem to go against you, and yet God may be with you. The Lord does not promise you that you shall have what looks like prosperity, but you shall have what is real prosperity in the best sense.

Now, what did God's being with Joseph do for him? First, *it saved him from gross sin*. He flees, he shuts his ears: he flees and conquers; for God is with him. O young friend, if God is with you in the hour of temptation, you will want no better, no grander result than to remain perfectly pure, with garments unspotted by the flesh.

God was with him, and the next result was it *enabled him to act grandly*. Wherever he is he does the right thing, does it splendidly. If he is a slave his master finds that he never had such a servant before; if he is in prison, those dungeons were never charmed by the presence of such a ministering angel before; if he is exalted to be with Pharaoh, Pharaoh never had such a chancellor of the exchequer in Egypt before, never was Egyptian finance so prosperous.

In such a manner did God help Joseph that he was enabled to *fulfill a glorious destiny*, for if Noah be the world's second father, what shall we say of Joseph, but that he was its foster nurse? The human race had died of famine if Joseph's foresight had not laid by in store the produce of the seven plenteous years, for there was a famine over all lands. The breasts of Joseph nourished all mankind. It was no mean position for the young Hebrew to occupy, to be manager of the commissariat of the whole known world. If God be with us we shall fulfill a noble destiny too. It may not be so widely known, so visible to human eye, but life is always ennobled by the presence of God.

Also *it gave him a very happy life*, for taking the life of Joseph all through, it is an enviable one. Nobody would think of putting him down among the miserable. If we had to make a selection of unhappy men, we certainly should not think of Joseph. No, it was a great life and a happy life; and such will yours be if God be with you.

And, to finish, God gave Joseph and his family *a double portion in Israel,* which never happened to any other of the twelve sons of Jacob. Jacob said, "And now thy two sons, Ephraim and Manasseh, which were born unto thee in the land of Egypt before I came unto thee into Egypt are mine; as Reuben and Simeon they shall be mine," thus making them into a tribe each. Ephraim and Manasseh each stood at the head of a tribe as if they had been actually sons of Jacob. Levi is taken out of the twelve, and provision is made for the Levites as servants of God, and then Ephraim and Manasseh are put in, so that Joseph's house figures twice among the twelve. There are two Josephs in Israel but only one Judah. Joseph has a double portion of the kingdom. Those who begin early with God, and stand fast to the end, and hold to God both in trouble and prosperity, shall see their children brought to the Lord, and in their children they shall possess the double, yes, the Lord shall render unto them double for all they may lose in honor for his name's sake. It may be they shall live to see the hand of the Lord upon their children and their children's children, and to them shall be fulfilled the word, "In thee shall Israel bless, saying, God make thee as Ephraim and as Manasseh." Let us seek after a double part with God's people by keeping heartily with them. Who is willing to suffer with them that he may reign with them? Who is willing to cast the riches of Egypt behind his back that he may have a double portion in the Promised Land, the land flowing with milk and honey? I think I hear some of you say, "Here I am, sir. I shall be glad enough to share with God's people, be it what it may." Carry Christ's cross and you shall wear Christ's crown. Go with him through the mire and through the slough, and you shall be with him in the palaces of glory; you shall share a double portion with him in the day of his appearing. This can only be because the Lord is with you: that must be the beginning and end of it. "The LORD was with Joseph"; O Lord, be with us. O thou, whose name is Emmanuel, God with us, be with us, henceforth and forever. Amen and amen.

Moses: Moses' Decision

Delivered on Lord's Day morning, July 28, 1872, at the Metropolitan Tabernacle, Newington. No. 1063.

> *By faith Moses, when he was come to years, refused to be called the son of Pharaoh's daughter; choosing rather to suffer affliction with the people of God, than to enjoy the pleasures of sin for a season; esteeming the reproach of Christ greater riches than the treasures in Egypt: for he had respect unto the recompense of the reward.*—HEBREWS 11:24–26

Last Sabbath day we spoke upon the faith of Rahab. We had then to mention her former unsavory character, and to show that, notwithstanding, her faith triumphed, and both saved her and produced good works. Now it has occurred to me that some persons would say, "This faith is, no doubt, a very suitable thing for Rahab and persons of that class; a people destitute of sweetness and light may follow after the gospel, and it may be a very proper and useful thing for them, but the better sort of people will never take to it." I thought it possible that, with a sneer of contempt, some might reject all faith in God, as being unworthy of persons of a higher condition of life and another manner of education. We have, therefore, taken the case of Moses, which stands as a direct contrast to that of Rahab, and we trust it may help to remove the sneer; though, indeed, that may be of small consequence, for if a man is given to sneering it is hardly worthwhile to waste five minutes in reasoning with him. The scorner is usually a person so inconsiderable that his scoffing deserves to be unconsidered. He who is great at sneering is good for nothing else, and he may as well be left to fulfill his vocation.

It occurred to me also that, peradventure, some might, in all seriousness, say, "I have, through the providence of God, and the circumstances which surround me, been kept from outward sin; moreover, I am not a member of the lowest ranks, and do not belong to the class of persons of whom Rahab would be a suitable representative. In fact, I have, by the providence of God, been placed in a choice position, and can, without egotism, claim a superior character." It is possible that such persons may feel as if they were placed under a disadvantage by this very superiority. The thought has passed over their mind, "The gospel is for sinners; it evidently comes to the chief of sinners and blesses them. We are free to admit that we are sinners, but peradventure, because we have not sinned so openly, we may not be so conscious of the sin, and consequently our mind may not be so well prepared to receive the abounding grace of God which comes to the vilest of the vile." I have known some who have almost wished that they were literally like the prodigal son in his wanderings, that they might be more readily like him in his return. It is altogether a mistake under which they labor, but it is by no means an uncommon one. Peradventure, as we introduce to their notice one of the heroes of faith, who was a man of noble rank, high education, and pure character, they may be led to correct their thoughts. Moses belonged to the noblest order of men, but he was saved by faith alone, even by the same faith which saved Rahab. This faith moved him to the faithful service of God and to a self-denial unparalleled. My earnest prayer is that you who are moral, amiable, and educated, may see in the action of Moses an example for yourselves. No longer despise a life of faith in God. It is the one thing which you lack, the one thing above all others needful. Are you young men of high position? Such was Moses. Are you men of spotless character? Such also was he. Are you now in a position where to follow out conscience will cost you dear? Moses endured as seeing him who is invisible, and though for a while a loser he is now an eternal gainer by the loss. May the Spirit of God incline you to follow in the path of faith, virtue, and honor, where you see such a man as Moses leading the way.

We shall first consider the decided action of Moses; and, second, the source of his decision of character—it was "by faith." Third, we shall look into those arguments by which his faith directed his action; after which we shall briefly reflect upon those practical lessons which the subject suggests.

I. And first let us observe *the decided action of Moses.*

"When he was come to years, he refused to be called the son of Pharaoh's daughter." We need not narrate the stories which are told by Josephus and other ancient writers with regard to the early days of Moses, such as, for instance, his taking the crown of Pharaoh and trampling upon it. These things may be true; it is equally possible that they are pure fiction. The Spirit of God has certainly taken no notice of them in holy Scripture, and what he does not think worth recording we need not think worth considering. Nor shall I more than hint at answers to the question why it was that Moses remained no less than forty years in the court of Pharaoh, and doubtless during that time was called "the son of Pharaoh's daughter," and, if he did not enjoy the pleasures of sin, at any rate, had his share in the treasures of Egypt. It is just possible that he was not a converted man up to the age of forty. Probably during his early days he was to all intents and purposes an Egyptian, an eager student, a great proficient in Egyptian wisdom, and also, as Stephen tells us in the Acts, "a man mighty in words and in deeds." During those early days he was familiar with philosophers and warriors, and perhaps in his engrossing pursuits he forgot his nationality.

We see the hand of God in his being forty years in the court of Pharaoh; whatever of evil or indecision in him may have kept him there we see the good result which God brought out of it, for he became by his experience and observation the better able to rule a nation, and a fitter instrument in the hand of God for fashioning the Israelitish state into its appointed form. Perhaps during the forty years he had been trying to do what a great many are aiming at just now; he was trying whether he could not serve God and remain the son of Pharaoh's daughter too. Perhaps he was of the mind of our brethren in a certain church who protest against but still remain in that church which gives to ritualism the fullest liberty. Perhaps he thought he could share the treasures of Egypt and yet bear testimony with Israel. He would be known as a companion of the priests of Isis and Osiris, and yet at the same time would bear honest witness for Jehovah. If he did not attempt this impossibility others in all ages have done so. It may be he quieted himself by saying that he had such remarkable opportunities for usefulness that he did not like to throw them up by becoming identified with the Israelitish dissenters of the period. An open avowal of his private sentiments would shut him out from good society, and especially from the court, where it was very evident that his influence was great and beneficial. It is just possible that the very feeling which still keeps so many good people in a wrong place may have operated upon Moses till he was forty years of age; but then, having reached the prime of his manhood, and having come under the influence of faith, he broke away from the ensnaring temptation, as I trust many of our worthy brethren will before long be able to do. Surely they will not always maintain a confederacy with the allies of Rome, but will be men enough to be free. If when Moses was a child he spoke as a child, and thought as a child, when he became a man he put away his childish ideas of compromise; if, when he was a young man, he thought he might conceal a part of the truth, and so might hold his position, when he came to ripe years enough to know what the truth fully was he scorned all compromise and came out boldly as the servant of the living God.

The Spirit of God directs our eye to the time when Moses came to years, that is to say, when his first forty years of life were over; then, without any hesitation he refused to be called the son of Pharaoh's daughter, and took his part with the despised people of God.

I beg you to consider first, *who he was that did this.* He was a man of education, for he was learned in all the wisdom of the Egyptians. Somebody says he does not suppose the wisdom of the Egyptians was anything very great. No, and the wisdom of the English is not much greater. Future ages will laugh as much at the wisdom of the English as we now laugh at the wisdom of the Egyptians. The human wisdom of one age is the folly of the next. Philosophy, so called, what is it but the concealment of ignorance under hard names, and the arrangement of mere guesses into elaborate theories? In comparison with the eternal light of God's Word, all the knowledge of men is "not light but darkness visible." Men of education, as a rule, are not ready to acknowledge the living God. Philosophy in its self-conceit despises the infallible revelation of the Infinite, and will not come to the light lest it be reproved. In all ages, when a man has considered himself to be wise, he has almost invariably condemned the infinite wisdom. Had he been truly wise, he would have humbly bowed before the Lord of all, but being only nominally so, he said, "Who is the Lord?" Not many great men after the flesh, not many mighty are chosen. Did not our Lord himself say it, and his word is for all time, "I thank thee, O Father, Lord of heaven and earth, that thou hast hid these things from the wise and prudent, and hast revealed them unto babes"? But yet, sometimes a man of education like Moses is led by the blessing of heaven to take the side of truth, and of the right, and when it is so, let the Lord be magnified!

Besides being a man of education, he was *a person of high rank.* He had been adopted by Thermuthis, the daughter of Pharaoh, and it is possible, though we cannot be sure of it, that he was the next heir by adoption to the Egyptian crown. It is said that the king of Egypt had no other child, and that his daughter had no son, and that Moses would, therefore, have become the king of Egypt. Yet, great as he was and mighty at court, he joined with the oppressed people of God. May God grant that we may see many eminent men bravely standing up for God and for his truth, and repudiating the religion of men, but if they do, it will be a miracle of mercy indeed, for few of the great ones have ever done so. Here and there in heaven may be found a king, and here and there in the church may be found one who wears a coronet and prays; but how hardly shall they that have riches enter into the kingdom of heaven. When they do so God be thanked for it.

In addition to this, remember that Moses was *a man of great ability.* We have evidence of that in the administrative skill with which he managed the affairs of Israel in the wilderness; for though he was inspired of God, yet his own natural ability was not superseded but directed. He was a poet: "Then sung Moses and the children of Israel this song unto the Lord." That memorable poem at the Red Sea is a very masterly ode, and proves the incomparable ability of the writer. The Ninetieth Psalm also shows the range of his poetic powers. He was both prophet, priest, and king in the midst of Israel, and a man second to no man save that Man who was more than man. No other man I know of comes so near in the glory of his character to Christ as Moses does, so that we find the two names linked together in the praise of heaven—"they sing the song of Moses the servant of God, and of the Lamb." Thus you see he was a truly eminent man, yet he cast in his lot with God's people. It is not many that will do this, for the Lord has usually chosen the weak things to confound the mighty, and the things that are not to bring to naught the things that are, that no flesh should glory in his presence. Yet here he, who will have mercy on whom he will have mercy, took this great man, this wise man, and gave him grace to be decided in the service of his God. Should I address such a one this morning I would anxiously pray that a voice from the excellent glory may call him forth to the same clear line of action.

Next, consider *what sort of society Moses felt compelled to leave.* In coming forth from Pharaoh's court he must separate from all the courtiers and men of high degree, some of whom may have been very estimable people. There is always a charm about the society of the great, but every bond was severed by the resolute spirit of Moses. I do not doubt that being learned in all the wisdom of Egypt, such a man as Moses would be always welcome in the various circles of science; but he relinquished all his honors among the elite of learning to bear the reproach of Christ. Neither great men nor learned men could hold him when his conscience had once pointed out the path. Be sure, also, that he had to tear himself away from many a friend. In the course of forty years one would suppose he had formed associations that were very dear and tender, but to the regret of many he associated himself with the unpopular party, whom the king sought to crush, and therefore no courtier could henceforth acknowledge him. For forty years he lived in the solitude of the desert, and he only returned to smite the land of Egypt with plague, so that his separation from all his former friendships must have been complete. But, O true-hearted spirit, should it break every fond connection, should it tear your soul away from all you love, if your God requires it, let the sacrifice be made at once. If your faith has shown you that to occupy your present position involves complicity with error or sin, then break away, by God's help, without further parley. Let not the nets of the fowler hold you, but as God gives you freedom, mount untrammeled and praise your God for liberty. Jesus left the angels of heaven for your sake; can you not leave the best of company for his sake?

But I marvel most at Moses when I consider not only who he was and the company he had to forgo, but *the persons with whom he must associate,* for in truth the followers of the true God were not, in their own persons, a lovable people at that time. Moses was willing to take upon himself the reproach of Christ, and to bear the affliction of God's people when, I venture to observe again, there was nothing very attractive in the people themselves. They were wretchedly poor; they were scattered throughout all the land as mere drudges, engaged in brick making, and this brick making, which was imposed upon them for the very purpose of breaking down their spirit, had done its work all too well. They were utterly spiritless, they possessed no leaders, and were not prepared to have followed them if they had arisen. When Moses, having espoused their cause, informed them that God had sent him, they received him at first, but when the prophet's first action prompted Pharaoh to double their toil by an enactment that they should not be supplied with straw, they upbraided Moses at once; even as forty years before, when he interfered in their quarrels, one of them said, "Wilt thou slay me as thou didst the Egyptian yesterday?" They were literally a herd of slaves, broken down, crushed and depressed. It is one of the worst things about slavery that it unmans men and unfits them even for generations for the full enjoyment of liberty. Even when slaves receive liberty we cannot expect them to act as those would do who were free born, for in slavery the iron enters into the very soul and binds the spirit.

Thus it is clear that the Israelites were not very select company for the highly educated Moses to unite with: though a prince he must make common cause with the poor; though a free man he must mingle with slaves; though a man of education he must mix with ignorant people; though a man of spirit he must associate with spiritless serfs. How many would have said, "No, I cannot do that; I know what church I ought to unite with if I follow Scriptures fully, and obey in all things my Lord's will; but then they are so poor, so illiterate, and their place of worship is so far from being architecturally beautiful. Their preacher is a plain, blunt man, and they themselves are not refined. Scarce a dozen of the whole sect can keep a carriage; I should be shut out of society if I joined with them." Have we not heard this base reasoning till we are sick of it, and yet it operates widely upon this brainless, heartless generation. Are there none left who love truth even when she wears no trappings? Are there none who love the gospel better than pomp and show? Where God raises up a Moses, what cares he how poor his brethren may be? "They are God's people," says he, "and if they are very poor, I must help them the more liberally. If they be oppressed and depressed, so much the more reason why I should come to their aid. If they love God and his truth, I am their fellow soldier, and will be at their side in the battle." I have no doubt Moses thought all this over, but his mind was made up, and he took his place promptly.

In addition to other matters, one mournful thing must be said of Israel, which must have cost Moses much pain. He found that among God's people there were some who brought no glory to God, and were very weak in their principles. He did not judge the whole body by the faults of some, but by their standards and their institutions: and he saw that the Israelites, with all their faults, were the people of God, while the Egyptians, with all their virtues, were not so. Now it is for each one of us to try the spirits by the Word of God, and then fearlessly to follow out our convictions. Where is Christ recognized as the head of the church? Where are the Scriptures really received as the rule of faith? Where are the doctrines of grace clearly believed? Where are the ordinances practiced as the Lord delivered them? For with that people will I go, their cause shall be my cause, their God shall be my God. We look not for a perfect church this side of heaven, but we do look for a church free from popery and sacramentalism and false doctrine; and if we cannot find one, we will wait until we can, but with falsehood and priestcraft we will never enter into fellowship. If there be faults with the brethren, it is our duty to bear with them patiently, and pray for grace to overcome the evil; but with papists and rationalists we must not join in affinity, or God will require it at our hands.

Consider now *what Moses left by siding with Israel.* He left honor—he "refused to be called the son of Pharaoh's daughter"; he left pleasure—for he refused to "enjoy the pleasures of sin for a season"; and, according to our apostle, he left wealth as well, for in taking up the reproach of Christ, he renounced "the treasures of Egypt." Very well, then, if it comes to this, if to follow God and to be obedient to him I have to lose my position in society and become a pariah; if I must abjure a thousand pleasures, and if I am deprived of emoluments and income, yet the demands of duty must be complied with. Martyrs gave their lives of old, are there none left who will give their livings? If there be true faith in a man's heart, he will not deliberate which of the two to choose, beggary or compromise with error. He will esteem the reproach of Christ to be greater riches than the treasures of Egypt.

Consider yet once more *what Moses espoused* when he left the court. He espoused abounding trial, "choosing rather to suffer affliction with the people of God"; and he espoused reproach, for he "esteemed the reproach of Christ greater riches than the treasures of Egypt." O Moses, if you must needs join with Israel there is no present reward for you; you have nothing to gain but all to lose; you must do it out of pure principle, out of love to God, out of a full persuasion of the truth, for the tribes have no honors or wealth to bestow. You will receive affliction, and that is all. You will be called a fool, and people will think they have good reason for so doing. It is just the same today. If any man today will go without the camp to seek the Lord, if he go forth unto Christ without the gate, he must do it out of love to God and to his Christ, and for no other motive. The people of God have no benefices or bishoprics to offer; they therefore beseech men to count the cost. When a fervent convert said to our Lord, "Lord, I will follow thee whithersoever thou goest," he received for answer, "Foxes have holes and the birds of the air have nests, but I, the Son of man, have not where to lay my head." To this hour truth offers no dowry but herself to those who will espouse her. Abuse, contempt, hard fare, ridicule, misrepresentation—these are the wages of consistency; and if better comes it is not to be reckoned on. If any man be of a noble enough spirit to love the truth for truth's sake, and God for God's sake, and Christ for Christ's sake, let him enlist with those of like mind; but if he seek anything over and above that, if he desire to be made famous or to gain power or to be well beneficed, he had better keep his place among the cowardly dirt eaters who swarm around us. The church of God bribes no man. She has no mercenary rewards to proffer, and would scorn to use them if she had. If to serve the Lord be not enough reward, let those who look for more go their selfish way: if heaven be not enough, let those who can despise it seek their heaven below. Moses, in taking up with the people of God, decidedly, and once for all, acted most disinterestedly, without any promise from the right side, or any friend to aid him in the change; for the truth's sake, for the Lord's sake, he renounced everything; content to be numbered with the downtrodden people of God.

II. Now, second, what was *the source of Moses' decision?*

Scripture says it was faith, otherwise some would insist upon it that it was the force of blood. "He was by birth an Israelite, and therefore," say they, "the instincts of nature prevailed." Our text assigns a very different reason. We know right well that the sons of godly parents are not led to adore the true God by reason of their birth. Grace does not run in the blood; sin may, but righteousness does not. Who does not remember sons of renowned lovers of the gospel, who are now far gone in ritualism? It was faith, not blood, which impelled Moses in the way of truth. Neither was it eccentricity which led him to espouse the side which was oppressed. We have sometimes found a man of pedigree and position who has associated with persons of quite another rank and condition, simply because he never could act like anybody else, and must live after his own odd fashion. It was not so with Moses. All his life through you cannot discover a trace of eccentricity in him: he was sober, steady, law abiding; what if I say he was a concentric man, for his center was in the right place, and he moved according to the dictates of prudence. Not thus can his decision be accounted for. Neither was he hurried on by some sudden excitement when there burned within his soul fierce patriotic fires which made him more fervent than prudent. No, there may have been some haste in his slaying the Egyptian on the first occasion, but then he had forty more years to think it over, and yet he never repented his choice, but held on to the oppressed people of God, and still refused to think of himself as the son of Pharaoh's daughter. It was faith then, faith alone, that enabled the prophet of Sinai to arrive at his decision, and to carry it out.

What faith had he? First, he had *faith in Jehovah.* It is possible that Moses had seen the various gods of Egypt, even as we see them now in the drawings which have been copied from their temples and pyramids. We find there the sacred cat, the sacred ibis, the sacred crocodile, and all kinds of creatures which were reverenced as deities; and in addition there were hosts of strange idols, compounded of man, and beast, and bird, which stand in our museums to this day, and were once the objects of the idolatrous reverence of the Egyptians. Moses was weary of all this symbolism. He knew in his own heart that there was one God, one only God, and he would have nothing to do with Amun, Pithah, or Maut. Truly, my very soul cries to God, that noble spirits may in these days grow weary of the gods of ivory and ebony and silver, which are adored under the name of crosses and crucifixes, and may come to abominate that most degrading and sickening of all idolatries in which a man makes a god with flour and water, bows down before it, and then swallows it, thus sending his god into his belly, and, I might say worse. The satirist said of the Egyptians, "O happy people, whose gods grow in their own gardens"; we may say with equal force, O happy people, whose gods are baked in their own ovens! Is not this the lowest form of superstition that ever debased the intellect of man. Oh, that brave and true hearts may be led to turn away from such idolatry, and abjure all association with it, and say, "No, I cannot, and dare not. There is one God that made heaven and earth, there is a pure Spirit who upholdeth all things by the power of his might, I will worship him alone; and I will worship him after his own law, without images or other symbols, for has he not forbidden them." Has he not said, "Thou shalt not make unto thee any graven image, or any likeness of anything that is in heaven above, or that is in the earth beneath, or that is in the water under the earth: thou shalt not bow down thyself to them, nor serve them: for I the LORD thy God am a jealous God"? Oh, that God would give to men faith to know there is but one God, and that the one God is not to be worshiped with man-ordained rites and ceremonies, for he is "a Spirit; and they that worship him must worship him in spirit and in truth"! That one truth, if it were to come with power from heaven into men's minds, would shiver St. Peter's and St. Paul's from their topmost cross to their lowest crypt; for what do these two churches teach us now but sheer clear idolatry, the one of rule and the other by permission, for now men who boldly worship what they call the "sacred elements" have leave and license to exercise their craft within the Church of England. Every man who loves his God should shake his skirts clear of these abominations, and I pray God that we may find many a Moses who shall do so.

The faith of Moses also *rested in Christ.* "Christ had not come," says one. No, but he was to come, and Moses looked to that coming One. He cast his eye through the ages that were to intervene, and he saw before him the Shiloh of whom dying Jacob sang. He knew the ancient promise which had been given to the fathers, that in the seed of Abraham should all the nations of the earth be blessed; and he was willing, in order to share in the blessing, to take his part in the reproach. Dear friends, we shall never have a thorough faith in God unless we have also faith in Jesus Christ. Men have tried long, and tried hard, to worship the Father apart from the Son; but there stands it, and it always will be so: "No man cometh unto the Father but by me." You get away from the worship of the Father if you do not come through the mediation and atonement of the Son of God. Now, though Moses did not know concerning Christ all that is now revealed to us, yet he had faith in the coming Messiah, and that faith gave strength to his mind. Those are the men to suffer who have received Christ Jesus the Lord. If any man should ask me what made the Covenanters such heroes as they were; what made our Puritan forefathers fearless before their foes; what led the Reformers to protest and the martyrs to die; I would reply, it was faith in the invisible God, coupled with faith in that dear Son of God who is God incarnate. Believing in him they felt such love within their bosoms, that for love of him they could have died a thousand deaths.

But then, in addition to this, Moses had faith *in reference to God's people.* Upon that I have already touched. He knew that the Israelites were God's chosen, that Jehovah had made a covenant with them, that despite all their faults, God would not break his covenant with his own people, and he knew, therefore, that their cause was God's cause, and being God's cause it was the cause of right, the cause of truth. Oh, it is a grand thing when a man has such faith that he says, "It is nothing to me what other people do or think or believe; I shall act as God would have me. It is nothing to me what I am commanded to do by my fellow creatures, nothing to me what fashion says, nothing to me what my parents say, as far as religion is concerned; the truth is God's star, and I will follow wherever it may lead me. If it should make me a solitary man, if I should espouse opinions which no one else ever believed in, if I should have to go altogether outside the camp, and break away from every connection, all this shall be as immaterial to me as the small dust of the balance; but if a matter be true, I will believe it, and I will propound it, and I will suffer for its promulgation; and if another doctrine be a lie, I will not be friends with it, no, not for a solitary moment; I will not enter into fellowship with falsehood, no, not for an hour. If a course be right and true, through floods and flames if Jesus leads me, I will pursue it." That seems to me to be the right spirit, but where do you find it nowadays? The modern spirit mutters, "We are all right, every one of us." He who says yes is right, and he who says no is also right. You hear a man talk with mawkish sentimentality which he calls Christian charity. "Well, I am of opinion that if a man is a Muslim or a Catholic or a Mormon, or a Dissenter, if he is sincere, he is all right." They do not quite include devil worshipers, thugs, and cannibals yet, but if things go on they will accept them into the happy family of the Broad Church. Such is the talk and cant of this present age, but I bear my witness that there is no truth in it, and I call upon every child of God to protest against it, and, like Moses, to declare that he can have no complicity with such a confederacy. There is truth somewhere, let us find it; the lie is not of the truth, let us abhor it. There is a God, let us follow him, and it cannot be that false gods are gods too. Surely truth is of some value to the sons of men, surely there must be something worth holding, something worth contending for, and something worth dying for; but it does not appear nowadays as if men thought so. May we have a respect for God's true church in the world which abides by the apostolic word and doctrine. Let us find it out, and join with it, and at its side fight for God and for his truth!

Once again, Moses had faith in the "recompense of the reward." He said thus within himself, "I must renounce much, and reckon to lose rank, position, and treasure; but I expect to be a gainer notwithstanding, for there will be a day when God shall judge the sons of men; I expect a judgment throne with its impartial balances, and I expect that those who serve God faithfully shall then turn out to have been the wise men and the right men, while those who truckled and bowed down to gain a present ease, shall find that they missed eternity while they were snatching after time, and that they bartered heaven for a paltry mess of pottage." With this upon his mind, you could not persuade Moses that he ought to compromise, and must not be uncharitable, and ought not to judge other good people, but should be large minded, and remember Pharaoh's daughter, and how kindly she had nurtured him, and consider what opportunities he had of doing good where he was; how he might befriend his poor brethren, what influence he might have over Pharaoh, how he might be the means of leading the princes and the people of Egypt in the right way, and perhaps God had raised him up on purpose to be there, who could tell, and so on, and so on, and so on—you know the Babylonian talk, for in these days you have all read or heard the plausible arguments of the deceivableness of unrighteousness, which in these last days teaches men to do evil that good may come. Moses cared for none of these things. He knew his duty, and did it, whatever might be the consequences. Every Christian man's duty is to believe the truth, and follow the truth, and leave results with God. Who dares do that? He is a king's son. But again I say it, who dares do that in these days?

III. Third, we are going to run over in our minds some of the *arguments which supported Moses* in his decided course of following God.

The first argument would be, he saw clearly that God was God and therefore must keep his word, must bring his people up out of Egypt and give them a heritage. Now he said within himself, "I desire to be on the right side. God is almighty, God is all truthful, God is altogether just. I am on God's side, and being on God's side I will prove my truthfulness by leaving the other side altogether."

Then, second, we have it in the text that he perceived the pleasures of sin to be but for a season. He said to himself, "I may have but a short time to live, and even if I live to a good old age, life at the longest is still short; and when I come to the close of life what a miserable reflection it will be that I have had all my pleasure, it is all over, and now I have to appear before God as a traitorous Israelite who threw up his birthright for the sake of enjoying the pleasures of Egypt." Oh, that men would measure everything in the scales of eternity! We shall be before the bar of God all of us in a few months or years, and then think you, how shall we feel? One will say, "I never thought about religion at all," and another, "I thought about it, but I did not think enough to come to any decision upon it. I went the way the current went." Another will say, "I knew the truth well enough, but I could not bear the shame of it; they would have thought me fanatical if I had gone through with it." Another will say, "I halted between two opinions. I hardly thought I was justified in sacrificing my children's position for the sake of being out and out a follower of truth." What wretched reflections will come over men who have sold the Savior as Judas did! What wretched deathbeds must they have who have been unfaithful to their consciences and untrue to their God! But oh! with what composure will the believer look forward to another world! He will say, "By grace I am saved, and I bless God I could afford to be ridiculed, I could bear to be laughed at. I could lose that situation; I could be turned out of that farm, and could be called a fool, and yet it did not hurt me. I found solace in the society of Christ; I went to him about it all, and I found that to be reproached for Christ was a sweeter thing than to possess all the treasures of Egypt. Blessed be his name! I missed the pleasures of the world, but they were no miss to me. I was glad to miss them, for I found sweeter pleasure in the company of my Lord, and now there are pleasures to come which shall never end." O brethren, to be out and out for Christ, to go to the end with him, even though it involve the loss of all things, this will pay in the long run. It may bring upon you much disgrace for the present, but that will soon be over, and then comes the eternal reward.

And, then, again, he thought within himself that even the pleasures, which did last for a season, while they lasted were not equal to the pleasure of being reproached for Christ's sake. This ought also to strengthen us, that the worst of Christ is better than the best of the world, that even now we have more joy as Christians, if we are sincere, than we could possibly derive from the sins of the wicked.

I have only this to say in closing. First, we ought all of us to be ready to part with everything for Christ, and if we are not we are not his disciples. "Master, you say a hard thing," says one. I say it yet again, for a greater Master has said it: "He that loveth son or daughter more than me is not worthy of me." "Unless a man forsake all that he has he cannot be my disciple." Jesus may not require you actually to leave anything, but you must be ready to leave everything if required.

The second observation is this: We ought to abhor the very thought of obtaining honor in this world by concealing our sentiments or by making compromises. If there be a chance of your being highly esteemed by holding your tongue, speak at once and do not run the risk of winning such dishonorable honor. If there be a hope of people praising you because you are so ready to yield your convictions, pray God to make you like a flint never to yield again; for what more damning glory could a man have than to be applauded for disowning his principles to please his fellowmen! From this may the Lord save us!

The third teaching is that we ought to take our place with those who truly follow God and the Scriptures, even if they are not altogether what we should like them to be. The place for an Israelite is with the Israelites, the place for a

Christian man is with Christian men. The place for a thorough-going disciple of the Bible and of Christ is with others who are such, and even if they should happen to be the lowest in the land, and the poorest of the poor, and the most illiterate and uneducated persons of the period, what is all this if their God loves them and if they love God? Weighed in the scales of truth the least one among them is worth ten thousand of the greatest ungodly men.

Lastly, we must all of us look to our faith. Faith is the main thing. You cannot make a thorough character without sincere faith. Begin there, dear hearer. If you are not a believer in Christ, if you believe not in the one God, may the Lord convert you, and give you now that precious gift! To try and raise a character which shall be good without a foundation of faith is to build upon the sand, and to pile up wood and hay and stubble; wood, hay, and stubble are very good things as wood, hay, and stubble, but they will not bear the fire; and as every Christian character will have to bear fire, it is well to build on the rock, and to build with such graces and fruits as will endure trial. You will have to be tried, and if you have, by sneaking through life as a coward, avoided all opposition and all ridicule, ask yourself whether you really are a disciple of that master of the house whom they called Beelzebub, whether you are truly a follower of that crucified Savior who said, "except a man take up his cross daily and follow me, he cannot be my disciple." Suspect the smooth places; be afraid of that perpetual peace which Christ declares he came to break. He says, "I came not to send peace on the earth, but a sword." He came to being fire upon the earth; and "what will I," said he, "if it be already kindled."

Must I be carried to the skies
On flowery beds of ease,
While others fought to win the prize,
And sailed through bloody seas.

Sure I must fight if I would reign,
Increase my courage, Lord,
I'd bear the toil, endure the pain,
Supported by thy Word. Amen.

Joshua: Strengthening Medicine for God's Servants

Delivered at the Metropolitan Tabernacle, Newington. Published in 1875. No. 1214.

I will not fail thee, nor forsake thee.—JOSHUA 1:5

No doubt God had spoken to Joshua before. He had been a man of faith for many years, and his faith enabled him to distinguish himself by such simple truthfulness of character and thoroughly faithful obedience to the Lord's will, that he and another were the only two left of the whole generation that came up out of Egypt. "Faithful among the faithless found," he survived where all else died; standing erect in full vigor, he might have been compared to a lone tree which spreads its verdant branches untouched by the axe which has leveled its fellows with the ground. But now Joshua was about to enter upon a new work: he had become king in Jeshurun instead of Moses, from a servant he had risen to be a ruler, and it now fell to his lot to lead the people across the Jordan, and marshal their forces for the conquest of the Promised Land. On the threshold of this high enterprise the Lord appears to his servant and says, "As I was with Moses, so I will be with thee: I will not fail thee, nor forsake thee." When God's people come into fresh positions, they shall have fresh revelations of his love. New dangers will bring new protections; new difficulties, new helps; new discouragements, new comforts; so that we may rejoice in tribulations also, because they are so many newly opened doors of God's mercy to us. We will be glad of our extremities, because they are divine opportunities. What the Lord said to Joshua was particularly encouraging, and it came precisely when he needed it. Great was his peril, and great was the consolation of that word from the Lord of hosts, "Have not I commanded thee? Be strong and of a good courage; be not afraid, neither be thou dismayed: for the Lord thy God is with thee whithersoever thou goest."

We will waste no time in preface, but at once consider the divine promise. "I will not fail thee, nor forsake thee."

I. Observe here, first, *the suitability of the consolation which these words gave to Joshua.* "I will not fail thee, nor forsake thee."

This must have been very cheering to him *in reference to himself.* He knew Moses, and he must have had a very high esteem for him. He was a great man, one of a thousand; scarcely among all that have been born of woman has there arisen a greater than Moses. Joshua had been his servant, and no doubt considered himself to be very far inferior to that great lawgiver. A sense of his own weakness comes over a man all the more from being associated with a grander mind. If you mingle with your inferiors you are apt to grow vain; but closely associated with superior minds there is a far greater probability that you will become depressed, and may think even less of yourself than humility might require; for humility is, after all, only a right estimate of our own powers. Joshua, therefore, may possibly have been somewhat despondent under a very pressing sense of his own deficiencies; and this cheering assurance would meet his case, "*I* will not fail thee: though thou be less wise, or meek, or courageous than Moses, *I* will not fail thee, nor forsake thee." If God be with our weakness it waxes strong; if he be with our folly it rises into wisdom; if he be with our timidity it gathers courage. It matters not how conscious a man may be of being nothing at all in himself, when he is conscious of the divine presence he even rejoices in his infirmity because the power of God doth rest upon him. If the Lord say unto the weakest man or woman here, "I will not fail thee, nor forsake thee," no craven thought will cross that ennobled Spirit; that word will nerve the trembler with a lionlike courage which no adversary will be able to daunt.

The consolation given to Joshua would be exceedingly suitable *in the presence of his enemies*. He had spied out the land, and he knew it to be inhabited by giant races, men famous both for stature and strength. The sons of Anak were there, and other tribes, described as "great, and many, and tall." He knew that they were a warlike people, and expert in the use of destructive implements of war, such as brought terror upon men, for they had chariots of iron. He knew, too, that their cities were of colossal dimensions—fortresses whose stones at this very day surprise the traveler, so that he asks what wondrous skill could have lifted those masses of rock into their places. The other spies had said that these Canaanites dwelled in cities that were walled up to heaven; and, though Joshua did not endorse that exaggeration, he was very well aware that the cities to be captured were fortresses of great strength, and the people to be exterminated were men of ferocious courage and great physical energy.

Therefore the Lord said, "I will not fail thee, nor forsake thee." What more was needed? Surely, in the presence of God, Anakim become dwarfs, strongholds become as a lodge in a garden of cucumbers, and chariots of iron are as thistledown upon the hillside driven before the blast. What is strong against the most High? What is formidable in opposition to Jehovah? "If God be for us, who can be against us?" They that be with us are more than they that be against us, when once the Lord of hosts is seen in our ranks. "Therefore will we not fear, though the earth be removed, the mountains be carried into the midst of the sea." Though a host should encamp against us, our heart shall not fear: though war should rise against us, in this will we be confident.

This consolation, too, was *sufficient for all supplies*. Perhaps Joshua knew that the manna was no longer to fall. In the wilderness the supply of heavenly bread was continuous, but when they crossed the Jordan they must quarter on the enemy; and with the myriads of people that were under Joshua's command, the matter of providing for them must have been no trifle. According to some computations, nearly three millions of people came up out of Egypt: I scarcely credit the computation and am inclined to believe that the whole matter of the numbers of the Old Testament is not yet understood, and that a better knowledge of the Hebrew tongue will lead to the discovery that the figures have been frequently misunderstood; but still a very large number of people came with Joshua to the edge of the wilderness, and crossed the Jordan into the land of Canaan. Who was to provide for all these hungry bands? Joshua might have said, "Shall all the flocks and the herds be slain for this great multitude, and will the sea yield up her fish, when the manna ceases? How shall these people be fed?" "I will not fail thee, nor forsake thee" was a supply which would meet all the demands of the commissariat. They might eat to the full, for God would find them food; their clothes might wax old upon them now that the miracle of the wilderness would cease, for new garments would be found for them in the wardrobes of their enemies. When the Lord opens all his granaries none shall lack for bread, and when he unlocks his wardrobes none shall go bare. So that there was no room for anxiety in Joshua's mind. As for himself, if weak, this made him strong; as for his enemies, if they were powerful, this promise made him stronger than they; and as for the needs of Israel, if they were great, this promise supplied them all.

Surely this word must often have brought charming consolation to the heart of the son of Nun *when he saw the people failing him*. There was only the venerable Caleb left of all his comrades with whom he had shared the forty years' march through the great and terrible wilderness; Caleb and he were the last two sheaves of the great harvest, and they were both like shocks of corn fully ripe for the garner. Old men grow lonely, and small wonder is it if they do. I have heard them say that they live in a world where they are not known, now that, one by one, all their old friends are gone home, and they are left alone—like the last swallow of autumn when all its fellows have sought a sunnier clime. Yet the Lord says, "I will not forsake thee: I shall not die: I am ever with thee. Thy Friend in heaven will live on as long as thou dost." As for the generation which had sprung up around Joshua, they were very little better than their fathers; they turned back in the day of battle, even the children of Ephraim, when they were armed and carried bows. They were very apt to go aside into the most provoking sin. Joshua had as hard a task with them as Moses had, and it was enough to break the heart of Moses to have to do with them. The Lord seems to bid him put no confidence in them, neither to be discomfited if they should be false and treacherous: "I will not fail thee: *they* may, but *I* will not. I will not forsake thee. They may prove cowards and traitors, but I will not desert thee." Oh, what a blessed thing it is in a false and fickle world, where he that eats bread with us lifts up his heel against us, where the favorite counselor becomes an Ahithophel, and turns his wisdom into crafty hate, to know that "there is a friend that sticketh closer than a brother," One who is faithful and gives us sure tokens of a love which many waters cannot quench.

I might thus dwell upon this point, and show that the consolatory promise has as many facets as a well-cut diamond, each one reflecting the light of divine consolation upon the eye of Joshua's faith. But we will come to other matters.

II. Second, *at what times may we consider this promise to be spoken to ourselves?*

It is all very well to listen to it, as spoken to Joshua, but, O God, if you would speak thus to us how consoled would we be! Do you ever do so? May *we* be so bold as to believe that thus you comfort *us*? Beloved, the whole run of Scripture speaks to the same effect to men of like mind with Joshua. No Scripture is of private interpretation: no text has spent itself upon the person who first received it. God's comforts are like wells, which no one man or set of men can drain dry, however mighty may be their thirst. A well may be opened for Hagar, but that well is never closed, and any other wanderer may drink at it. The fountain of our text first gushed forth to refresh Joshua, but if we are in Joshua's position, and are of his character, we may bring our water pots and fill them to the brim.

Let me mention when I think we may safely feel that God says to us, "I will not fail thee, nor forsake thee." Surely it is when we are *called to do God's work*. Joshua's work was the Lord's work. It was God who had given the country to the people, and who had said, "I will drive out the Canaanite from before thee," and Joshua was God's executioner, the sword in the hand of the Lord for the driving out of the condemned races. He was not entering upon a quixotic engagement of his own choosing and devising; he had not elected himself, and selected his own work, but God had called him to it, put him in the office and bidden him do it, and therefore he said to him, "I will not fail thee, nor forsake thee." Brother, are you serving God? Do you live to win souls? Is it your grand object to be the instrument in God's hand of accomplishing his purposes of grace to the fallen sons of men? Do you know that God has put you where you are and called you to do the work to which your life is dedicated? Then go on in God's name, for, as surely as he called you to his work, you may be sure that to you also he says, as indeed to all his servants, "I will not fail thee, nor forsake thee."

But I hear some of you say, "We are not engaged in work of such a kind that we could precisely call it 'work for God.'" Well, brethren, but are you *engaged in a work which you endeavor to perform to God's glory*? Is your ordinary and common trade one which is lawful—one concerning which you have no doubt as to its honest propriety, and in carrying it on do you follow right principles only? Do you endeavor to glorify God in the shop? Do you make the bells on the horses holiness to the Lord? It would not be possible for all of us to be preachers, for where would be the hearers? Many would be very much out of place if he were to leave his ordinary calling, and devote himself to what is so unscripturally called "the ministry." The fact is, the truest religious life is that in which a man follows the ordinary calling of life in the spirit of a Christian. Now, are you so doing? If so, you are as much ministering before God in measuring out yards of calico or weighing pounds of tea, as Joshua was in slaying Hivites and Jebusites and Hittites. You are as much serving God in looking after your own children and training them up in God's fear, and minding the house, and making your household a church for God, as you would be if you had been called to lead an army to battle for the Lord of hosts. And you may take this promise for yourself, for the path of duty is the path where this promise is to be enjoyed. "I will not fail thee, nor forsake thee."

Now, mark you, if you are living for yourself, if you are living for gain, if selfishness be the object of life, or if you are pursuing an unhallowed calling, if there is anything about your mode of business which is contrary to the mind and will of God and sound doctrine, you cannot expect God to aid you in sin, nor will he do it. Neither can you ask him to pander to your lusts and to assist you in the gratification of your own selfishness. But if you can truly say, "I live to the glory of God, and the ordinary life that I lead I desire to consecrate to his glory entirely," then may you take this promise home to yourself, "I will not fail thee, nor forsake thee."

But, mark you, there is another matter. We must, if we are to have this promise, *take God into our calculations*. A great many persons go about their supposed life-work without thinking about God. I have heard of one who said everybody had left him, and someone said, "But surely, as a Christian, God has not failed you?" "Oh," said he, "I forgot God." I am afraid there are many who call themselves Christians, and yet forget God in common life. Among all the forces that a man calculates upon when he engages in an enterprise, he should never omit the chief force: but often it is so with us. We inquire, "Am I competent for such a work? I ought to undertake it, but am I competent?" And straightaway there is a calculation made of competences. And in these competences there is no item put down—"Item, the promise of a living God. Item, the guidance of the Spirit." These are left out of the calculation. Remember that if you willfully omit them you cannot expect to enjoy them. You must walk by faith if you are to enjoy the privileges of the faithful. "The just shall live by faith," and if you begin to live by sense, you shall join the weeping and the wailing of those who have gone to broken cisterns and have found them empty; and your lips shall be parched with thirst, because you have forgotten the Fountain of living waters to which you should have gone. Do you, brethren and sisters, habitually take God into your calculations? Do you calculate upon omniscient direction and omnipotent aid?

I have heard of a certain captain who had led his troops into a very difficult position, and he knew that on the morrow he should want them all to be full of courage; and so, disguising himself, at nightfall he went around their tents, and listened to their conversations, until he heard one of them say, "Our captain is a very great warrior, and has won many victories, but he has this time made a mistake; for see, there are so many thousands of the enemy, and he has only so many infantry, so many cavalry, and so many guns." The soldier made out the account, and was about to sum up the scanty total when the captain, unable to bear it any longer, threw aside the curtain of the tent, and said, "And how many do you count me for, sir?"—as much as to say, "I have won so many battles that you ought to know that my skill can multiply battalions by handling them." And so the Lord hears his servants estimating how feeble they are, and how little they can do, and how few are their helpers; and I think I hear him rebukingly say, "But how many do you count your God for? Is he never to come into your estimate? You talk of providing, and forget the God of providence; you talk of working, but forget the God who works in you to will and to do of his own good pleasure."

How often in our enterprises have prudent people plucked us by the sleeve, and said we have gone too far? Could we reckon upon being able to carry out what we had undertaken? No, we could not reckon upon it, except that we believed in God, and with God all things are possible. If it be his work, we may venture far beyond the shallowness of prudence into the great deeps of divine confidence, for God who warrants our faith, will honor it before long. O Christian, if you can venture, and feel it to be no venture, then may you grasp the promise, "I will not fail thee, nor forsake thee." When you are on your own feet, you may dash against a stone; when you are running in your own strength, you may faint; but "they that wait upon the Lord shall renew their strength; they shall mount up with wings as eagles; they shall run, and not be weary; and they shall walk, and not faint."

Now, remember, that we may take this promise when we are engaged in God's work, or when we turn our ordinary business into God's work, and when we do really by faith take God into our calculations; but *we must also be careful that we walk in God's ways*. Observe that the next verse to the text runs thus, "Be strong, and of a good courage," and then the seventh verse is a singular one, "Only be thou strong and very courageous, that thou mayest observe to do according to all the law, which Moses my servant commanded thee: turn not from it to the right hand or to the left, that thou mayest prosper whithersoever thou goest."

"Be strong and very courageous." What for? To obey! Does it want courage and strength to obey? Why, nowadays, that man is thought to be courageous who will have no laws of God to bind him; and he is thought to be strong minded who ridicules revelation. But let us rest assured that he is truly strong of mind and heart who is content to be thought a fool, and sticks to the good old truth, and keeps the good old way. There are enough nowadays of "intellectual" preachers; some of us may be excused from this vaunted intellectualism that we may preach the simple gospel. There are enough who can becloud theology with the chill fogs of "modern thought"; we are satisfied to let the Word speak for itself without misting it with our thinkings. I believe it wants more courage and strength of mind to keep to the old things, than to follow after novel and airy speculations. We must not expect the God of truth to be with us if we go away from God and his truth.

Be careful how you dive. To watch every putting down of your foot is a good thing. Be exact and precise as to the divine rule, careless about man's opinion, and even defying it wherein it is error; but dutiful to God's law, bowing before it, yielding your whole nature in cheerful subservience to every command of the most High. He that walketh uprightly, walketh surely, and to him the promise is "I will not fail thee, nor forsake thee." Begin your life-course with a policy of your own, and you may get through it how you can; be wise in your own conceit, and trust to your own judgment, and the promotion of fools will be your reward; but be simple enough to do God's will only, to leave consequences and to follow truth, and integrity and uprightness will preserve you. Go on doing right at all costs, and the right will repay you all it costs you, and the righteous Lord will be true to his word: "I will not fail thee, nor forsake thee." These, then, I think, are the conditions under which any believing man may take to himself the words of our text.

III. But now, third, let us consider *what this promise does not preclude.*

"I will not fail thee, nor forsake thee." We must not misunderstand this gracious word, lest we be disappointed when things happen contrary to our expectations.

This promise does not exclude effort. A great many mistakes are made about the promises of God. Some think that if God is to be with them they will have nothing to do. Joshua did not find it so. He and his troops had to slay every Amorite and Hittite and Hivite that fell in battle. He had to fight and use his sword arm just as much as if there had been no God at all. The best and the wisest thing in the world is to work as if it all depended upon you, and then trust in God, knowing that it all depends upon him. He will not fail us, but we are not therefore to fold our arms and sit still. He will not forsake us; we are not therefore to go upstairs to bed and expect that our daily bread will drop into our mouths. I have known idle people who have said "Jehovah-Jireh," and sat with their feet over the fender, and their arms folded, and been lazy and self-indulgent; and generally their presumption has ended in this: God has provided them rags and jags, and a place in the county jail before long; the very best provision, I think, that can be made for idle people, and the sooner they get it the better for society. Oh, no, no, no, no, God does not pander to our laziness, and any man who expects to get on in this world with anything that is good, without work, is a fool. Throw your whole soul into the service of God, and then you will get God's blessing if you are resting upon him. Even Muhammad could appreciate this. When one of his followers said, "I will turn my camel loose, and trust in Providence," "No, no," said Muhammad, "tie him up as tightly as you can, and then trust in Providence." Oliver Cromwell had a commonsense view of this truth too. "Trust in God," said he, as they went to battle, "but keep your powder dry." And so must we. I do not believe that God would have his servants act like fools. The best judgment a man has should be employed in the service of God. Common sense is, perhaps, as rare a thing among Christian people as salmon in the Thames. The devil's servants have more wisdom in their generation than the children of light have, but it ought not so to be. If you want to succeed, use every faculty you have, and put forth all your strength; and if it is a right cause, you may then fall back on the promise, "I will not fail thee, nor forsake thee."

Neither does this promise preclude occasional disaster. After Joshua had received this promise he went up to Ai, and suffered a terrible defeat there, because the regulations of the war had been violated. They had defrauded the Lord of a part of the spoil of Jericho, which was hidden in Achan's tent, and this troubled Israel. Yes, and without the violation of any law, the best man in the world must expect in the most successful enterprise that there will be some discouragements. Look at the sea: it is rolling in, it will rise to full tide before long, but every wave that comes up dies upon the shore, and after two or three great waves which seem to capture the shingle there comes a feebler one which sucks back. Very well, but the sea will win, and reach its fullness. So in every good work for God there is a back-drawing wave every now and then. In fact, God often makes his servants go back that they may have all the more room to run and take a huger leap than they could have taken from the place where they stood before. Defeats in the hand of faith are only preparations for victory. If we are beaten for a little, we grind our swords the sharper, and the next time we take more care that our enemies shall know how keen they are. Do not, therefore, let any temporary disappointments dismay you; they are incidental to humanity, and needful parts of our education. Go on. God will certainly test you, but he will not fail you, nor forsake you.

Nor, again, does this promise preclude frequent tribulations and testings of faith. In the autobiography of the famous Francke of Halle, who built and, in the hand of God, provided for the orphan house of Halle, he says, "I thought when I committed myself and my work to God by faith, that I had only to pray when I had need, and that the supplies would come; but I found, that I had sometimes to wait and pray for a long time." The supplies did come, but not at once. The pinch never went so far as absolute want; but there were intervals of severe pressure. There was nothing to spare. Every spoonful of meal had to be scraped from the bottom of the barrel, and every drop of oil that oozed out seemed as if it must be the last; but still it never did come to the last drop, and there was always just a little meal left. Bread shall be given us, but not always in quarter loaves; our water shall be sure, but not always a brook full; it may only come in small cups. God has not promised to take any of you to heaven without trying your faith. He will not fail you, but he will bring you very low. He will not forsake you, but he will test you and prove you. You will frequently need all your faith to keep your spirits up; and unless God enables you to trust without staggering, you will find yourself sorely disquieted at times. Now are any of you brought to the verge of famine in God's work? It is a state in which I have often been—thank God, very often—and I have always been delivered, and, therefore, I can from experience say the Lord is to be trusted, and he will not allow the faithful to be confounded. He has said it, and he will perform it: "I will not fail thee, nor forsake thee."

Dear friends, I would like to say, once more, about this, that *this promise does not preclude our suffering very greatly*, and our dying, and perhaps dying a very sad and terrible death, as men judge. God never left Paul, but I have seen the spot where Paul's head was smitten off by the headsman. The Lord never left Peter, but Peter, like his Master, had to die by crucifixion. The Lord never left the martyrs, but they had to ride to heaven in chariots of fire. The Lord has never left his church, but oftentimes his church has been trodden as straw is trodden for the dunghill; her blood has been scattered over the whole earth, and she has seemed to be utterly destroyed. Still, you know, the story of the church is only another illustration of my text; God has not failed her, nor forsaken her; in the deaths of her saints we read not defeat, but victory; as they passed away one by one, stars ceasing to shine below, they shone with tenfold brilliance in the upper sky because of the clouds through which they passed before they reached their celestial spheres. Beloved, we may have to groan in a Gethsemane, but God will not fail us: we may have to die on a Golgotha, but he will not forsake us. We shall rise again, and, as our Master was triumphant through death, even so shall we through the greatest suffering and the most terrible defeats rise to his throne.

IV. I must pass on again, and occupy you for a few moments over a fourth point, which is this: *what, then, does the text mean, if we may have all this trial happening to us?*

It means to those to whom it belongs, first, *no failure for your work*; second, *no desertion for yourself.*

"I will not fail thee." *Your labor shall not be in vain in the Lord.* What is it? Is it the great work of preaching the gospel to thousands? God will not fail you in that. I remember how twenty years ago I was preaching the gospel in the simplicity of my heart, and some little stir was made, but the wise men made light of it and said it was all to end in six months' time. We went on, did we not? And by and by, when we had still greater crowds listening to us, it was "a temporary excitement, a sort of religious spasm"; it would all end like a mere flash in the pan. I wonder where those prophets are now. If there are any of them here, I hope they feel comfortable in the unfulfilled prophecy, which they can now study with some degree of satisfaction. Thousands on earth and hundreds in heaven can tell what God hath wrought. Is it another kind of work, dear brother, that you are engaged in? A very quiet, unobtrusive, unobserved effort? Well, I should not wonder that, little as it is, somebody or other sneers at it. There is scarcely a David in the world without an Eliab to sneer at him. Press on, brother! Stick to it, plod away, work hard, trust in your God, and your work will not fail. We have heard of a minister who added only one to his church through a long year of very earnest ministry—only one, a sad thing for him; but that one happened to be Robert Moffatt, and he was worth a thousand of most of us. Go on. If you bring but *one* to Christ, who shall estimate the value of the one? Your class is very small just now; God does not seem to be working. Pray about it, get more scholars into the class, and teach better, and even if you should not see immediate success do not believe that it is all a failure. Never was a true gospel sermon preached yet, with faith and prayer, that was a failure. Since the day when Christ our Master first preached the gospel, unto this day—I dare to say it—there was never a true prayer that failed, nor a true declaration of the gospel made in a right spirit that fell to the ground without prospering according to the pleasure of the Lord. Fire away, brother. Every shot tells somewhere, for in heavenly as well as earthly warfare, "every bullet has its billet."

And then there shall be *no desertion as to yourself*, for your heavenly Friend has said, "I will not *forsake* thee." You will not be left alone or without a helper. You are thinking of what you will do in old age. Do not think of that: think of what God will do for you in old age. Oh, but your great need and long illness will wear out your friends, you say. Perhaps you may wear out your friends, but you will not wear out your God, and he can raise up new helpers if the old ones fail. Oh, but your infirmities are many and will soon crush you down: you cannot live long in such circumstances. Very well, then you will be in heaven; and that is far better. But you dread pining sickness. It may never come; and, suppose it should come, remember what will come with it: "I will make all thy bed in thy sickness." "I will never leave thee, nor forsake thee"—so runs the promise. "Fear thou not, for I am with thee; be not dismayed, for I am thy God." "'The mountains may depart, and the hills be removed; but the covenant of my love shall not depart from thee,' saith the Lord, that hath mercy on thee." You shall not be a lone one. You shall not wring your hands in despair, and say, "I am utterly wretched, like the pelican of the wilderness—utterly forsaken like the owl of the desert." The mighty God of Jacob forsaketh not his own.

V. And so this brings me to the last point, which is this: *why may we be quite sure that this promise will be fulfilled to us?*

I answer, first, we may be quite sure because it is God's promise. Did ever any promise of God fall to the ground yet? There be those in the world who are challenging us continually, and saying, "Where is your God?" They deny the efficacy of prayer; they deny the interpositions of Providence. Well, I do not wonder that they do so deny, because the bulk of Christians do not realize either the answer of prayer or the interposition of Providence, for this reason, that they do not live in the light of God's countenance, or live by faith. But the man who walks by faith will tell you that he notices Providence, and never is deficient of a Providence to notice; that he notices answers to his prayer, and never is without an answer to his prayer. What is a wonder to others becomes a common fact of everyday life to the believer in Christ. Where God has given his word, "I will not fail thee, nor forsake thee," let us believe it; for

His very word of grace is strong
As that which built the skies;
The voice that rolls the stars along
Speaks all the promises.

Rest ye well assured that if a man be called to do God's work, God will not fail him, because *it is not after the manner of the Lord to desert his servants*. David in the dark day of his sin bid Joab place Uriah, the Hittite, in the forefront of the battle, and leave him there to die by the hand of the children of Ammon. Was it not cruel? It was base and treacherous to the last degree. Can you suspect the Lord of anything so unworthy? God forbid. My soul has known what it is to plead with the Lord my God after this fashion: "Lord, thou hast placed me in a difficult position, and given me service to perform far beyond my capacity. I never coveted this prominent place, and if thou dost not help me now why hast thou placed me in it?" I have always found such argument to be prevalent with God. He will not push his servants into severe conflicts, and then fail them.

Besides, remember that *should God's servants fail*, if they are really God's servants, *the enemy would exult and boast against the Lord himself*. This was a great point with Joshua in after days. He said, "The Canaanites and all the inhabitants of the land shall hear of it, and shall environ us round, and cut off our name from the earth: and what wilt thou do unto thy great name?" If the Lord raises up Luther, and does not help Luther, then it is not Luther that fails; it is God that fails, in the estimation of the world. If the Lord sends a man to bear witness to a truth, and that man's testimony utterly breaks down, then in the estimation of men it is the truth that breaks down, and consequently dishonor is cast upon God and his truth; and he will not have it so. If he uses the weakest instrumentality, he will laugh to scorn his adversaries by it, and they shall never say that the Lord was overcome.

Besides, if God has raised you up, my brother or sister, to accomplish a purpose by you, *do you think he will be defeated*? Were ever any of his designs frustrated? I have heard preachers talk about God being defeated by the free will of man and disappointed by man's depravity, and I do not know what. But such a God is no God of mine. My God is one who has his will and will have it; who, when he designs a thing, accomplishes it; he is a God whose omnipotence none can resist, concerning whom it may be said, "Who shall stay his hand, or say unto him, What doest thou?" The mighty God of Jacob puts his hand to a design and carries it through as surely as he begins; the weakness of the instrument in his hand does not hinder him, nor the opposition of his enemies deter him. Only believe in him, and weak as you are, you shall perform wonders, and in your feebleness the strength of God shall be glorified.

Besides, my brethren, if we trust God, and live for God, *he loves us much too well to leave us*. It is not as though we were aliens and strangers and foreigners—mercenary troops whom the prince who hires them leaves to be cut in pieces: no, we are his own dear children. God sees his own self in all his servants. He sees in them the members of the body of his dear Son. The very least among them is dear to him as the apple of his eye, and beloved as his own soul. It is not to be imagined that he will ever put a load upon his own children's shoulders without giving them strength to bear the burden, or send them to labors for which he will not give them adequate resources. Oh, rest in the Lord, you faithful. "Rest in the LORD, and wait patiently for him," for he will appear unto your rescue. Has he not said, "I will not fail thee, nor forsake thee"?

As I have thus been bringing forth marrow and fatness from the Word, I have been thinking of some of you, poor souls, who cannot eat thereof, and have no share in it. I am glad to see you here, especially on Thursday night, for it is not every unconverted person that will come to these weeknight services. You must have a hungering after these good things, or you would not be here in such numbers. I hope your mouths are watering after the good things of the covenant. I hope, as you see the promises of God on the table, and see how rich they are, you will say to yourself, "Would God I had a share in them!" Well, poor soul, if God gives you an appetite, I can only say, the food is free to you. If you would have God to be your Helper—if you would indeed be saved by Christ—come and welcome, for you are the soul that he desires to bless. If you have half a wish toward God, he has a longing toward you. If you desire him, you have not the start of him; depend upon it, he has long before desired you. Come you to him, rest in him, accept the atonement which his Son has presented, begin the life of faith in real earnest, and you shall find that what I have said is all true, only it falls short of the full truth, for you will say, like the queen of Sheba when she had seen Solomon's glory, "The half hath not been told me." Blessed be the Lord forever, who has taught my poor heart to believe in himself, and to live upon unseen realities, and rest in a faithful God! There is no peace or joy like it, or worthy to be mentioned in the same day. God grant it to each one of you, beloved, for his name's sake. Amen.

Gideon: The Dream of the Barley Cake

Delivered on Lord's Day morning, at the Metropolitan Tabernacle, Newington, November 22, 1885. No. 1873.

> *And when Gideon was come, behold, there was a man that told a dream unto his fellow, and said, "Behold, I dreamed a dream, and, lo, a cake of barley bread tumbled into the host of Midian, and came unto a tent, and smote it that it fell, and overturned it, that the tent lay along." And his fellow answered and said, "This is nothing else save the sword of Gideon the son of Joash, a man of Israel: for into his hand hath God delivered Midian, and all the host."*—JUDGES 7:13–14

The Midianites were devastating the land of Israel. These wandering tribes purposely kept away during the times of plowing and sowing, and allowed the helpless inhabitants to dream that they would be able to gather in a harvest; but no sooner did there come to be anything eatable by man or beast, than these Bedouin hordes came up like locusts, and devoured everything. Imagine a country like Israel, which had at one time been powerful, so greatly reduced as to be unable to keep off these desert rangers; brought so low that the cities and villages were empty, and the inhabitants were hidden in the hillsides, in the watercourses, and in the huge caverns of the rocks. God had forsaken them for their sins, and therefore their own manhood had forsaken them, and they hid themselves from enemies, whom, in better days, they had despised.

In her extremity, the guilty nation began to cry to Jehovah her God; and the answer was not long delayed. An angel came to Gideon and announced to him that the Lord had delivered Midian into his hand, and that he should smite them as one man. Gideon was a man of great faith: his name shines among the heroes of great faith in the eleventh chapter of the epistle to the Hebrews; and you and I will do well if we attain to the same rank in the peerage of faith as he did. But for all that, the best of men are men at the best; and men of strong faith are often men of strong conflicts; and so it was with Gideon. This man's great faith and great weakness of faith both showed themselves in a desire for signs. Once assure him that God is with him, and Gideon has no fear, but hastens to the battle, bravest of the brave. With a handful of men, he is quite prepared to go against a host of adversaries; but he pines for a sign. Again and again he asks it. The anxious question seems to be constantly recurring to him, "Is the LORD with us? If the LORD is with us, where are all his miracles which our fathers told us of, saying, 'Did not the LORD bring us up from Egypt?'" Hence his frequent prayer is, "If now I have found grace in thy sight, show me a sign." He began with this, and this ill beginning colored his whole after career. I have known many persons like this son of Joash; they say, "Let me but know that God is with me, and my fear is gone"; but their repeated question is, "Is the LORD with me? Is Jesus mine, and am I his? Let me but know that I am a true believer, and I am sure that I shall not perish, for God will not forsake his own; but then, am I a believer? Have I the marks and evidences of a child of God?" Hence the practice of severe self-examination, and hence also the weakening habit of craving for tokens and feelings. How many are crying "we see not our signs," when they ought to say, "but we see Jesus!" How many are praying "show me a token for good," when the Lord Jesus has given himself for them, and has thereby given the best token of his grace?

So it happened unto Gideon, that the Lord, knowing his hunger for signs and yet knowing the sincerity of his faith, bade him, on the night of the great battle which was to rout Midian, go down as a spy into the camp with his servant, and there he should receive a token for good, which would effectually quiet all his fears.

I picture Gideon and his attendant creeping down the hill in the stillness of the night, when the camp was steeped in slumber. It was about the end of the first watch, when they were soon to change sentinels. The two brave men, with stealthy footsteps, drew near the pickets, and even passed them. From long habit they had learned to make no more sound with their footfalls than if they had been cats. As they move along, they come near to a couple of men who are talking together, and they listen to their conversation. Whether they were inside the tent, lying on their beds, or whether they were sitting by the campfire whiling away the last half hour of their weary watch, we do not know: but there they were, and Gideon remained breathless to hear their talk. One of them told his fellow that he had dreamed a dream, and he began the telling of it. Then the other ventured an interpretation, and Gideon must have been awestricken when he heard his own name mentioned, and his own success foretold. Do you not see him with streaming eyes and clasped hands silently worshiping God? His assurance overflows, and motioning to his servant, they steal away through the shadows and quietly ascend the hill to the place where the little band of three hundred lay in hiding. They look down upon the sleeping camp, and Gideon cries, "The LORD hath delivered into your hands the hosts of Midian." Obedient to their leader they descend with their trumpets, and with torches covered over with pitchers. At a signal they break the pitchers, display the lights, sound the trumpets, and shout, "The sword of the LORD and of Gideon." Imagining that a vast army is upon them, the tribes of the desert run for their lives, and in the darkness fall foul of one another. Midian is scattered: Israel is free.

In quiet contemplation let us now play the part of spies. With all our wits about us, let us thread our way among the sleepers, and listen to this dream and the interpretation thereof.

I. The first thing that I shall bring under your observation is *the striking providence* which must have greatly refreshed Gideon.

Just as he and Phurah stealthily stole up to the tent, the Midianite was telling a dream, bearing an interpretation so appropriate to Gideon. It may appear to be a little thing, but an occurrence is nonetheless wonderful because it appears to be insignificant. The microscope reveals a world of marvels quite as surprising as that which is brought before us by the telescope. God is as divine in the small as in the stupendous, as glorious in the dream of a soldier as in the flight of a seraph.

Now observe, first, the providence of God that this man should have dreamed just then, and that he should have dreamed that particular dream. Dreamland is chaos, but the hand of the God of order is here. What strange romantic things our dreams are!—fragments of this, and broken pieces of the other, strangely joined together in absurd fashion.

How many monstrous forms in sleep we see,
That neither were, nor are, nor e'er can be!

Yet observe that God holds the brain of this sleeping Arab in his hand, and impresses it as he pleases. Dreams often come of previous thoughts; see then the providence which had taken this man's mind to the hearth and the cake baking. The Lord prepares him when he is awake to dream aright when he is asleep. God is omnipotent in the world of mind as well as in that of matter: he rules it when men are awake, and does not lose his power when men fall asleep. The heathen ascribed dreams to their gods; we read of one, that

Pallas poured sweet slumbers on his soul,
And balmy dreams, the gift of soft repose.

Thin as the air, inconstant as the wind, the stuff that dreams are made of is vanity of vanities; and yet the Lord fashions it according to his own good pleasure. The man must dream, must dream then and there, and dream that dream which should convey confidence and courage to Gideon. Oh, believe it, God is not asleep when we are asleep: God is not dreaming when we are. I admire the providence of God in this; do not you? Is it not specially well ordered that this man shall dream, and therein declare a truth as deep as any in the compass of philosophy?

Further, I cannot but admire *that this man should be moved to tell his dream to his fellow*. It is not everybody that tells his dream at night; he usually waits till the morning. We are grossly foolish sometimes, but we are not always so: and hence we do not hurry to tell such disjointed visions as that which this Arab had just seen. What was there in it? Many a time, no doubt, this son of the desert would have cried, "I have had a dream—past the wit of man to say what dream it was." But this time he cannot shake it off. It burdens him, and he must tell it to his comrade by the campfire. Look you into the face of Gideon as he catches every syllable.

Now, if this dream telling had been arranged by military authority, and if it had been part of a program that Gideon should be present at the nick of time to hear it, there would have been a failure somehow or other. If the man had known that he had a listener, he might not have been punctual with his narrative; but he did not know a word about being overheard, and yet he was punctual to the tick of a clock. God rules men's idle tongues as well as their dreaming brains, and he can make a talkative soldier in the camp say just as much and just as little as will subserve the purposes of wisdom. It is remarkable that *the man should tell his dream just when Gideon and Phurah had come near*. Just think a minute of the many chances against such a thing. We are on the side of the hill, and we glide down among the trees and the great rocks till we are nearly in the grasslands in the valley. Here lie the Midianites in their long lines of black tents, and the hush of deep slumber is over all, save where a few maintain a sleepy watch. Why does Gideon go to that particular part of the camp? Going there, why does he happen to drop on this particular spot where two men are talking? If he was spying out the camp, he would naturally wander along where there was most quiet, in order that he might not be discovered; for if the warriors had suddenly started up and snatched their spears these two men would have had small chance of life. It was singular that out of tents so countless Gideon should alight upon the very one in which were the two wakeful sentinels, and that he should come just as they were talking to one another about Gideon the son of Joash, a man of Israel. Considering that there were fifty thousand other things that they might have talked of, and considering that there were fifty thousand other persons upon whom Gideon might have lighted, there were so many chances against Gideon's hearing that singular talk, that I do not hesitate to say, this is the finger of God. If this were but one instance of the accuracy of Providence it might not so much surprise us; but history bristles with such instances: I mean not only public history, but our own private lives. Men sometimes make delicate machines where everything depends upon the touching of a certain pin at a certain instant, and their machinery is so arranged that nothing fails. Now our God has so arranged the whole history of men, and angels, and the regions of the dead, that each event occurs at the right moment so as to effect another event, and that other event brings forth a third, and all things work together for good.

I think if I had been Gideon, I should have said to myself, "I do not so much rejoice in what this dreamer says as I do in the fact that he has told his dream at the moment when I was lurking near him: I see the hand of the Lord in this, and I am strengthened by the sight. Verily, I perceive that the Lord works all things with unfailing wisdom, and fails not in his designs. He that has ordered this matter can order all things else." O child of God, when you are troubled it is because you fancy that you are alone; but you are not alone; the eternal Worker is with you. Listen, and you will hear the revolution of those matchless wheels which are forever turning according to the will of the Lord. These wheels are high and dreadful, but they move with fixed and steady motion, and they are all "full of eyes roundabout." Their course is no blind track of a car of juggernaut, but the eyes see, the eyes look toward their end, the eyes look upon all that comes within the circuit of the wheels. Oh, for a little heavenly eye salve to touch our eyes that we may perceive the presence of the Lord in all things! Then shall we see the mountain to be full of horses of fire and chariots of fire around about the prophets of the Lord. The stars in their courses are fighting for the cause of God. Our allies are everywhere. God will summon them at the right moment.

II. But now, second, I want to say something to you about *the comfortable trifle* which Gideon had thus met with.

It was a dream, and therefore a trifle or a nothing, and yet he took comfort from it. He was solaced by a dream, a gipsy's dream, and a poor dream at that. He took heart from an odd story of a barley bannock [cake] which overturned a tent. It is a very curious thing that some of God's servants do draw a very great deal of consolation from comparatively trivial things. We are all the creatures of sentiment as well as of reason, and hence we are often strongly affected by little things. Gideon is cheered by a dream of a barley cake. When Robert Bruce had been frequently beaten in battle, he despaired of winning the crown of Scotland; but when he lay hidden in the loft among the hay and straw, he saw a spider trying to complete her web after he had broken the thread many times. As he saw the insect begin again, and yet again, until she had completed her net for the taking of her prey, he said to himself, "If this spider perseveres and conquers, so will I persevere, and succeed." There might not be any real connection between a spider and an aspirant to a throne; but the brave heart made a connection, and thereby the man was cheered. If you and I will but look about us, although the adversaries of God are as many as grasshoppers, yet we shall find consolation. I hear the birds sing, "Be of good cheer," and the leafless trees bid us trust in God and live on, though all visible signs of life be withered. If a dream was sufficient to encourage Gideon, an everyday fact in nature may equally well serve the same purpose to us.

But what a pity it is that we should need such little bits of things to cheer us up, when we have matters of far surer import to make us glad! Gideon had already received, by God's own angel, the word, "Surely I will be with thee, and thou shalt smite the Midianites as one man." Was not this enough for him? Whence is it that a boy's dream comforts him more than God's own word. O child of God, how you degrade yourself and your Master's word, when you set so much store by a small token! Your Lord's promise—is that little in your eyes? What surer pledge of love do you desire than the blood of Jesus spilled for you? When Jesus says, "Verily, verily, I say unto you," what more can you require? Is not the word of the Lord absolute truth? What seal do you want to the handwriting of God? The Lord may grant us further tokens for good, but we ought not to require them.

I have said that our gracious God does condescendingly grant us even trifles, when he sees that they will cheer us, and this, I think, calls for adoring gratitude, and also for practical use of this comfort. God grant us grace to do great things, as the result of that which to others may seem a trifle. Let us not make a sluggard's bed out of our tokens; but let us hasten to the fight as Gideon did. If you have received a gleam of comfort, hasten to the conflict before the clouds return; go to your consecrated labor before you have lost the fervor of your spirit. May the Holy Ghost lead you so to do.

III. I have been brief upon that point, because I want you to notice, third, *the cheering discovery.*

Gideon had noticed a striking providence, he had received a comfortable trifle, but he also made a very cheering discovery; which discovery was that the enemy dreamed of disaster. You and I sometimes think about the hosts of evil, and we fear we shall never overcome them, because they are so strong, and so secure. Hearken: we overestimate them. The powers of darkness are not so strong as they seem to be. The subtlest infidels and heretics are only men. What is more, they are bad men; and bad men at bottom are weak men. You fret because in this war you are not angels; be comforted to think that the adversaries of the truth are men also. You sometimes grow doubtful; and so do they. You half despair of victory; and so do they. You are at times hard put to it; so are they. You sometimes dream of disaster; so do they. It is natural to men to fear, and doubly natural to bad men. It must have been a great comfort to Gideon to think that the Midianites dreamed about him, and that their dreams were full of terror to themselves. He did not think much of himself; he reckoned himself to be the least of all his father's house, and that his father's house was little in Israel—but the foes of Israel had taken another gauge of Gideon—they had evidently the notion that he was a great man, whom God might use to smite them; and they were afraid of him. He that interpreted the dream made use of the name of "Gideon the son of Joash," evidently knowing a great deal more about Gideon than Gideon might have expected. "This," said the soldier, "is the sword of Gideon the son of Joash, a man of Israel: for into his hand hath God delivered Midian, and all the host." Notice how his words tallied with those which the Lord had spoken to Gideon. The enemy had begun to dream, and to be afraid of him who now stood listening to their talk. A dread from the Lord had come upon them. Let us say to ourselves, "Why should we be afraid of sinners? They are afraid of us." A Christian man, the other day, was afraid to speak about his Lord to one whom he met. It cost him a deal of trouble to screw his courage up to speak to a skeptic; but when he had spoken, he found that the skeptic had all along been afraid that he would be spoken to. It is a pity when we tremble before those who are trembling because of us. By want of faith in God we make our enemies greater than they are.

Behold the host of doubters and heretics and revilers who, at the present time, have come up into the inheritance of Israel, hungry from their deserts of rationalism and atheism! They are eating up all the corn of the land. They cast a doubt upon all the verities of our faith. But we need not fear them; for if we heard their secret counsels, we should perceive that they are afraid of us. Their loud blusterings and their constant sneers are the index of real fear. Those who preach the cross of our Lord Jesus are the terror of modern thinkers. In their heart of hearts they dread the preaching of the old-fashioned gospel, and they hate what they dread. On their beds they dream of the coming of some evangelist into their neighborhood. What the name of Richard was to the Saracens, that is the name of Moody to these boastful intellects. They wish they could stop those Calvinistic fellows and those evangelical old fogies. Brethren, so long as the plain gospel is preached in England, there will always be hope that these brigands will yet be scattered, and the church be rid of their intrusion. Rationalism, Socinianism, ritualism, and universalism will soon take to their legs, if the clear, decided cry of "the sword of the LORD and of Gideon" be once more heard.

There is nothing of which a child of God need be afraid either on the earth or under it. I do not believe that in the lowest depths of hell we should hear or see anything that need make a believer in the Lord Jesus to be afraid. On the contrary, tidings of what the Lord has worked have made the enemy to tremble. Goodness wears in her innocence a breastplate of courage, but sin genders to cowardice. Those who follow after falsehood have a secret monitor within, which tells them that theirs is a weak cause, and that truth must and will prevail over them. Let them alone; the beating of their own hearts will scare them. The Lord lives, and while he lives let none that trust in his word suffer his heart to fail him; for the mountains shall depart, and the hills be removed, but the word of the Lord endureth forever. Our adversaries are neither so wise, nor so brave, nor so influential as we think them to be. Only have courage and rely upon God, and you will overcome them. David, you need not fear the giant because of his size; the vastness of his shape will only make him an easier target for your smooth stone. His very bulk is his weakness; it were hard to miss so huge a carcass. Be not afraid, but run to meet him; the Lord has delivered him into your hand. Why should the servants of the Lord speak doubtfully when their God pledges his honor that he will aid them? Let us change our manner of speech, and say with the psalmist, "Ascribe ye strength unto God: his excellency is over Israel. Let God arise, let his enemies be scattered; let them also that hate him flee before him." We have received a kingdom which cannot be moved. We have believed the faith once delivered unto the saints, and we will display it as a banner because of the truth. Yet shall this song be sung in our habitations: "The LORD gave the word: great was the company of those that published it. Kings of armies did flee apace: and she that tarried at home divided the spoil."

IV. Last, and most important of all, let us think for a little of *the dream itself and of its interpretation.*

The Midianite in his dream saw a barley cake. Barley cakes were not much valued as food in those days, any more than now. People ate barley when they could not get wheat; but they would need to be driven to such food by poverty or famine. Barley meal was rather food for dogs or cattle than for men; and therefore the barley cake would be the emblem of a thing despised. A barley cake was generally made upon the hearth. A hole was made in the ground and paved with stones; in this a fire was made, and when the stones were hot, a thin layer of barley meal was laid upon them, covered over with the ashes, and thus quickly and roughly baked. The cake itself was a mere biscuit. You must not interpret the dream as having in it a large quarter loaf of barley bread, tumbling down the hill and smashing up the tent with its own weight. No, it was only a cake, that is to say, a biscuit, of much the same form and thinness as we see in the Passover cakes of the Jews. It may have been a long piece of thin crust, and it was seen in the dream moving onward and waving in the air something like a sword. It came rolling and waving down the hill till it came crash against the pavilion of the prince of Midian, and turned the tent completely over, so that it lay in ruins. Perhaps driven by a tremendous wind, this flake of barley bread cut like a razor through the chief pole of the pavilion, and over went the royal tent. That was his vision: an odd, strange dream enough. His fellow answered, "The dream means mischief for our people. One of those barley cake eaters from the hills will be upon us before long. That man Gideon, whom we have heard of lately, may fall upon us on a sudden, and break down our power." That was the interpretation: the barley biscuit the ruin of the pavilion.

Now, what we have to learn from it is just this, *God can work by any means*. He can never be short of instruments. For his battles he can find weapons on the hearth, weapons in the kneading trough, weapons in the poor man's basket. Omnipotence has servants everywhere. For the defense of his cause God can enlist all the forces of nature, all the elements of society, all the powers that be. His kingdom cannot fail, since the Lord can defend it even by the cakes which are baking upon the coals. Gideon, who threshes corn today, will thresh the Lord's enemies tomorrow. Preachers of the Word are being trained everywhere.

God can work by the feeblest means. He can use a cake which a child can crumble to smite Midian, and subdue its terrible power. Alas, sirs! we often consider the means to be used, and forget to go onward to him who will use them. We often stop at the means and begin to calculate their natural force, and thus we miss our mark. The point is to get beyond the instruments, to the God who uses the instruments. I think I have heard that a tallow candle fired from a rifle will go through a door: the penetrating power is not in the candle, but in the force impelling it. So in this case, it was not the barley biscuit, but the almighty impulse which urged it forward, and made it upset the pavilion. We are nothing; but God with us is everything. "He giveth power to the faint; and to them that have no might he increaseth strength."

By using weak means our Lord gets to himself all the glory, and hides pride from men. The Lord had said to Gideon in the early part of this chapter, "The people are yet too many for me to give the Midianites into their hands, lest Israel vaunt themselves against me, saying, 'Mine own hand hath saved me.'" Their oppression was a punishment for sin, and their deliverance must be an act of mercy. They must be made to see the Lord's hand, and they cannot see it more clearly than by being delivered by feeble means. Out of jealousy for his own glory it often pleases God to set aside likely means and use those which we looked not for. Now I know how it is today: men think that if the world is to be converted it must be done by learned men, men of noble family, or at least of eminent talent. But is this the Lord's usual way? Is there anything in the Acts of the Apostles, or in the life of Christ, that should lead us to look to human wisdom or talent or prestige? Does not everything look in the contrary direction? The lake of Galilee was Christ's apostolic college. Has not God always acted upon his own declaration that he has hid these things from the wise and prudent and has revealed them unto babes? Is it not still true that the Lord has chosen the weak things of the world to confound the things which are mighty; and base things of the world, and things which are despised has God chosen, yes, and things which are not, to bring to naught things that are? Are we not on the wrong track altogether when we look to men, and means and measures, instead of considering the right hand of the most High? Brethren, let us never forget that out of the mouth of babes and sucklings has the Lord ordained strength because of his enemies, that he might still the enemy and the avenger.

The Lord employs feeble means, that so he may have an opening for you and for me. If he used only the great, the wise, the strong, we should have to lie in the corner. Then might the men of one talent be excused for hiding it. But now the least among us may through God's grace aspire to usefulness. Brothers, let not your weakness keep you back from the Lord's work: you are at least as strong as barley cakes. I find that the original text suggests a noise, such as might be made by chestnuts or corn when roasting in the fire. The dreamer marked that it was a noisy cake which tumbled into the host of Midian. More noise than force, one would say. It was like a coal which dies out of the fire, makes a little explosion, and is never more heard of. Thus have many of God's most useful servants been spoken of at the first. They were nine-day wonders, mere flashes in the pan, much ado about nothing, and so forth. And yet the Lord smites his enemies by their feeble means. My brother, perhaps you have begun to make a little stir by faithfully preaching the gospel, and this has opened the mouths of the adversaries, who are indignant that such a nobody as you should be useful. "Why, there is nothing in the fellow: it is sheer impudence for him to suppose that he has any right to speak." Never mind. Go on with your work for the Lord. Cease not because you are of such small account, for by such as you are God is pleased to work.

Never are his adversaries so shamefully beaten as when the Lord uses feeble instrumentality. The Lord smote the hosts of Jabin by the hand of a woman, and the hosts of Philistia by the hand of Shamgar the plowman. It was to their everlasting reproach that the Lord put his foes to the rout with pitchers and trumpets in the hand of the little band who followed the thresher of Abiezer. The Lord will tread Satan under our feet shortly, even under our feet, who are less than the least of all saints.

Note, next, *God uses unexpected means*. If I wanted to upset a tent, I certainly should not try to overturn it by a barley cake. If I had to cannonade an encampment, I should not bombard it with biscuits. Yet how wonderfully God hath wrought by the very persons whom we should have passed over without a thought. O paganism, your gigantic force and energy, with Caesar at their head, shall be vanquished by fishermen from the sea of Galilee! God willed it so, and so it was done. Rome's papal met a singular downfall from reformers rude of speech and poor in estate. Expect the unexpected. Thus the Lord works to call men's attention to what he does. If he does what men commonly reckon upon, they take no notice of his doings, however splendid they may be in themselves; but if he steps aside and does that which none could have looked for, then is their attention arrested, and they consider that the hand of the Lord is in it. Then also they admire and feel somewhat of awe of him. For the tent to fall seems nothing, but for the tent to fall by being smitten with a barley cake is something to be marveled at. For souls to be saved is in itself remarkable, but for them to be saved by some simple childlike evangelist who can scarcely speak grammatically, this is the talk of the town. For the Lord to call out a thief or a blasphemer and speak by his lips, is a thing to make men feel the greatness of God. Then they cry, "How unsearchable are his ways!" For an error to be blasted and dried up is a blessed thing—and yet it is all the more miraculous when this is done, not by reasoning, nor by eloquent argument, but by the simple declaration of gospel truth. O sirs, we never know what the Lord will do next. He can raise up defenders of the faith from the stones of the river. I despair not for the grand old cause. No, I hope against hope. Driven back as we may be, I see the very dust breeding warriors, and the grass of the field hardening into spears. Courage! Courage! Stand still, and see the salvation of God!

But the dream has more in it than this: *God uses despised means*. This man Gideon is likened to a cake, and then only to a barley cake; but the Lord styles him "a mighty man of valor." God loves to take men whom others despise, and use them for his glorious ends. "He is a fool," they say, "an uneducated man, one of the very lowest class of minds. He has no taste, no culture, no thought. He is not a person of the advanced school." My dear brother, I hope no one among you will be influenced by this kind of silly talk. The "mashers" in our churches talk in this fashion; but who cares for their proud nonsense? It is time that men who despise others should be themselves despised, and be made to know that they are so. Those who boast their intellect are of small account with God. The whole tenor of this inspired Book is that way; it speaks kindly of things that are despised, but it has no word of reverence for the boastful and pretentious. Therefore, you despised ones, let the proud unbelievers laugh at you, and sing concerning you their song of a barley cake; but do you in patience possess your souls, and go on in the service of your Lord. They think to render you contemptible; but the scorn shall return upon the scorners. You shall yet by the Lord's strength have such force and vigor put into you, that you shall put to flight the armies of the aliens. Say you with Paul, "When I am weak, then am I strong." "Fear not, little flock; for it is your Father's good pleasure to give you the kingdom." "He hath put down the mighty from their seats, and exalted them of low degree."

But, then, *God ever uses effectual means*. This cake of barley bread came unto a tent and smote it, that it fell, and overturned it, that the tent lay along. The Lord never does his work by halves. Even if he works by barley cakes, he makes a clean overthrow of his enemy. A cannonball could not have done its work better than did this barley cake. Friend, if the Lord uses you for his own purpose, he will do his work by you as effectually and surely as if he had selected the best possible worker. He lifts our weakness out of itself, and elevates it to a level of power and efficacy little dreamed of by us. Wherefore, be not afraid, you servants of God, but commit yourselves into the hands of him who, out of weakness, can bring forth strength.

I shall be done when I have made an application of all this to certain practical purposes. Brethren, do you not think that this smiting of the tent of Midian by the barley cake, and afterward the actual overthrow of the Midianite hordes by the breaking of the pitchers, the blazing of the torches, and the blowing of the trumpets, all tends to comfort us as to those powers of evil which now cover the world? I am appalled sometimes as I think of the power of the enemy, both in the matter of impurity and falsehood. At this present moment you seem as if you could do nothing: you cannot get in to strike a blow. Sin and error have so much the upper hand that we know not how to strike them. The two great parties in England, the Puritan and the Cavalier, take turn about, and just now the Cavalier rules most powerfully. At one time sound doctrine and holy practice had sway; but in these days loose teaching and loose living are to the fore. But our duty clearly lies in sticking to the Word of the Lord and the gospel of our fathers. God forbid that we should glory save in the cross of our Lord Jesus Christ. By this sign we shall conquer yet. The impurity of the age will never be cleansed except by the prevalence of the gospel; and the infidelity of the period will never die before any assault but that of the pure truth of the living Lord. We must tell of pardon bought with blood, of free forgiveness according to the riches of divine grace, and of eternal power changing fallen human nature, and making men new creatures in Christ Jesus. They call this a worn-out doctrine: let us put its power to the test on the largest scale, and we shall see that it is the power of God unto salvation to everyone that believeth.

As for me, I shall preach the gospel of the grace of God, and that only, even if I be left alone. The hosts of Israel are melting away, and they will melt much more. As in Gideon's day, out of the whole host twenty and two thousand have gone altogether away from true allegiance to the cause, and many more have no stomach for the fight. Let them go. The thousands and the hundreds. Let the thirty thousand who came at the trumpet call decrease to the three hundred men that lap in haste as a dog laps, because they are eager for the fray. When we are thinned out, and made to see how few we are, we shall be hurled upon the foe with a power not our own. Our weapon is the torch of the old gospel, flaming forth through the breaking of our earthen vessels. To this we add the trumpet sound of an earnest voice. Ours is the midnight cry: "Behold he cometh!" We cannot get victory by any might or skill of ours, and yet in the end the foe shall be defeated, and the Lord alone shall be exalted. Were things worse than they are, we would still cry, "The sword of the LORD and of Gideon," and stand each man in his place till the Lord appeared in strength.

Another lesson would I draw from the text as to our inward conflicts. Dear friend, you are feeling in your heart the great power of sin. The Midianites are encamped in your soul; in the little valley of Esdraelon [Jezreel] which lies within your bosom, there are countless evils, and these, like the locusts, eat up every growing thing, and cause comfort and strength and joy to cease from your experience. You sigh because of these invaders. I counsel you to try what faith can do. Your own earnest efforts appear to make you worse; try faith. Neither tears nor prayers nor vows nor self-denials have dislodged the foe; try the barley cake of faith. Believe in the Lord Jesus Christ. In him you are saved; in him you have power to become a child of God. Believe this and rejoice. Poor sinner! try faith. Poor backslider! try faith. Poor desponding heir of heaven! try faith. This barley cake of faith will smite the power of sin and break the dominion of doubt, and bring you victory. Remember that ancient Scripture, "Call upon me in the day of trouble, and I will deliver thee, and thou shalt glorify me." Make bold to believe. Say at once,

I do believe, I will believe,
That Jesus died for me.

This seems a very poor means of getting the victory, as poor as the barley cake baked on the coals—but God has chosen it, and he will bless it, and it will overthrow the throne of Satan within your heart, and work in you holiness and peace.

Once again, still in the same vein: let us, dear friends, try continually the power of prayer for the success of the gospel, and the winning of men's souls. Prayer will do anything—will do everything. It fills the valleys and levels the mountains. By its power men are raised from the door of hell to the gate of heaven. What is to become of London? What is to become of heathen nations? I listen to a number of schemes, very visionary, and very hard to work out. But I put these aside. There remains to believers but one scheme: our Lord has said, "Go ye into all the world and preach the gospel to every creature." This, therefore, we must do, and at the same time we must cry mightily unto God by prayer that his Holy Spirit may attend the proclamation of the Word. Let us more and more prove the power of prayer, resting assured that the Lord is able to do exceeding abundantly above what we ask or even think. Let each man stand with the flaming torch of truth in his hand, and the trumpet of the gospel at his lips, and so let us compass the army of the aliens. This is our war cry—Christ and him crucified! God forbid that we should know anything else among men, but the death, the blood, the resurrection, the reign, the coming, the glory of Christ. Let us not lose faith in our calling, nor in our God; but rest assured that the Lord reigns and his cause must triumph. Where sin abounded grace doth much abound. We shall see better and brighter days than these. Grant it, O Lord, for thy Son's sake. Amen.

Samuel: An Example of Intercession

Delivered on Lord's Day morning, May 9, 1880, at the Metropolitan Tabernacle, Newington. No. 1537.

> *Moreover as for me, God forbid that I should sin against the* Lord *in ceasing to pray for you: but I will teach you the good and the right way.*
> —1 Samuel 12:23

It is a very great privilege to be permitted to pray for our fellowmen. Prayer in each man's case must necessarily begin with personal petition, for until the man is himself accepted with God, he cannot act as an intercessor for others; and herein lies part of the excellence of intercessory prayer, for it is to the man who exercises it aright a mark of inward grace, and a token for good from the Lord. You may be sure that your King loves you when he will permit you to speak a word to him on behalf of your friend. When the heart is enlarged in believing supplication for others, all doubts about personal acceptance with God may cease; he who prompts us to love has certainly given us that love, and what better proof of his favor do we desire? It is a great advance upon anxiety for our own salvation when we have risen out of the narrowness of dread about ourselves into the broader region of care for a brother's soul. He who in answer to his intercession has seen others blessed and saved may take it as a pledge of divine love, and rejoice in the condescending grace of God. Such prayer rises higher than any petition for ourselves, for only he who is in favor with the Lord can venture upon pleading for others.

Intercessory prayer is an act of communion with Christ, for Jesus pleads for the sons of men. It is a part of his priestly office to make intercession for his people. He has ascended up on high to this end, and exercises this office continually within the veil. When we pray for our fellow sinners we are in sympathy with our divine Savior, who made intercession for the transgressors.

Such prayers are often of unspeakable value to those for whom they are offered. Many of us trace our conversion, if we go to the root of it, to the prayers of certain godly persons. In innumerable instances the prayers of parents have availed to bring young people to Christ. Many more will have to bless God for praying teachers, praying friends, praying pastors. Obscure persons confined to their beds are often the means of saving hundreds by their continual pleadings with God. The book of remembrance will reveal the value of these hidden ones, of whom so little is thought by the mass of Christians. As the body is knit together by bands and sinews, and interlacing nerves and veins, so is the whole body of Christ converted into a living unity by mutual prayers; we were prayed for, and now in turn we pray for others. Not only the conversion of sinners, but the welfare, preservation, growth, comfort, and usefulness of saints are abundantly promoted by the prayers of their brethren; hence apostolic men cried, "Brethren, pray for us"; he who was the personification of love said, "Pray one for another that ye may be healed," and our great Lord and Head ended his earthly career by a matchless prayer for those whom the Father had given him.

Intercessory prayer is a benefit to the man who exercises it, and is often a better channel of comfort than any other means of grace. The Lord turned again the captivity of Job when he prayed for his friends. Even where such prayer does not avail for its precise object, it has its results. David tells us that he prayed for his enemies: he says, in PSALM 35:13, "As for me, when they were sick, my clothing was sackcloth: I humbled my soul with fasting." And he adds, "my prayer returned into mine own bosom." He sent forth his intercession, like Noah's dove, but as it found no rest for the sole of its foot, and no blessing came of it, it returned to him who sent it, and brought back with it an olive leaf plucked off, a sense of peace to his own spirit; for nothing is more restful to the heart than to have prayed for those who despitefully use us and persecute us. Prayers for others are pleasing to God and profitable to ourselves; they are no waste of breath, but have a result guaranteed by the faithful Promiser.

I. Let us first dwell upon *his habit of intercession,* for it was most manifest in Samuel.

We gather this from the text. He says, "God forbid that I should sin against the LORD in ceasing to pray for you." It is clear, therefore, that he had been in the continual habit and practice of praying for Israel; he could not speak of ceasing to pray if he had not hitherto continued in prayer. Samuel had become so rooted in the habit of prayer for the people that he seems to start at the very thought of bringing his intercession to an end. The people, measuring the prophet by themselves, half suspected that he would be irritated with them, and would, therefore, deny them his prayers; therefore in verse 19 we read, "All the people said unto Samuel, 'Pray for thy servants unto the LORD thy God, that we die not.'" They greatly valued his prayers, and felt as if their national life, and perhaps their personal lives, depended upon his pleadings:

therefore they urged him as men who plead for their lives that he would not cease to pray for them, and he replied, "God forbid that I should." The denial of his prayers does not seem to have entered his thoughts. To my mind the words represent him as astonished at the idea, horrified and half indignant at the suggestion—"What I, Samuel, I who have been your servant from my childhood, since the day when I put on the little ephod, and waited for you in the house of the Lord; I that have lived for you and have loved you, and was willing to have died in your service, shall I ever cease to pray for you?" He says, "God forbid." It is the strongest expression that one can well imagine, and this, together with his evident surprise, shows that the prophet's habit of intercession was rooted, constant, fixed, abiding, a part and parcel of himself.

If you will read his life you will see how truly this was the case. Samuel was born of prayer. A woman of a sorrowful spirit received him from God and joyfully exclaimed, "For this child I prayed." He was named in prayer, for his name Samuel signifies, *"asked of God."* Well did he carry out his name and prove its prophetic accuracy, for having commenced life by being himself asked of God, he continued asking of God, and all his knowledge, wisdom, justice, and power to rule were things which came to him because "asked of God." He was nurtured by a woman of prayer at the first, and when he left her it was to dwell in the house of prayer all the days of his life. His earliest days were honored by a divine visitation, and he showed even then that waiting, watchful spirit which is the very knee of prayer. "Speak, LORD, for thy servant heareth" is the cry of a simple, sincere heart, such as the Lord ever accepts.

We all think of Samuel under that little figure so often painted and sculptured, in which a sweet child is seen in the attitude of prayer. We all seem to know little Samuel, the praying child: our boys and girls know him as a familiar friend, but it is as kneeling with clasped hands. He was born, named, nurtured, housed, and trained in prayer, and he never departed from the way of supplication. In his case the text was fulfilled, "Out of the mouth of babes and sucklings thou hast perfected praise"; and he so persevered in prayer that he brought forth fruit in old age, and testified of God's power to those who came after him. So famous did Samuel become as an intercessor that, if you will turn to the Ninety-ninth Psalm, at the sixth verse, you will read a short but very fragrant eulogy of him: "Moses and Aaron among his priests, and Samuel among them that call upon his name." If Moses and Aaron are selected as being consecrated men, leaders of God's Israel in service and sacrifice, Samuel is selected as the praying man, the man who calls upon God's name. All Israel knew Samuel was an intercessor as well as they knew Aaron as a priest. Perhaps even more notably you get the same inspired estimate of him in Jeremiah 15, at the first verse, where he is again classed with Moses: "Then said the LORD unto me, 'Though Moses and Samuel stood before me, yet my mind could not be toward this people: cast them out of my sight, and let them go forth.'" Here there is no doubt an allusion to the prevalent prayer of Moses, when in the agony of his heart he cried, "If not, blot me, I pray thee, out of thy book which thou hast written." This was a high form of pleading, but such is God's valuation of Samuel as an intercessor that he puts him side by side with Moses, and by way of threatening to sinful Israel he tells Jeremiah that he would not even listen to Moses and Samuel if they stood before him. It is well to learn the art of prayer in our earliest days, for then we grow up to be proficient in it. Early prayer grows into powerful prayer.

Hear this, you young people, and may the Lord now make Samuels of you. What an honor to be called to intercede for others, to be the benefactor of our nation, or even the channel of blessing to our own households. Aspire to it, my dear young friends. Perhaps you will never preach, but you may pray. If you cannot climb the pulpit, you may bow before the mercy seat, and be quite as great a blessing.

As to the success of Samuel's prayers, read his life, and you will find that wrought great deliverances for the people. In the seventh chapter of this book we find that the Philistines grievously oppressed Israel, and Samuel bravely called the people together, to consider their condition, and bade them turn from idolatry, and worship the only true God, and promised them his prayers as a boon which they greatly valued. These are his words: "Gather all Israel to Mizpeh, and I will pray for you unto the LORD." He then took a lamb, and offered it up for a burnt offering wholly unto the Lord, "and Samuel cried unto the LORD for Israel, and the LORD heard him." This is one of the grand events of his life, and yet it is fairly descriptive of his whole career. He cried, and the Lord heard. In this instance the Israelites marched to battle, but Jehovah went before them, in answer to the prophet's prayer. You could hear the rolling of the drums in the march of the God of armies, and see the glittering of his spear, for so is the history of the battle recorded: "And as Samuel was offering up the burnt offering, the Philistines drew near to battle against Israel: but the LORD thundered with a great thunder on that day upon the Philistines, and discomfited them; and they were smitten before Israel. And the men of Israel went out of Mizpeh, and pursued the Philistines, and smote them." The conclusion of the whole is "So the Philistines were subdued"; that is to say, the prayer of Samuel was the conquering weapon, and Philistia crouched beneath its power. O you who know the power of prayer, write this on your banners, "So the Philistines were subdued."

Samuel's prayers were so prevalent that the very elements were controlled by him. Oh, the power of prayer! It has been ridiculed: it has been represented as an unscientific and an unpractical thing, but we who daily try it know that its power cannot be exaggerated, and do not feel even a shadow of doubt concerning it. There is such power in prayer that it "moves the arm that moves the world." We have but to know how to pray, and the thunder shall lift up its voice in answer to our cry, and Jehovah's arrows shall be scattered abroad to the overthrowing of his adversaries. How should those be able to judge of prayer who never ask at all, or never ask in faith? Let those bear witness to whom prayer is a familiar exercise, and to whom answers from God are as common as the day. Over a father's heart no power has so great a control as his child's necessity, and in the case of our Father who is in heaven it is especially so. He must hear prayer, for he cannot dishonor his own name or forget his own children.

When in his old age the people began to turn against Samuel, and to express dissatisfaction with his unworthy sons, it is beautiful to notice how Samuel at once resorted to prayer. Look at the eighth chapter, the fifth verse: the people "said unto him, 'Behold, thou art old, and thy sons walk not in thy ways: now make us a king to judge us.'" The old man was sorely grieved; it was natural that he should be. But look at the next words. Did Samuel scold the people? Did he send them home in a huff? No. It is written, "And Samuel prayed unto the LORD." He told his Master about them, and his Master said to him, "Hearken unto the voice of the people in all that they say unto thee: for they have not rejected thee,"—do not lay it to heart as if it were a personal affront to you—"but they have rejected me, that I should not reign over them." This slight upon God's servant was a rejection of God himself, and he would not have Samuel lay to heart their ingratitude to him, but think of their wicked conduct to the Lord their God.

Thus, you see, Samuel was a man of abundant prayer, and in the twenty-first verse we read that, after he had entered his protest, and told the people of all that they would have to suffer from a king, how he would tax them and oppress them and take their sons to be soldiers and their daughters to wait in his palace, and take their fields and vineyards, though they still persisted in saying, "Nay, but we will have a king," he made no angry answer but returned to his God in secret communion, "Samuel heard all the words of the people, and he rehearsed them in the ears of the LORD." Oh, that we were wise enough to do the like! Instead of going about and telling one and another of the opprobrious things that have been said about us, it were well to go straight away to our closet and rehearse them in the ears of the Lord. Samuel was thus, you see, throughout his whole official life, a man mighty in prayer, and when the people left him and followed after their new-made king, our text shows that he did not cease to intercede for them. He says, "God forbid that I should cease to pray to God for you."

Nor was this all, when Saul had turned aside and become a traitor to his divine Lord, Samuel made intercession for him. One whole night he spent in earnest entreaty, though it was all in vain; and many a time and often did he sigh for the rejected prince. The old man had been, from his youth up, an intercessor, and he never ceased from the holy exercise till his lips were closed in death. Now, beloved, you are not judges of the land, else would I plead with you to pray much for the people whom you rule. You are not all pastors and teachers, else would I say that if we do not abound in prayer the blood of souls will be upon our skirts. Some of you, however, are teachers of the young: do not think that you have done anything for your classes till you have prayed for them. Be not satisfied with the hour or two of teaching in the week, be frequent in your loving supplications. Many of you are parents. How can you discharge your duty toward your children except you bear their names upon your hearts in prayer? Those of you who are not found in these relationships have nevertheless some degree of ability, some measure of influence, some position in which you can do good to your fellows, and these demand your dependence upon God. You cannot discharge your responsibilities as relatives, as citizens, as neighbors, no, as Christian men, unless you often make supplication for all ranks and conditions. To pray for others must become to you a habit from which you would not cease even if they provoked you to the utmost degree; for you would only cry out, God forbid that I should cease to pray for you, for it would be a great sin in the sight of the most High.

II. Now, second, I call you to notice in Samuel's case *his provocation to cease from intercession,* which provocation he patiently endured.

The first provocation was *the slight which they put upon himself.* The grand old man who had all the year round made his circuit from place to place to do justice had never looked at a bribe. He had done everything for them without fee or reward. Though he had a right to his stipend, yet he did not take it; in the generosity of his spirit he did everything gratuitously, like Nehemiah in after days who said, "The former governors that had been before me were chargeable unto the people, and had taken of them bread and wine, beside forty shekels of silver; yea, even their servants bare rule over the people: but so did not I, because of the fear of God." Samuel throughout a long life had kept the land in peace, and innumerable blessings had come to Israel through his leadership; but now he was getting old and somewhat infirm, though he was far from being worn out, and they seized on this excuse for setting up a king. The old man felt that there was life and work in him yet; but they clamored for a king, and therefore their aged friend must give up his office and come down from his high position. It displeases him when he first hears their demand, but after a little time spent in prayer he resigns his position very pleasantly, and all his anxiety is to find the right man for the throne. When the man is found he is full of care that the Lord's anointed shall be guided aright in the kingdom; and without a thought about himself he rejoices at the sight of one whose opening days promised so well. His deposition was a hard thing, mark you, an unkind, ungenerous thing; but he did not pray one atom the less for the people because of it; probably he prayed much more; for as his mother prayed most when the sorrow of her heart was greatest, so was it with him.

Beyond the provocation which came from slight upon himself he felt wounded *by their utter rejection of his solemn protest.* He stood before them and reasoned with them in the clearest possible manner: "What do you want a king for?" he seemed to say. "This will be the manner of the king that shall reign over you: he will take your sons and appoint them for himself, for his chariots, and to be his horsemen; and some shall run before his chariots. He will take your daughters to be confectionaries, and to be cooks, and to be bakers; and he will take your fields, and your vineyards, and your olive yards, even the best of them, and give them to his servants. He will take the tenth of your seed, and of your vineyards, and give to his officers, and to his servants; and he will take your menservants, and your maidservants, and your goodliest young men, and your asses, and put them to his work. He will take the tenth of your sheep; and ye shall be his servants; and ye shall cry out in that day because of your king which ye shall have chosen you; and the LORD will not hear you in that day." There was sound common sense in all these, and every word turned out to be true in fact before long, and yet they would not listen. They said, "Nay, but we will have a king over us; that we also may be like all the nations; and that our king may judge us, and fight our battles." Despite their rejection of his warning, the venerable man did not grow testy. It is sometimes the infirmity of wise men of years and weight, that when they have presented a clearer case, presented it earnestly in all simplicity of heart, and the thing looks as plain as that twice two make four, then if their hearers deliberately persist in defying their warning they grow peevish, or perhaps it is more fair to say they exhibit a justifiable indignation. Samuel is always hopeful, and if they will not do the best thing possible, he will try to lead them to do the second best. If they will not abide under the direct rule of the Lord, as their King, he hopes that they will do well under a human king who shall be a viceroy under God, and so he continues hopefully to pray for them, and to make the best he can of them.

At last it came to this, that the nation must have a king, and their king must be crowned. They must go to Gilgal to settle the kingdom, and then Samuel stood up and in the words which I read to you just now he declared how he had dealt with them, how he had never defrauded nor oppressed, nor taken anything from them, and he told them that their choice of a king was to some extent a rejection of God, that they were putting aside the best of rules and the most honorable of governments to go down to the level of the nations. Still, *they rejected his last appeal,* and it is beautiful to my mind to see how calmly he drops the question when he has given his last address, and made his most solemn appeal to heaven. Their obstinate adherence to their whim did not cause him to restrain prayer on their behalf.

The practical lesson of this is that when you are tempted to cease from pleading for certain persons you must not yield to the suggestion. They have ridiculed your prayers: they tell you that they do not want them: they have even made a taunt and a jest of your pious wishes on their behalf. Never mind. Retaliate by still greater love. Do not cease to wrestle with God for them. It may be you have been very much disappointed in them; your heart breaks to see how they have gone aside, yet go with your deep anxieties to the mercy seat, and cry out again for them. What will become of them if you leave them to themselves? Do not leave off interceding, though you are provoked to do so in ten thousand ways.

It may be that you think, partly in unbelief, and partly through trembling anxiety, that really their doom is sealed, and they will go on to perdition. Let this rather increase the intensity of your prayer than in the least degree diminish it. Till sinners are in hell cry to God for them. As long as there is breath in their bodies and your body cause the voice of our supplication to be heard. Your husband, good woman, what if he does grow more drunken and more profane, pray for him still; for God, who can draw out leviathan as with a hook, can yet take this great sinner and make a saint of him. What if your son does seem to be more profligate than ever, follow him with many entreaties, and weep before God about him still. Loving mother and gracious father, join your fervent cries day and night at the mercy seat and you shall yet obtain your desire.

III. I come, in the third place, briefly to notice Samuel in his *persevering intercession.*

Though the people thus provoked him, he did not cease from prayer for them; for, first, there and then, he offered fresh supplication for them, and that cry was heard, and Saul was dowried with a rich measure of favor to start with. Samuel did not cease his prayer for Saul when Saul had gone far astray, for we find this passage: "Then came the word of the LORD to Samuel, saying, 'It repenteth me that I have set up Saul to be king, for he has turned back from following me, and hath not performed my commandment'; and it grieved Samuel, and he cried unto the LORD all night." *All night.* I think I see the old man in an agony for Saul, whom he loved. Old men need sleep, but the prophet forsook his bed, and in the night watches poured out his soul unto the Lord. Though he received no cheering answer, he still continued to cry; for we read, a little further on, that the Lord said to him, "How long wilt thou mourn for Saul?" He was pushing the case as far as ever he could push it, till the Lord gave him warning that there was no use in it. "How long wilt thou mourn for Saul?"

It is to be admired in Samuel, that, even though Saul may have committed the sin which is unto death, and Samuel had some fear that his fate was fixed, yet he prayed on in desperate hope. The apostle John puts the case thus: "If any man see his brother sin a sin which is not unto death, he shall ask, and he shall give him life for them that sin not unto death. There is a sin unto death: I do not say that he shall pray for it." He does not in such a case forbid our prayers, neither does he encourage them, but I take it that he gives us a permit to pray on. We do not know for certain that the most guilty person has indeed passed the bound of mercy, and therefore we may intercede with hope. If we have a horrible dread upon us that possibly our erring relative is beyond hope, if we are not commanded to pray, we are certainly not forbidden, and it is always best to err on the safe side, if it be erring at all. We may still go to God, even with a forlorn hope, and cry to him in the extremity of our distress. We are not likely to hear the Lord say to us, "How long wilt thou mourn for Saul?" We are not likely to hear him say, "How long will you pray for your boy? How long will you mourn over your husband? I do not intend to save them."

When the prophet knew that Saul was hopelessly rejected, he did not cease to pray for the nation, but went down to Bethlehem and anointed David, and when David was pursued by the malice of Saul we find him harboring David at Ramah, and exhibiting the power of prayer in his own house and in the holy place; for when Saul came down thinking to seize David, even in the seer's house, there was a prayer meeting being held, and Saul was so struck with it that he took to prophesying himself, and lay down all night among them disrobed and humbled. Men exclaimed, "Is Saul also among the prophets?" The malicious king could not venture to touch Samuel. The prophet was a gentle, mild, loving man; and yet the black-hearted Saul always had an awe of him, so that he took hold of his skirts for protection, and after he was dead wickedly sought to his supposed spirit for guidance. The man of God had evidently impressed the tall reprobate with the weight of his holy character. It is written that God was with him, and did let none of his words fall to the ground; and this was because he was a praying man. He who can prevail with God for man can always prevail with man for God. If you can overcome heaven by prayer, you can overcome earth by preaching: if you know the art of speaking to the Eternal, it will be a small thing to speak to mortal men. Rest assured that the very essence of all true power over men for their good must lie in power with God in secret: when we have waited upon the Lord, and prevailed, our work is well-nigh done.

I pray you, therefore, still persevere in supplication, and be supported in your perseverance by the knowledge that it would be a sin to cease to pray for those who have been the subjects of your petitions. Samuel confesses that it would have been sinful on his part to abstain from intercession. How so? Why, if he ceased to pray for that people, he would be neglecting his office, for God had made him a prophet to the nation, and he must intercede for them or neglect his duty. It would show a want of love to the Lord's chosen people if he did not pray for them. How could he teach them if he was not himself taught of God? How could he possibly hope to sway them if he had not enough affection for them to cry to God on their behalf? It would be in his case, too, a sin of anger. It would look as if he were in a pet [petulance] with them and with God too, because he could not be all that he would wish to be. "God forbid," he said, "I should harbor such anger in my bosom as to cease to pray for you." It would have been a neglect of the divine glory; for whatever the people might be, God's name was wrapped up in them, and if they did not prosper, the Lord would not be glorified in the eyes of the heathen. He could not give up praying for them, for their cause was the cause of God. It would have been a cruelty to souls if he who possessed such power in prayer had restrained it. Now, brethren and sisters, it will be sin on your part if you neglect the mercy seat. You will grieve the Holy Spirit, you will rob Christ of his glory, you will be cruel to souls dead in sin, and you will be false and traitorous to the Spirit of grace, and to your sacred calling.

IV. Our last point is that Samuel showed *his sincerity in intercession* by corresponding action.

For he says in the words of the text, "God forbid that I should sin against the LORD in ceasing to pray for you: but I will teach you the good and the right way." So far from leaving off praying, he would be doubly diligent to teach them: and he did so. He taught them by reminding them of God's promises, that he would not forsake his people: by directing them how to act—"serve God in truth with all your heart"; by urging motives upon them—"consider the great things he hath done for you"; and by adding a solemn warning, "if you shall still do wickedly, ye shall be consumed, both ye and your king." After praying for your friends, do try as well as you can to answer your own prayer by using the means which God ordinarily blesses. Some persons make idle prayers, for they use no effort for obtaining their requests. If a husbandman asks for a harvest, he also plows and sows, for else his supplications would be hypocritical. If we wish to see our neighbors converted, we shall labor for it in all ways. We shall invite them to go with us where the gospel is faithfully preached, or we shall place a good book in their way, or we shall speak with them personally about eternal things. If I knew where gold was to be had for the picking up, and I wanted my neighbor to be rich, I would tell him of the precious deposit and ask him to come and gather some of the treasure with me. But many never think of inviting a neighbor or a friend who is a Sabbath breaker to go with them to the house of God; and there are thousands in London who only want an invitation and they would be sure to come, once, at any rate, and who can tell but that once might lead to their conversion?

If I desire the salvation of anyone, I ought to tell him as best as I can what his condition is, and what the way of salvation is, and how he may find rest. All men are approachable at some time or in some way. It is very imprudent to rush at everybody as soon as you see them, without thought or ordinary prudence, for you may disgust those whom you wish to win: but those who earnestly plead for others, and bestir themselves to seek them, are generally taught of God, and so they are made wise as to time, manner, and subject. A man who wishes to shoot birds will, after a while, become expert in the sport, because he will give his mind to it: he will after a little practice become a noted marksman and know all about guns and dogs. A man who wants to catch salmon has his heart set upon his angling, and becomes absorbed in the pursuit. He soon learns how to use his rod and how to manage his fish. So he who longs to win souls, and puts his heart into it, finds out the knack of it by some means, and the Lord gives him success. I could not teach it to you, you must practice in order to find out; but this I will say, no man is clear of his fellows' blood simply because he has prayed to be so. Suppose we had around this parish of Newington a number of people who were dying of hunger, and we were to have a prayer meeting that God would relieve their wants: would it not be hypocrisy worthy to be ridiculed and held up to reprobation if, after having prayed for these people, we all went home and ate our own dinners and did not give them a farthing's worth of bread? The truly benevolent man puts his hand in his pocket and says, "What can I do that my prayer may be answered?" I have heard of one who prayed in New York for a certain number of very poor families that he had visited, and he asked the Lord that they might be fed and clothed. His little son said, "Father, if I were God I should tell you to answer your own prayer, for you have plenty of money." Thus the Lord might well say to us when we have been interceding, "Go and answer your own prayer by telling your friends of my Son." Do you sing, "Fly abroad, thou mighty gospel"? Then give it wings covered with silver. Do you sing, "Waft, waft, ye winds, his story"? Then spend your breath for it. There is a power in your gifts; there is a power in your speech; use these powers. If you cannot personally do much, you can do a great deal by helping another to preach Christ: but chief and first you ought to do somewhat by your own hand, heart, and tongue. Go and teach the good and right way, and then shall your prayers be heard.

David: Encouraging Himself *in* God

Delivered on Lord's Day morning, June 26, 1881, at the Metropolitan Tabernacle, Newington. No. 1606.

> *And David was greatly distressed; for the people spake of stoning him, because the soul of all the people was grieved, every man for his sons and for his daughters: but David encouraged himself in the* LORD *his God. . . . And David inquired at the* LORD*, saying, "Shall I pursue after this troop? shall I overtake them?" And he answered him, "Pursue: for thou shalt surely overtake them, and without fail recover all."*—1 SAMUEL 30:6, 8

We ought to be deeply grateful to God for the inspired history of the life of his servant David. It was a great life, a vigorous life, a life spent in many positions and conditions. I almost rejoice that it was not a faultless life, for its failings and errors are instructive. It is the life of a man after God's own heart; but still, the life of one who went astray, like a lost sheep, and was recovered by the great Shepherd's grace. By this fact he comes all the nearer to us poor, faulty men and women. I would venture to apply to David the description which has been applied to the world's own poet—

> *A man so various, that he seemed to be*
> *Not one, but all mankind's epitome.*

Each one may find something like himself in the long, eventful, and checkered life of the son of Jesse. Among other things we learn this, that where there is faith there is sure to be trial; for David, though he trusted God so heartily, had good need of all the faith he possessed. In his early days he was hunted like a partridge upon the mountains by Saul and was constantly in jeopardy of his life. He had so choice a treasure of faith about him, that Satan was forever trying to plunder him of it. Still, the worst trials that David suffered arose not out of his faith, but out of his want of it. That which he did to avoid trouble brought him into deeper distress than ordinary providences ever caused him. He left the country where he was so ill at ease, which was, nevertheless, your land, O Emmanuel, and he went away into the land of the Philistines, expecting there to escape from further turmoil. In so doing he transgressed, and fresh trials came upon him, trials of a worse kind than those which had happened to him from the hand of Saul. Brethren, the poet said—

> *The path of sorrow, and that path alone,*
> *Leads to the land where sorrow is unknown,*

and he spoke truly; for "in the world ye shall have tribulation." If you have faith, it must be tried, and should that faith fail, you must be tried still more. There is no discharge from this war: difficulties must be faced. This is the day of battle, and you must fight if you would reign. You are like men thrown into the sea, you must swim or drown. It is useless to expect ease where your Lord had none. If you adopt the paltry shifts suggested by unbelief, not even then shall you avoid affliction; the probabilities are that you will be taken among the thorns and scourged with the briars of the wilderness. However rough the king's highway may be, the bypaths are far worse; therefore keep the way of the commandment and bravely face its trials.

Another lesson is this: though we shall be tried, yet faith in God is an available resource at all times. Faith is a shield which you may use for warding off every kind of arrow, yes, even the fiery darts of the great enemy; for this shield cannot be penetrated even by javelins of fire. You cannot be cast into a condition in which faith shall not help you. There is a promise of God suitable for every state, and God has wisdom and skill and love and faithfulness to deliver you out of every possible jeopardy; and therefore you have only to confide in God, and deliverance is sure to come. Mainly note this: that *even when your trouble has been brought upon you by your own fault, faith is still available.* When your affliction is evidently a chastisement for grievous transgression, still trust in the Lord. The Lord Jesus prayed for erring Peter that his faith might not fail him: his hope of recovery lay there. Faith under a sense of guilt is one of those noble kinds of faith at which some are staggered. To my mind the faith of a saint is comparatively easy; it is the faith of a sinner that is hard. When you know that you have walked uprightly before God, and have not stained your garments, then you can trust him without difficulty: but, oh, when you have stepped aside, and when at last the heavenly Father makes you smart under his rod—to cast yourself upon him then is faith indeed. Do not fail to exercise it, for this is the faith which saves. What faith is that which first of all brings men into possession of a good hope but the faith of a sinner? Often in life, when our sinnership becomes more manifest to us than usual, we shall be driven to that first sort of faith, in which, being unworthy, we trust entirely in pardoning grace. It would be wise always to live by this same faith.

If any of you at this time are in great distress, and are conscious that you richly deserve all your troubles because of your folly, still trust in the mercy of the Lord. Do not doubt the Lord your Savior, for he invites his backsliding children to return unto him. Though you have fallen by your iniquity, yet take with you words and return unto the Lord. May the Holy Spirit give you renewed trust in the Lord, who forgives iniquity, transgression, and sin, and retains not his anger forever, because he delights in mercy.

Let this stand as our preface, and the whole of the sermon will tend to illustrate it. We notice: first, David's distress—"David was greatly distressed"; second, David's encouragement—"David encouraged himself in the LORD his God"; third, David's inquiry—"And David inquired at the LORD"; and then, fourth, David's answer of peace—the Lord said, "Pursue: for thou shalt surely overtake them, and without fail recover all."

I. First, then, let us look at *David's distress*—"David was greatly distressed."

His city was burned, his wives were gone, the sons and daughters of his comrades were all captive, and little Ziklag, where they had made a home, smoked before them in blackened ruins. The men of war, wounded in heart, mutinied against their leader, and were ready to stone him. David's fortunes were at their lowest ebb. To understand his position we must go a little further back in his history.

David was greatly distressed for *he had been acting without consulting his God*. It was his general habit to wait upon the Lord for direction, for even as a shepherd lad it was his joy to sing, "He leadeth me"; but for once David had gone without leading, and had chosen a bad road. Worn out by the persecution of Saul, in an evil moment his heart failed him, and he said, "I shalt surely fall one day by the hand of Saul." This was a dangerous mood. Always be afraid of being afraid. Failing faith means failing strength. Do not regard despondency as merely a loss of joy, view it as draining away your spiritual life. Struggle against it, for it often happens that when faith ebbs sin comes to the flood. He who does not comfortably trust God will soon seek after comfort somewhere else, and David did so: without asking divine direction he fled to the court of the Philistine chieftain Achish, hoping to be quiet there. See what came of it! When he stood among the ashes of Ziklag, he began to understand what an evil and bitter thing it is to lean to our own understanding, to forget God who guides us, and to become a law unto ourselves. Perhaps some of you are in distress in the same way: you have chosen your own path, and now you are caught in the tangled bushes which tear your flesh. You have carved for yourselves, and you have cut your own fingers; you have obtained your heart's desire, and while the meat is yet in your mouth a curse has come with it. You say you "did it for the best"; yes, but it has turned out to be for the worst. David never made a heavier rod for himself than when he thought to avoid all further discomfort by leaving his true place.

Worse than this, if worse can be, *David had also followed policy instead of truth*. The Oriental mind was, and probably still is, given to lying. Easterners do not think it wrong to tell an untruth; many do it habitually. Just as an upright merchant in this country would not be suspected of a falsehood, so you would not in the olden time have suspected the average Oriental of ever speaking the truth if he could help it, because he felt that everybody else would deceive him and so he must practice great cunning. The golden rule in David's day was, "Do others, for others will certainly do you." David in his early days was not without the taint of his times. He became the commander of the bodyguard of Achish, king of Gath, and he lived in the royal city. As he found himself rather awkwardly situated in that idolatrous town, he said to the king, "If I have now found grace in thine eyes, let them give me a place in some town in the country, that I may dwell there: for why should thy servant dwell in the royal city with thee?" Achish appears to have been almost a convert to the worship of Jehovah, and certainly shines brilliantly in the narrative before us. At David's request he gave him the town of Ziklag.

David and his men warred with the various tribes of Canaanites who dwelled in the south of Palestine, and took from them great spoil; but he greatly erred in making Achish believe that he was fighting against Judah. We read, "And Achish believed David, saying, 'He hath made his people Israel utterly to abhor him; therefore he shall be my servant forever.'" This was the result of David's acted and uttered lie, and lest the falsehood should be found out, David spared none of those whom he conquered, saying "Lest they should tell on us, saying, 'So did David.'" So that beginning with policy he went on to falsehood, and from one falsehood he was driven to another, and his course became far other than that which a man of God should have pursued. How different was such false conduct from the usual character of the man who said, "He that worketh deceit shall not dwell within my house: he that telleth lies shall not tarry in my sight." See the fruit of his falsehood! Ziklag is burned with fire: his wives are captives; and his men speak of stoning him.

If you and I ever get away from living by straightforward truth, we shall wander into a maze from which it will be hard to extricate ourselves. We should each feel that we can die but we cannot lie, we can starve but we cannot cheat, we can be ground into the dust but we cannot do an unrighteous thing. If it be so, we may count upon the help of God, and may go bravely on under every difficulty. David had left the highway of righteousness, and was stumbling among the dark mountains of craft and deceit. He was plotting and scheming likc the worst of worldlings, and he must be made to see his error, and taught to abhor the way of lying; hence in one moment the Lord launches at him bereavement, plunder, mutiny, danger of life, that he might be driven to his God, and made to hate the way of cunning. What wonder that David was greatly distressed?

Yet was his distress the more severe on another account, for *David had sided with the enemies of the Lord's people.* He had gone to the Philistines, and their prince had said to him, "I will make thee keeper of mine head forever." Think of David keeping the head of a Philistine! When Achish gathered the Philistine army to battle with Israel, we read with shame, "And the lords of the Philistines passed on by hundreds, and by thousands: but David and his men passed on in the reward with Achish." How dreadfully troubled David must have felt in this false position. Think of David, who was ordained to be king of Israel, marching his armed band to fight his own countrymen! How gracious was the Lord in bringing him out of that perilous position. The Philistine princes suspected him, as well they might, and said to Achish, "What do these Hebrews here?" They were jealous of the high office to which David had been promoted, and fearful of his turning against them during the fight. "And the princes of the Philistines were wroth with Achish; and the princes of the Philistines said unto him, 'Make this fellow return, that he may go again to his place which thou hast appointed him, and let him not go down with us to battle, lest in the battle he be an adversary to us: for wherewith should he reconcile himself unto his master? should it not be with the heads of these men? Is not this David, of whom they sang, one to another in dances, saying, "Saul slew his thousands, and David his ten thousands?"'" Though the Philistine king, like the true man that he was, smoothed it down, he was forced to send David away. What a relief David must have felt! Well might he pen the words of Psalm 124, "Our soul is escaped as a bird out of the snare of the fowlers: the snare is broken, and we are escaped." What a horror would have been upon him if he had actually gone with the Philistines to the battle in which Saul and Jonathan were slain. It would have been a stain upon David all his life. The Lord delivered him, but he made him to feel his rod at the same time, for no sooner had David reached Ziklag, than he saw that the hand of the Lord was gone out against him, desolation smoked around him, and we do not marvel that David was greatly distressed.

Picture the position of David, in the center of his band. He has been *dri-*

ven away by the Philistine lords with words of contempt; his men have been sneered at—"What do these Hebrews here? Is not this David?" When he walked with God he was like a prince, and no man dared to sneer at him, but now he has been flouted by the uncircumcised Philistines, and has been glad to sneak back to his little city, ashamed of himself. It is terrible when a man of God falls into such a position that he gives the enemy opportunity to blaspheme God, and to despise his servant. It is terrible when even worldlings scout the inconsistency of the professed follower of Jesus. "What do these Hebrews here?" is the sarcastic question of the world. "How comes a professing Christian to be acting as we do? Look, he is trying to cultivate our acquaintance, and pass for one of ourselves, and yet he calls himself a servant of God!" They begin to point, as they did at Peter—"Thou also wast with Jesus of Nazareth, for thy speech betrayeth thee." "What doest thou here, Elijah?" is the voice which comes from God's mouth, and the lips of his adversaries repeat it. When the child of God feels that he is in that predicament, and in great trouble too, it is not strange that he is greatly distressed.

At the back of this came *bereavement*. His wives were gone. He was a man of a large, affectionate, tender heart, and what grief it must have been to him! Nor was he a solitary mourner; but all those brave fellows who were joined with him were bereaved too. Hark to the common chorus of grief! They weep, until they have no more power to weep. It must have been a dread day for their leader to feel his own personal sorrow merged and drowned in the flood of grief which swept over his companions. As for his worldly possessions, he was now as *poor* as he possibly could be; for all that he had was taken away, and his habitation was burned with fire, and the rovers were gone he knew not whither. Worst of all, he was now *forsaken* by his followers. Those who had been with him in his worst fortunes now upbraided him with their calamity. Why did he leave the city to go off to help these enemies of the Lord, the uncircumcised Philistines? He might have known better; and they grew indignant, and one said, "Let us stone him"; to which others answered, "Let us do it at once." They were evidently in a great rage. He stands there faint with weeping, a friendless, forsaken man, with *his very life in danger* from furious mutineers. Do you wonder that it is written, "And David was greatly distressed"? He is surrounded with sorrow; but he has no need to gather ashes as the emblems of his woe; for ashes are everywhere about him, the whole place is smoking. He mourns greatly for his wives, and his soldiers mourn for their children, for they are as if they were slain with the sword. It is a case of deep distress, with this added sting—that he had brought it upon himself.

There is the picture before you: now let us see a fairer scene as we observe what David did under the circumstances. When he was at his worst he was seen at his best.

II. Second, let us consider *David's encouragement*: "And David encouraged himself."

That is well, David! He did not at first attempt to encourage anybody else; but he encouraged *himself.* Some of the best talks in the world are those which a man has with himself. He who speaks to everybody except himself is a great fool. I think I hear David say, "Why art thou cast down, O my soul, and why art thou disquieted within me? hope thou in God; for I will yet praise him." David encouraged himself. But he encouraged himself "in the LORD his God," namely, in Jehovah. That is the surest way of encouraging yourself. David might have drawn, if he had pleased, a measure of encouragement from those valiant men who joined him just about this particular time; for it happened, according to 1 Chronicles 12:19–22, that many united with his band at that hour. Let us read the passage. "And there fell some of Manasseh to David, when he came with the Philistines against Saul to battle; but they helped them not: for the lords of the Philistines upon advisement sent him away, saying, 'He will fall to his master Saul to the jeopardy of our heads.' As he went to Ziklag, there fell to him of Manasseh, Adnah, and Jozabad, and Jediael, and Michael, and Jozabad, and Elihu, and Zilthai, captains of the thousands that were of Manasseh. And they helped David against the band of the rovers: for they were all mighty men of valor, and were captains in the host. For at that time day by day there came to David to help him, until it was a great host, like the host of God." These newcomers had not lost their wives and children, for they had not been in Ziklag; but David did not look around to them and beg them to stand by him, and put down the mutiny. No, he had by this time become sick of men, and weary of trusting to himself. God was beginning to cure his servant by a bitter dose of distress, and the evidence of the cure was that he did not encourage himself by his new friends, or by the hope of others coming; but he encouraged himself in the Lord his God.

Do you not feel a wind from the hills? The air blows strong and fresh from the everlasting mountains, now that the man of God is looking to God alone. Before, David was down there in the valleys, with his policy and his craft, in the stagnant atmosphere of self-trust and worldliness; but now he stands in Ziklag, a friendless man, but free and true. How grand he is amid the rains! He rises to his full height, while his fortunes fall! He reminds you of his youthful days when he said, "The LORD that delivered me out of the paw of the lion, and out of the paw of the bear, he will deliver me out of the hand of this Philistine." He is no longer in bondage to craft, but he is a man again, strong in the strength of God; for he casts himself away from all earthly trusts, and encourages himself in the Lord.

He did not sit down in sullen despair, nor did he think, as Saul did, of resorting to wrong means for help; but he went, sinner as he was, confessing all his wrongdoing, straightaway to his God, and asked for the priest to come that he might speak with him in the name of the most High. Brothers and sisters, if you are in trouble, and your trouble is mixed with sin, if you have afflicted yourselves by your backslidings and perversities, nevertheless I pray you look nowhere else for help but to the God whom you have offended. When he lifts his arm, as it were, to execute vengeance, lay hold upon it and he will spare you. Does he not himself say, "Let him lay hold on my strength"? I remember old Master Quarles has a strange picture of one trying to strike another with a flail, and how does the other escape? Why, he runs in and keeps close, and so he is not struck. It is the very thing to do. Close in with God. Cling to him by faith; hold fast by him in hope. Say, "Though he slay me, yet will I trust in him." Resolve, "I will not let thee go." Guilty as you are, it is good for you to draw nigh unto God.

Let us try to conceive of the way in which David would encourage himself in the Lord his God. Standing amid those ruins, he would say, "Yet the Lord does love me, and I love him. Though I have wandered, yet my heart cannot rest without him. Though I have had but little fellowship with him of late, yet he has not forgotten to be gracious, nor has he in anger shut up his bowels of compassion." He would look back upon those happy days when he kept sheep, and sang psalms unto the Lord his God amid the pastures of the wilderness. He would recollect those peaceful hours of happiest communion and long to have them over again. His own psalms would tend to comfort him as he saw how his heart had once been glad. He would say to himself: "My experience of divine love is not a dream. I know it is not a myth or a delusion. I have known the Lord, and I have had near and dear intercourse with him, and I know that he changes not, and therefore he will help me. His mercy endureth forever. He will put away my transgression." Thus he encouraged himself in the Lord his God.

Then he went further, and argued, "Hath not the Lord chosen me? Has he not ordained me to be king in Israel? Did he not send his prophet Samuel, who poured oil upon my head, and said, 'This is he'? Surely the Lord will not change his appointment or suffer his word to fail. I have been separated from my kinsfolk and hunted by Saul and driven from rock to cave and from cave to wilderness, and I have known no rest, and all because I was ordained to be king in Saul's place; surely the Lord will carry out his purpose, and will set me on the throne. He has not chosen and ordained and anointed me in mockery."

Brethren, do you need an interpretation of this parable? Can you not see its application to yourselves? Are you not saying, "The Lord called me by his grace, brought me out from my love of the world, and made me a priest and a king unto himself, and can he leave me? Is not the oil of his Spirit still upon me? Can he cast me off? He separated me to himself, and gave me to know that my destiny was not like that of the ungodly world, but that he had ordained me and chosen me to be his servant forever—will he leave me to perish? Shall his enemy rejoice over me?" Thus may you encourage yourself in God.

Then he would go over all the past deliverances which he had experienced. I see the picture which passed like a panorama before David's eye. He saw himself when he slew the lion and the bear. Did God deliver him then, and will he not deliver him now? He pictured himself going out to meet the giant Goliath, with nothing but a sling and a stone, and coming back with the monster's head in his hand; and he argued, "Will he not rescue me now?" He saw himself in the courts of Saul, when the mad king sought to pin him to the wall with a javelin, and he barely escaped. He saw himself let down by the kindness of Michal from the window, when her father sought to slay him in his bed.

He saw himself in the cave of Engedi, and upon the tracks of the wild goats, pursued by his remorseless adversary, but always strangely guarded from his cruel hand. He cheers himself, as one had done before him, with the inference, "If the Lord had meant to destroy me, he would not have showed me such things as these."

Come, now, dear children of God, take down your diaries and refer to the days when the Lord helped you again and again. How many times has he blessed you? You could not count them, for God has been so gracious and tender that he has aided you ten thousand times already. Has he changed in love, in faithfulness, in power? God forbid that we should indulge such a wicked thought. He is still the same, and so let us encourage ourselves in him.

"Alas," say you, "I have done wrong." I know you have; but *he* has not. If your confidence were in yourself, that wrong of yours might crush your hope; but since your confidence is in God, and he has not changed, why should you fear? "Oh, but I am so sinful." Yes; I know you are, and so you were when he first looked upon you in love. If his love had sought to come to you by the way of merit, it never would have reached you; but it comes to you by way of free, rich, sovereign grace, and therefore it will come to you evermore. Do you not feel refreshed this morning as you think of what the Lord has done? And do you not feel that after doing so much it would be wrong now to distrust him? Will you not even now encourage yourself in your God?

Perhaps David at that moment perceived that this crushing blow was sent in infinite tenderness to clean him right out of the condition into which he had fallen. The Lord seems to say to David, "All that you have ever got of Achish is this village of Ziklag, and I have caused it to be burned up, so that you have nothing left to be a tie between you and Philistia. The princes said, 'I send this fellow away,' and they have sent you away; and now the town that Achish gave you is utterly destroyed; there is no link left between you and the Philistines, and you have come back to your natural standing." The hardest blow that our God ever strikes, if it puts us right and separates us from self and sin, and carnal policy, is a coup de grâce, a blow of love. If it ends our life of selfishness, and brings us back into the life of trust, it is a blessed blow. When God blesses his people most it is by terrible things in righteousness. He smote David to heal him. He fetched him out from the snare of the Philistine fowler, and delivered him from the noisome pestilence of heathen association, by a way that brought the tears into his eyes till he had no more power to weep. Now the servant of the Lord begins to see the wonderful hand of God, and he shall yet say, "Before I was afflicted I went astray, but now have I kept thy word."

I, the preacher of this hour, beg to bear my little witness that the worst days I have ever had have turned out to be my best days, and when God has seemed most cruel to me he has then been most kind. If there is anything in this world for which I would bless him more than for anything else, it is for pain and affliction. I am sure that in these things the richest, tenderest love has been manifested toward me. I pray you, dear friends, if you are at this time very low and greatly distressed, encourage yourselves in the abundant faithfulness of the God who hides himself. Our Father's wagons rumble most heavily when they are bringing us the richest freight of the bullion of his grace. Love letters from heaven are often sent in black-edged envelopes. The cloud that is black with horror is big with mercy. We may not ask for trouble, but if we were wise we should look upon it as the shadow of an unusually great blessing. Dread the calm, it is often treacherous, and beneath its wing the pestilence is lurking. Fear not the storm, it brings healing in its wings, and when Jesus is with you in the vessel the tempest only hastens the ship to its desired haven. Blessed be the Lord, whose way is in the whirlwind, and who makes the clouds to be the dust of his feet. May some such thoughts as these help you to encourage yourself in God as David did.

III. And now, third, we have *David inquiring of God.*

"And David inquired at the LORD, saying, 'Shall I pursue after this troop? Shall I overtake them?'"

Note well that as soon as David had come to be right with God, he longed to know the Lord's mind as to his next action. You and I would have said, "Let us hasten after these marauders; let us not stop an instant, we can pray as we march, or at some other time. Haste! haste! for the lives of our wives and children are at stake." It was a time for hurry if ever there was; but, as the good proverb says, "Prayer and provender hinder no man's journey." David wisely stops. "Bring hither the ephod," cries he, and he waits till the oracle answers his inquiries. He will not march till the Lord shall give the word of command. This is well. It is a sweet frame of mind to be in to be brought to feel that you must now wait the Lord's bidding, that your strength is to sit still till God bids you go forward. Oh, that we could always keep up this submission of heart! Oh, that we never leaned to our own understanding, but trusted solely in God!

Observe that David takes it for granted that his God is going to help him. He only wants to know how it is to be done. "Shall I pursue? Shall I overtake?" When you, my brother, are inquiring of the Lord, do not approach him as if he would not help you, or could hardly be expected to aid you. You would not like your children to ask a favor of you as if they were afraid of their lives to speak to you. I am sure you would not like a dear child, whatever wrong he had been doing, to feel a suspicion of your love, and doubt your willingness to help; for whatever he has done he is your child still. David has encouraged himself in his God, and he is sure that God is ready to save him; all that he wants to know is how he is himself to act in the business.

It is to be remarked, however, that David does not expect that God is going to help him, without his doing his best. He inquires, "Shall I pursue? Shall I overtake?" He means to be up and doing. Sad as he is, and faint as he is, he is ready for action. Many who get into trouble seem to expect an angel to come and lift them up by the hair of their heads; but angels have other matters in hand. The Lord generally helps us by enabling us to help ourselves, and it is a way which does us double good. It was more for David's benefit that he should himself smite the Amalekites than that God should hurl hailstones out of heaven upon them, and destroy them. David will have their spoil for the wage of battle, and be rewarded for the forced march and the fight. Brother, you will have to work and labor to extricate yourself from debt and difficulty, and so the Lord will hear your prayer. The rule is to trust in God to smite the Amalekites, and then to march after them, as if it all depended upon yourself. There is a God-reliance which arouses all our self-reliance and yokes it to the chariot of providence, making the man ready for action because God is with him. It is instructive to notice that, although David was thus ready for action, trusting in God, he greatly distrusted his own wisdom; for he asked, "Shall I pursue them?" That man is wise who counts his own wisdom to be folly; and he who lays his judgment down at Jesus' feet is a man of soundest judgment. He who tarries till the divine wisdom shall guide him, he shall be expert and prudent in all things.

David also distrusted his own strength though quite ready to use what he had; for he said, "Shall I overtake?" Can my men march fast enough to overtake these robbers? And what a blessed state of heart that is when we have no strength of our own, but seek unto God! It is good to be insufficient, and to find God all-sufficient. I pause here a minute and pray God ever to keep you and me in just the condition into which he brought his servant David. I do not care so much about his overtaking the robbers, and all that: the glory was to have overtaken his God and to be waiting at his feet. He could not be brought to this without his city being burned, without his being bereaved, robbed, and ready to die by the hands of his own warriors; but it was worth all the cost to be brought to rest on the bare arm of God, and to wait in childlike dependence at the great Father's door. Let the proud lift up their heads, but let me rest mine on Jesus' bosom. Let the mighty raise their shields on high; as for me, the Lord is my Shield and my Defense, and he alone. When I am weak, then I am strong. "They that wait upon the LORD shall renew their strength." The old song of Hannah is still true: "He hath showed strength with his arm; he hath scattered the proud in the imagination of their hearts. He hath put down the mighty from their seats, and exalted them of low degree."

IV. We close our sermon with the fourth note, which is a note of jubilate and praise unto God, who helped his servant—*David's answer of peace.*

The Lord heard his supplication. He says, "In my distress I cried unto the LORD and he heard me." But mark this, he was not delivered without further trial. David marched with his six hundred men on foot after the foe, with all speed, and the band became so worn and weary that one third of them could not ford the brook Besor, which, though usually dry, was probably at that time flowing with a strong stream. Many a leader would have given up the chase with one out of three of his troop in hospital, but David pursued with his reduced force. When God means to bless us, he often takes away a part of the little strength we thought we had. We did not think our strength equal to the task, and the Lord takes away a portion even of the little power we had. Our

God does not fill till he has emptied. Two hundred men must be rent away from David's side before God could give him victory, for he meant to have David's whole force to be exactly equal to the four hundred Amalekites who fled, that he might make the victory the more memorable and renowned. Expect then, O troubled one, that you will be delivered, but know that your sorrow may yet deepen, that you may have all the greater joy by and by.

Leaving the two hundred men behind, David dashes ahead, and by forced marches overtakes the enemy; finds them feasting; smites them hip and thigh, and destroys them, and takes the spoil, but in such a way that manifestly it was the gift of God. He speaks of the spoil as "that which the LORD hath given us, who hath preserved us, and delivered the company that came against us into our hand." God will help his servants who trust him, but he will have all the honor of the victory. He will deliver them in such a way that they shall lift their psalms and hymns unto God alone, and this shall be the strain: "Sing unto the LORD, for he hath triumphed gloriously. We were unworthy, we were faint, we were distressed, but God has made us more than conquerors through his great love."

David's victory was perfect. We are told over and over again that "David recovered all." Nothing was lost: not a piece of money nor a garment, not an ox nor a sheep, much less a child, or one of womankind—"David recovered all." How well the Lord works when he once lays his hand to it. "He will perfect that which concerneth me." Salvation is of the Lord, and it is an everlastingly complete salvation. Trust in the Lord forever, for in the Lord Jehovah there is everlasting strength. He will work, and work perfectly, till he shall say, "It is finished." The battle is the Lord's, and his saints shall be more than conquerors.

Not only did God give David complete rescue, but he awarded him great spoil. "And they said, 'This is David's spoil.'" David became rich and able to send presents to his friends; but he was also the better man, the holier man, the stronger man, the more fit to wear that crown which was so soon to adorn his brow. O brothers and sisters, the deeper your trouble, the louder will be your song, if you can but trust in God and walk in fellowship with Jesus. Little skiffs that keep near the land carry but small cargoes, and their masters see little save the shore; but they that go down to the sea in ships, that do business in great waters, these see the works of the Lord and his wonders in the deep. It is something to be out on the wide main in a terrific storm, when the ship is tossed to and fro like a ball, when the heavens are mixed up with the ocean, and all is uproar. Then great thunder contends with the roaring of the sea, and the lightning flames are quenched by the boiling of the mighty waves. When you reach the shore again, you know a gladness which the landsman cannot feel, and you have a tale to tell to your children, and your children's children, of what you have seen in the deep, such as lubberly landsmen scarce can understand. As for those who dwell at ease, what do they see? You who have been in the battle can sing of victory, and, pointing to your experience, can exclaim, "This is David's spoil."

Trust in the Lord your God. Believe also in his Son Jesus. Get rid of sham faith, and really believe. Get rid of a professional faith, and trust in the Lord at all times, about everything. "What, trust him about pounds, shillings, and pence?" Assuredly. I dread the faith that cannot trust God about bread and garments—it is a lying faith. Depend upon it, that is not the solid, practical faith of Abraham, who trusted God about his tent and his cattle, and about a wife for his son. That faith which made David trust God about the sons and daughters and the spoil, that is the sort of faith for you and for me. If God cannot be trusted about loaves and fishes how shall he be trusted about the things of eternity and the glories which are yet to be revealed? Stay yourself on God with an everyday faith. Faith in God is the exercise of sanctified common sense. Somebody called me "superstitious" for trusting God as to his answering prayer, but I reply that he is superstitious who does not trust the living God. He who believes in the power of the greatest of all forces and trusts in the surest of all truths, is but acting rationally. The purest reason approves reliance upon God. The end shall declare the wisdom of believing God. At the last, when we with all believers shall lift up the great hallelujah unto the Lord God of Israel who reigns over all things for his people, it shall be known by all that faith is honorable and unbelief contemptible.

God bless you, brethren, and if any of you have never trusted God at all, nor rested in his dear Son, may you be brought to do so at once. May you see your self-righteousness burned like Ziklag, and all your carnal hopes carried away captive, and may you then encourage yourselves in Christ, for he will recover all for you, and give you spoil besides, and there shall be joy and rejoicing. The Lord be with you. Amen.

Job: The Turning of Job's Captivity

Delivered at the Metropolitan Tabernacle, Newington. Published in 1875. No. 1262.

The Lord *turned the captivity of Job, when he prayed for his friends: also the* Lord *gave Job twice as much as he had before.*—Job 42:10

Since God is immutable he acts always upon the same principles, and hence his course of action in the olden times to a man of a certain sort will be a guide as to what others may expect who are of like character. God does not act by caprice, nor by fits and starts. He has his usual modes and ways. The psalmist David uses the expression, "Then will I teach transgressors *thy ways*," as if God had well-known ways, habits, and modes of action; and so he has, or he would not be the unchangeable Jehovah. In that song of Moses the servant of God, and the song of the Lamb, which is recorded in the fifteenth chapter of the Revelation, we read, "Just and true are thy ways, thou King of saints."

The Lord has ways as high above our ways as the heavens are above the earth, and these are not fickle and arbitrary. These ways, although very different if we view them superficially, are really always the same when you view them with understanding. The ways of the Lord are right, though transgressors fall therein by not discerning them; but the righteous understand the ways of the Lord, for to them he makes them known, and they perceive that grand general principles govern all the actions of God. If it were not so, the case of such a man as Job would be of no service to us. It could not be said that the things which happened aforetime happened unto us for an example, because if God did not act on fixed principles we could never tell how he would act in any fresh case, and that which happened to one man would be no rule whatever, and no encouragement whatever, to another. We are not all like Job, but we all have Job's God. Though we have neither risen to Job's wealth, nor will, probably, ever sink to Job's poverty, yet there is the same God above us if we be high, and the same God with his everlasting arms beneath us if we be brought low; and what the Lord did for Job he will do for us, not precisely in the same form, but in the same spirit, and with like design. If, therefore, we are brought low tonight, let us be encouraged with the thought that God will turn again our captivity; and let us entertain the hope that after the time of trial shall be over, we shall be richer, especially in spiritual things, than ever we were before. There will come a turning point to the growing heat of affliction, and the fire shall cool. When the ebb has fallen to its lowest, the sea will return to its strength; when midwinter has come, spring will be near, and when midnight has struck, then the dawning will not be far away. Perhaps, too, the signal of our happier days shall be the very same as that of the patient patriarch, and when we pray for our friends, blessings shall be poured into our own bosoms.

Our text has in it three points very clearly; first, *the Lord can soon turn his people's captivity*: "The LORD turned the captivity of Job." Second, *there is generally some point at which he does this*: in Job's case he turned his captivity when he prayed for his friends. And, third, *believers shall never be losers by God*, for he gave Job twice as much as he had before.

I. First, then, *the Lord can soon turn his people's captivity.*

That is a very remarkable expression—"captivity." It does not say, "God turned his poverty," though Job was reduced to the extremity of penury, having lost all his property. We do not read that the Lord turned his sickness, though he was covered with sore boils. It does not say that he turned away the sting of bereavement, reproach, and calumny, although all those are included. But there is something more meant by the word *captivity*. A man may be very poor, and yet not in captivity; his soul may sing among the angels when his body is on a dunghill and dogs are licking his sores. A man may be very sick, and yet not be in captivity; he may be roaming the broad fields of covenant mercy though he cannot rise from his bed; and his soul may never enjoy greater liberty than when his body is scarcely able to turn from side to side. Captivity is bondage of mind, the iron entering into the soul. I suspect that Job, under the severe mental trial which attended his bodily pains, was, as to his spirit, like a man bound hand and foot and fettered, and then taken away from his native country, banished from the place which he loved, deprived of the associations which had cheered him, and confined in darkness. I mean that, together with the trouble and trial to which he was subjected, he had lost somewhat the presence of God; much of his joy and comfort had departed; the peace of his mind had gone, and the associations which he had formed with other believers were now broken: he was in all these respects like a lone captive. His three friends had condemned him as a hypocrite, and would not have association with him except to censure him, and thus he felt like one who had been carried into a far country, and banished both from God and man. He could only follow the occupation of a captive, that is, to be oppressed, to weep, to claim compassion, and to pour out a dolorous complaint. He hung his harp on the willows, and felt that he could not sing the Lord's song in a strange land. Poor Job! He is less to be pitied for his bereavements, poverty, and sickness than for his loss of that candle of the Lord which once shone about his head.

That is the worst point of all when trouble penetrates to the heart. All the bullets in the battle, though they fly thick as hail, will not distress a soldier like one which finds a lodging in his flesh. "To take arms against a sea of troubles, and by opposing end them" is a grand and manly thing; but when that sea of trouble fills the cabin of the heart, puts out the fires of inward energy, washes the judgment from the wheel, and renders the pumps of resolution useless, the man becomes very nearly a wreck. "A wounded spirit who can bear?" Touch a man in his bone, and in his flesh, and yet he may exult; but touch him in his mind—let the finger of God be laid upon his spirit—and then, indeed, he is in captivity. I think the term includes all the temporal distress into which Job came, but it chiefly denotes the bondage of spirit into which he was brought, as the combined result of his troubles, his sickness, the taunts of his friends, and the withdrawal of the divine smile. My point is that God can deliver us out of that captivity; he can both from the spiritual and the temporal captivity give us a joyful release.

The Lord can deliver us out of spiritual captivity, and that very speedily. I may be addressing some tonight who feel everything except what they want to feel. They enjoy no sweetness in the means of grace, and yet for all the world they would not give them up. They used at one time to rejoice in the Lord; but now they cannot see his face and the utmost they can say is, "Oh, that I knew where I might find him!" It little matters that some live in perpetual joy; the triumphs of others cannot cheer a man who is himself defeated. It is idle to tell a distressed soul that it ought to rejoice as others do. What one ought to do and what one can do are sometimes very different, for how to perform that which we would we find not. In vain do you pour your glad notes into a troubled ear. Singing songs to a sad heart is like pouring vinegar upon niter; the elements are discordant, and cause a painful effervescence. There are true children of God who walk in darkness and see no light; yes, some who are the excellent of the earth nevertheless are compelled to cry aloud, "My God, my God, why hast thou forsaken me?" Throughout all time some of these have been in the church, and there always will be such, let our perfect brethren condemn them as they please. The Lord will always leave his mourners; his church shall always have an afflicted and poor people in her midst. Let us all take warning, for we also may be tried and cast down before our day is over; it may be that the brightest eye among us may yet be dimmed, and the boldest heart may yet be faint, and he that dwells nearest to his God at this moment nary yet have to cry out in bitterness of soul, "O God, return unto me, and lift up the light of thy countenance upon me."

Therefore mark well this cheering truth, God can turn your captivity, and turn it at once. Some of God's children seem to think that to recover their former joy must occupy a long period of time. It is true, dear brother, that if you had to work your passage back to where you came from, it would be a weary voyage. There would have to be most earnest searchings of heart and purgings of spirit, struggling with inbred lusts and outward temptations, and all that, if joy were always the result of inward condition. There must needs be a great deal of scrubbing and cleansing and furbishing up of the house, before you could invite your Lord to come, if he and you dwelled together on terms of law. But albeit, that all this cleansing and purifying will have to be done, it will be done far better when you have a sense of his love than it ever can be if you do it in order to make yourself fit for it.

Do you not remember when first you sought him you wanted him to deal with you on the legal ground of making yourself better, and you prepared the house for him to come and dwell in it? But he would not come on such terms. He came to you just as you were, and when he came he himself drove out the intruders which profaned the temple of your soul, and he dwelled with you, in order to perfect the cleansing. Now he will vouchsafe to you the conscious enjoyment of his presence on the same terms as at first, that is, on terms of free and sovereign grace. Did you not at that time admit the Savior to your soul because you could not do without him? Was not that the reason? Is it not a good reason for receiving him again? Was there anything in you when you received him which could commend you to him? Say, were you not all over defilement and full of sin and misery? And yet you opened the door and said, "My Lord, come in, in your free grace, come in, for I must have you or I perish." My dear friend, dare you invite him now on other terms? Having begun in the Spirit, would you be made perfect in the flesh? Having begun to live by grace, would you go on to live by works? When you were a stranger, did you trust in his love, and now that you are his friend, will you appeal to the law? God forbid. O brother, Jesus loves you still, and in a moment he will restore you. O sister, Jesus would fain come back to your heart again, and that in an instant. Have you never read that joyful exclamation of the spouse, "Or ever I was aware, my soul made me like the chariots of Amminadib"? Why, can he not do the same with you now, and quicken and inspirit you even in a moment? After all, you are not worse than you were when he first visited you;

you are not in so sorry a plight after all, as your first natural state, for then you were dead in trespasses and sins altogether, and he quickened you, and now, though you say you feel dead, yet the very expression proves that there is some life lingering in you. Did I not hear you say,

Return, O Sacred Dove, return,
Sweet messenger of rest,
I hate the sins that made thee mourn,
And drove thee from my breast.

Why, friend, those sighs and groans are sweet to the Lord, and they would not have been in you if he had not put them there; they are sure tokens that his grace has not been altogether taken from thee. Know you not, O child of God, that the grace of God is intended to meet all your sins after conversion as well as before conversion? Do you not know that the Lord loved you of old, despite your sins, and he loves you still? Understand you not that the ground of your salvation is not your standing or your character, but the standing of Christ before God, and the character and work of Christ in the presence of God? Believe you firmly that still he loves you, for so indeed he does. Cast your eyes upon those dear wounds of his, and read his love still written there. O unbelieving Thomas, do not put your finger into your own wounds, for that will not help you, but place them in the wounds of Jesus. Come close to him, and you shall cry with ecstasy of spirit, "My Lord and my God."

Well do I know what it is to feel this wondrous power of God to turn our captivity. When one is constantly engaged in ministry, it sometimes happens that the mind wanders, the spirit flags, and the energy is damped, yet, all in a minute, the Lord can quicken us into vigorous activity; the tow catches fire and blazes gloriously, when the Holy Spirit applies the fire. We have heard a hymn sung, and we have said, "I cannot join in that as I could wish," and yet, on a sudden, a mighty rushing wind has borne us away with the song right into heaven. The Lord does not take days, months, weeks, or even hours, to do his work of revival in our souls. He made the world in six days, but he lit it up in an instant with one single word. He said, "light be," and light was, and cannot he do the same for us, and chase away our gloom before the clock ticks again? Do not despair, no, do not even doubt your God. He can turn your captivity as the streams in the south.

Beloved, *he can do the same as to our temporal captivity*. We do not often say much about temporals when we are preaching; I fear we do not say enough about them, for it is wonderful how the Old Testament is taken up with the narration of God's dealings with his people as to temporal things. Many people imagine that God has a great deal to do with their prayer closet, but nothing to do with their store closet; it would be a dreadful thing for us if it were so. Indeed, my brethren, we ought to see as much the hand of our Lord on the table in the kitchen when it is loaded as we do at the communion table, for the same love that spreads the table when we commemorate our Savior's dying love, spreads the table which enables us to maintain the bodily life without which we could not come to the other table at all. We must learn to see God in everything, and praise him for all that we have.

Now it may be I address some friend who has been a great sufferer through pecuniary losses. Dear friend, the Lord can turn your captivity. When Job had lost everything, God readily gave him all back. "Yes," say you, "but that was a very remarkable case." I grant you that, but then we have to do with a remarkable God, who works wonders still. If you consider the matter, you will see that it was quite as remarkable a thing that Job should lose all his property as it was that he should get it back again. If you had walked over Job's farm at first and seen the camels and the cattle, if you had gone into his house and seen the furniture and the grandeur of his state—if you had seen how those who passed him in the street bowed to him, for he was a highly respected man, and if you had gone to his children's houses, and seen the comfort in which they lived, you would have said, "Why, this is one of the best-established men in all the land of Uz." There was scarcely a man of such substance to be found in all that region, and if somebody had foretold that he would in one day lose all this property—all of it—and lose all his children, why you would have said, "Impossible! I have heard of great fortunes collapsing, but then they were built on speculations. They were only paper riches, made up of bills and the like; but in the case of this man, there are oxen, sheep, camels, and land, and these cannot melt into thin air. Job has a good substantial estate, I cannot believe that ever he will come to poverty." Why, when he went out into the gate where the magistrates sat to administer justice, they rose up and gave him the chief seat on the bench. He was a man whose flocks could not be counted, so great were his possessions—possessions of real property, not of merely nominal estate: and yet suddenly, marvelously, it all took to itself wings and disappeared. Surely, if God can scatter, he can gather. If God could scatter such an estate as that, he could, with equal ease, bring it back again. But this is what we do not always see. We see the destructive power of God, but we are not very clear about the upbuilding power of God. Yet, my brethren, surely it is more consonant with the nature of God that he should give than take, and more like him that he should caress than chastise. Does he not always say that judgment is his strange work? I feel persuaded that it was strange work with God to take away all Job's property from him and bring him into that deep distress; but when the Lord went about to enrich his servant Job again, he went about that work, as we say, *con amore*—with heart and soul. He was doing then what he delights to do, for God's happiness is never more clearly seen than when he is distributing the largesses of his love. Why can you not look at your own circumstances in the same light? It is more likely that God will bless you and restore to you than it was ever likely that he would chasten you and take away from you. He can restore you all your wealth, and even more.

This may seem to be a very trite observation, commonplace, and such as everybody knows, but, beloved, the very things that everybody knows are those which we need to hear, if they are most suitable to our case. Those old things which we did not care about in our prosperity are most valued when we are cast down by the terrible blows of tribulation. Let me then repeat the truism, the Lord who takes away can as easily restore. "The Lord maketh sore, *and bindeth up*; he woundeth, *and his hands make whole*. He killeth, *and he maketh alive*." Believe that he will put forth his right hand soon if the left has been long outstretched, and, if you can believe it, it will not be long before you will be able to say, "He hath regarded the low estate of his servant. He hath lifted the poor from the dunghill and set him among princes, even the princes of his people. For the Lord putteth down the mighty from their seat, but he exalteth them that are of low degree." I leave with you this simple truth: The Lord can turn the captivity of his people. You may apply the truth to a thousand different things. You Sunday school teachers, if you have had a captivity in your class, and no good has been done, God can change that. You ministers, if for a long time you have plowed and sowed in vain, the Lord can turn your captivity there. You dear wives who have been praying for your husbands, you fathers who have been pleading for your children, and have seen no blessing yet, the Lord can turn your captivity in those respects. No captivity is so terrible but God can bring us back from it; no chain is so fastened but God can strike it off, and no prison house is so strong but God can break the bars and set his servants free.

II. I pass on to our second remark, which is this: *there is generally some point at which the Lord interposes to turn the captivity of his people.*

In Job's case, I have no doubt, the Lord turned his captivity, as far as the Lord was concerned, because *the grand experiment which had been tried on Job was now over.*

The suggestion of Satan was that Job was selfish in his piety—that he found honesty to be the best policy, and, therefore, he was honest—that godliness was gain, and therefore he was godly. "Hast thou not set a hedge about him and all that he hath?" said the old accuser of the brethren. The devil generally does one of two things. Sometimes he tells the righteous that there is no reward for their holiness, and then they say, "Surely, I have cleansed my heart in vain and washed my hands in innocence"; or else he tells them that they only obey the Lord because they have a selfish eye to the reward. Now it would be a calamity if the devil could charge the Lord with paying his servants badly: it would have been an ill thing if the fiend had been able to say, "There is Job, a perfect and an upright man, but thou hast set no hedge about him. Thou hast given him no reward whatever." That would have been an accusation against the goodness and justice of God; but, as the devil cannot say that, he takes the other course and says—"Thou hast set a hedge about him and all that he has; he serves thee for gain and honor; he has a selfish motive in his integrity."

By God's permission the matter was tested. The devil had said, "Put forth now thy hand and touch his bone and his flesh, and he will curse thee to thy face." But Job had done no such thing. In his extremity he said, "The Lord gave and the Lord hath taken away; blessed be the name of the Lord." God puts his servants sometimes into these experiments that he may test them, that Satan himself may know how truehearted God's grace has made them, and that the world may see how they can play the man. Good engineers, if they build a bridge, are glad to have a train of enormous weight go over it. You remember when the first Great Exhibition was built, they marched regiments of soldiers, with a steady tramp, over the girders, that they might be quite sure that they would be strong enough to bear any crowd of men; for the regular tramp of well-disciplined soldiers is more trying to a building than anything else. So our wise and prudent Father sometimes marches the soldiery of trouble right over his people's supports, to let all men see that the grace of God can sustain every possible pressure and load. I am sure that if any of you had invented some implement requiring strength, you would be glad to have it tested, and the account of the successful trial published abroad. The gunsmith does not object to a charge being fired from the barrel at the proof house far greater than any strain which it ought ordinarily to bear; for he knows that it will endure the proof. "Do your worst or do your best; it is a good instrument; do what you like with it"; so the maker of a genuine article is accustomed to speak; and the Lord seems to say the same concerning his people. "My work of grace in them is mighty and thorough. Test it, Satan; test it, world; test it by bereavements, losses, and reproaches; it will endure every ordeal." And when it is tested, and bears it all, then the Lord turns the captivity of his people, for the experiment is complete.

Most probably there was, in Job's character, some fault from which his trial was meant to purge him. If he erred at all, probably it was in having a somewhat elevated idea of himself and a stern manner toward others. A little of the elder-brother spirit may, perhaps, have entered into him. A good deal that was sour came out of Job when his miserable comforters began to tease him—not a hundredth part as much as would come out of me, I warrant you, or, perhaps, out of you; but, still, it would not have come out if it had not been in. It must have been in him or otherwise all the provocation in the world would not have brought it out; and the Lord intended by his trials to let Job have a view of himself from another standpoint, and discover imperfections in his character which he would never have seen if he had not been brought into a tried condition. When through the light of trial, and the yet greater light of God's glorious presence, Job saw himself unveiled, he abhorred himself in dust and ashes. Probably Job had not humbled himself of late, but he did it then, and now, if any sort of selfishness lurked in him, it was put away, for Job began to pray for his cruel friends. It would take a good deal of grace to bring some men to pray for such friends as they were. To pray for one's real friends, I hope, comes natural to us; but to pray for that Bildad and the other two, after the abominable things they had spoken and insinuated—well, it showed that there was a large amount of sweetness and light in Job's character, and abounding grace deep down in his soul, or he would scarcely have interceded for such ungenerous tramplers upon a fallen friend. Now, behold, Job has discovered his fault, and he has put it away, and the grand old man bows his knee to pray for men who called him hypocrite—to pray for men who cut him to the very soul. He pleads with God that he would look in mercy upon men who had no mercy upon him, but had pitilessly heaped all kinds of epithets upon him, and stung him in his tenderest places, just when they ought to have had pity upon him. His misery alone ought to have stopped their mouths, but it seems as if that misery egged them on to say the most cruel things that could possibly have been conceived—the more cruel because they were, all of them, so undeserved. But now Job prays for his friends. You see the trial had reached its point. It had evidently been blessed to Job, and it had proved Satan to be a liar, and so now the fire of the trial goes out, and like precious metal the patriarch comes forth from the furnace brighter than ever.

Beloved friends, the point at which God may turn your captivity may not be the same as that at which he turned Job's, for yours may be a different character. I will try and indicate, briefly, when I think God may turn your trial.

Sometimes he does so *when that trial has discovered to you your special sin.* You have been putting your finger upon diverse faults, but you have not yet touched the spot in which your greatest evil is concentrated. God will now help you to know yourself. When you are in the furnace, you will begin to search yourself, and you will cry, "Show me wherefore thou contendest with me." You will find out three or four things, perhaps, in which you are faulty, and you will commit yourself to the Lord and say, "Give me grace, good Lord, to put away these evil things." Yes, but you have not come to the point yet, and only a greater trial will guide you to it. The anger of the Lord smokes against your house, not for this or that, but for another evil, and you have need to institute another search, for the images may be under the seat whereon a beloved Rachel sits. The evil in your soul may be just at the point where you think that you are best guarded against temptation. Search, therefore, and look, dear brother, for when the sin has been found out, and the Achan has been stoned, then the valley of Achor shall be a door of hope, and you shall go up to victory, the Lord going with you.

Perhaps, too, your turning point will be *when your spirit is broken.* We are by nature a good deal like horses that want breaking in, or, to use a scriptural simile, we are as "bullocks unaccustomed to the yoke." Well, the horse has to go through certain processes in the ménage until at last it is declared to be "thoroughly broken in," and we need similar training. You and I are not yet quite broken in, I am afraid. We go very merrily along, and yield to the rein in certain forms of service; but if we were called to other sorts of work, or made to suffer, we should need the kicking strap put on, and require a sharper bit in our mouths. We should find that our spirit was not perfectly broken. It takes a long time of pain and sickness to bring some down to the dust of complete resignation to the divine will. There is something still in which they stick out against God, and of many it is true, "Though thou shouldest bray a fool in a mortar among wheat with a pestle, yet will not his foolishness depart from him." We have been brayed in that mortar, and with that pestle day after day, and week after week, and yet we are still foolish. When our soul shall cheerfully say, "Not as I will, but as thou wilt," then our captivity will be almost over, if not quite. While we cry, "It must not be so, I will not have it so," and we struggle and rebel, we shall only have to feel that we are kicking against the pricks, and wounding our foot every time we kick; but when we give up all that struggling, and say, "Lord, I leave it entirely with thee, thy will be done"—then will the trial cease, because there will be no necessity for it any longer. That is with some the culmination and turning point of trouble. Their Gethsemane ends when, like the Lord Jesus, they cry, "Nevertheless, not as I will, but as thou wilt."

Sometimes, again, trial may cease *when you have learned the lesson which it was intended to teach you, as to some point of gospel truth*. I think I have sometimes said that many truths of the gospel are like letters written with sympathetic ink. If you have ever had a letter written with that preparation, when you look at it you cannot see anything whatever: it is quite illegible. The proper thing to do is to hold the writing up to the fire. As it warms at the fire, the acid writing becomes manifest, and the letters are before you. Many of God's promises need to be held before the scorching fires of adversity and personal trouble, and then we read the precious secret of the Spirit's consolation. You cannot see the stars in the daytime upon the surface of the earth, but if you go down into a well you can, and when you go down the deep well of trouble it often happens that you see a beauty and luster in the promise which nobody else can see, and when the Lord has brought you into a certain position in which you can see the glory of his grace as you never could have seen it anywhere else, then he will say, "It is enough; I have taught my child the lesson, and I will let him go."

I think, too, it may be with some of us that *God gives us trouble until we obtain a sympathetic spirit*. I should not like to have lived forty years in this world without ever having suffered sickness. "Oh," you say, "that would have been very desirable." I grant you it appears so. When I met with a man that never had an ache or a pain or a day's sickness in his life, I used to envy him, but I do not now because I feel very confident that he is a loser by his unvarying experience. How can a man sympathize with trouble that he never knew? How can he be tender in heart if he has never been touched with infirmity himself? If one is to be a comforter to others, he must know the sorrows and the sicknesses of others in his measure. It was essential to our Lord, and, certainly, what was essential to him is necessary to those who are to be shepherds of others, as he was. Now it may be that by nature some of us are not very sympathetic; I do not think Job was: it is possible that though he was kind, and generous to the poor, yet he was rather hard, but his troubles taught him sympathy. And, perhaps, the Lord may send you trouble till you become softer in heart, so that afterward you will be one who can speak a word in season to the weary. As you sit down by the bedside of the invalid, you will be able to say, "I know all the ins and outs of a sick man's feelings, for I have been sore sick myself." When God has worked that in you, it may be he will turn your captivity.

In Job's case, the Lord turned his captivity *when he prayed for his friends.* Prayer for ourselves is blessed work, but for the child of God it is a higher exercise to become an intercessor, and to pray for others. Prayer for ourselves, good as it is, has just a touch of selfishness about it: prayer for others is delivered from that ingredient. Herein is love, the love which God the Holy Spirit delights to foster in the heart, when a man's prayers go up for others. And what a Christlike form of prayer it is when you are praying for those who have ill-treated you and despitefully used you. Then are you like your master. Praying for yourselves, you are like those for whom Jesus died; but praying for your enemies, you are like the dying Jesus himself. "Father, forgive them, for they know not what they do" has more of heaven in it than the songs of seraphs, and your prayer when offered for those who have treated you ill is somewhat akin to the expiring prayer of your Lord. Job was permitted to take a noble revenge, I am sure the only one he desired, when he became the means of bringing them back to God. God would not hear them, he said, for they had spoken so wrongly of his servant Job, and now Job is set to be a mediator, or intercessor, on their behalf: thus was the contempt poured upon the patriarch turned into honor. If the Lord will only save the opposer's soul through your prayer, it will be a splendid way of returning bitter speeches. If many unkind insinuations have been thrown out, and wicked words said, if you can pray for those who used such words, and God hears you and brings them to Jesus, it will be such a triumph as an angel might envy. My brother, never use any other weapon of retaliation than the weapon of love. Avenge not yourself in anywise by uttering anything like a curse, or desiring any hurt or mischief to come to your bitterest foe, but inasmuch as he curses, overwhelm him with blessings. Heap the hot coals of your good wishes and earnest prayers upon his head, and if the Lord give you to bring him to a state of salvation, he shall be praised, and you shall have happiness among the sons of men.

Perhaps some of you are in trouble now because you cannot be brought sincerely to pray for your enemies. It is a grievous fault when Christian men harbor resentments; it is always a sad sign when a man confesses, "I could not heartily pray for So-and-So." I would not like to live an hour at enmity with any man living, be he who he may; nor should any Christian man, I think. You should feel that however treacherous, dishonorable, unjust, and detestable the conduct of your enemy may have been to you, yet still it is forgiven, quite forgiven in your heart, and, as far as possible, forgotten, or wherein remembered, remembered with regret that it should have occurred, but with no resentment to the person who committed the wrong. When we get to that state, it is most probable that the Lord will smile upon us and turn our captivity.

III. The last word I have to say—the third word—is this: that *believers shall not be losers for their God.*

God, in the experiment, took from Job all that he had, but at the end he gave him back twice as much as he had—twice as many camels and oxen, and twice as many of everything, even of children. I heard a very sweet remark about the children the other day, for somebody said, "Yes, God did give him twice as many children, because his first family were still his. They were not lost but gone before." So the Lord would have his people count their children that are gone to heaven, and reckon them as belonging to the family still, as the child did in Wordsworth's pretty poem, "Master, we are seven." And so Job could say of his sons and daughters, as well as of all the other items, that he had twice as many as before. True, the first family were all gone, but he had prayed for them in the days of their feasting, he had brought them together and offered sacrifice, and so he had a good hope about them, and he reckoned them as still his own. Tried brother, the Lord can restore to you the double in temporal things if he pleases. If he takes away, he can as certainly give, and that right early. He certainly can do this in spiritual things; and if he takes away temporals and gives spirituals we are exceedingly great gainers. If a man should take away my silver and give me twice the weight in gold in return, should I not be thankful? And so, if the Lord takes away temporals and gives us spirituals, he thus gives us a hundred times more than he takes away.

Dear brethren, you shall never lose anything by what you suffer for God. If, for Christ's sake, you are persecuted, you shall receive in this life your reward; but if not, rejoice and be glad, for great is your reward in heaven. You shall not lose anything by God's afflicting you. You shall, for a time, be an apparent loser; but a real loser in the end you shall never be. When you get to heaven you will see that you were a priceless gainer by all the losses you endured. Shall you lose anything by what you give to God? Never. Depend on it, he will be no man's debtor. There dwells not in earth or heaven any man who shall be creditor to the most High. The best investment a man makes is that which he gives to the Lord from a right motive. Nothing is lost which is offered to the cause of God. The breaking of the alabaster box of precious ointment was not a wasteful thing, and he who should give to the Lord all that he had would have made a prudent use of his goods. "He that giveth to the poor lendeth to the Lord," and he that giveth to the Lord's church and to the Lord himself lays up his treasure in heaven, where it shall be his forever.

Beloved, we serve a good Master, and if he chooses to try us for a little we will bear our trial cheerfully, for God will turn our captivity before long. In closing, I wish I could feel that this subject had something to do with you all, but it is not the case. Oh no, there are some of you who have felt no captivity, but you have a dreadful captivity to come, and there is no hope of God's ever turning that captivity when once you get into it. Without God, without Christ, strangers from the commonwealth of Israel, you are in bondage until now, and there will before long come upon you bondage that will never end. You cannot pray for your friends: you have never prayed for yourself. God would not hear you if you did pray for others, for, first of all, you must be yourself reconciled to him by the death of his Son. Oh, that you would mind these things and look to Jesus Christ alone for your salvation, for if you do he will accept you, for he has promised to cast out none who come to him. And then look at this: after all is right between God and your soul, you need not fear what happens to you in the future, for, come sickness or health, come poverty or wealth, all is right, all is safe, all is well. You have put yourself into the hand of God, and wherever God may lift that hand, you are still within it, and therefore always secure and always blessed; and, if not always consciously happy, yet you have always the right to be so, seeing you are true to God, and he delights in you. God bless you, and give you all salvation, for Jesus Christ's sake. Amen.

Isaiah: Messengers Wanted

Delivered on Sunday morning, April 22, 1866, at the Metropolitan Tabernacle, Newington. No. 687.

> *Also I heard the voice of the* Lord, *saying, "Whom shall I send, and who will go for us?" Then said I, "Here am I; send me."*
> —Isaiah 6:8

God's great remedy for man's ruin of man is the sacrifice of his dear Son. He proclaims to the sons of men that only by the atonement of Jesus can they be reconciled unto himself. In order that this remedy should be of any avail to any man, he must receive it by faith, for without faith men perish even under the gospel dispensation. There is at the present moment great lack of men to tell out the story of the cross of Jesus Christ, and many considerations press that lack upon our hearts. Think how many voices all mingle into this one—"Who will go for us?" Listen to the wounds of Jesus, as they plaintively cry, "How shall we be rewarded? How shall the precious drops of blood be made available to redeem the souls of men, unless loving lips shall go for us to claim by right those who have been redeemed by blood?" The blood of Jesus cries like Abel's blood from the ground, "Whom shall I send?" and his wounds repeat the question, "who will go for us?" Does not the purpose of the eternal Father also join with solemn voice in this demand? The Lord has decreed a multitude unto eternal life. He has purposed, with a purpose which cannot be changed or frustrated, that a multitude whom one man can number shall be the reward of the Savior's travail; but how can these decrees be fulfilled except by the sending forth of the gospel, for it is through the gospel, and through the gospel alone, that salvation can come to the sons of men. I think I hear the awful voice of the purpose mingling with the piercing cry of the cross, appealing to us to declare the word of life. I see the handwriting of old Eternity bound in one volume with the crimson writing of Calvary, and both together write out most legibly the pressing question: who shall go for us to bring home the elect and redeemed ones?

The very sins of men, horrible as they are to think upon, may be made an argument for proclaiming the gospel. Oh, the cruel and ravenous sins which destroy the sons of men, and rend their choicest joy in pieces! When I see monstrous lusts defiling the temple of God, and gods many and lords many usurping the throne of the Almighty, I can hear aloud the cry, "Who will go for us?" Do not perishing souls suggest to us the question of the text? Men are going down to the grave, perishing for lack of knowledge; the tomb engulfs them, eternity swallows them up, and in the dark they die without a glimmer of hope. No candle of the Lord ever shines upon their faces. By these perishing souls we implore you this morning to feel that heralds of the cross are wanted, wanted lest these souls be ruined everlastingly; wanted that they may be lifted up from the dunghill of their corruption, and made to sit among princes redeemed by Christ Jesus. The cry wells into a wail of mighty pathetic pleading; all time echoes it, and all eternity prolongs it, while heaven and earth and hell give weight to the chorus.

Beloved, there are two forms of missionary enterprise, conducted by two classes of agents. I so divide them merely for the occasion; they are really not divided by any rigid boundary. The first is the agency of those specially dedicated to the ministry of the word, who give themselves wholly to it, who are able by the generous effort of the Christian church, or by their own means, to set their whole time apart for the great work of teaching the truth. As there are but few in this assembly who can do this, I shall not translate my text in its reference to ministers, although it has a loud voice to such, but I shall rather refer to another and equally useful form of agency, namely, the Christian church as a whole; the believers who, while following their secular avocations, are heralds for Christ and missionaries for the cross. Such are wanted here, such are needed in our colonies, such might find ample room in the great world of heathendom, men and women, who, if they did not stand up beneath the tree to address the assembled throng, would preach in the workshop; who, if they did not teach the hundreds, would at the fireside instruct the twos and threes.

We want both sorts of laborers, but I may do more good on this present occasion by stirring up this second sort. You may all be teachers of Christ in another sense; you can all give yourself to the work of God in your own calling, and promote your Master's glory perseveringly in your daily avocations. I lift up an earnest cry in God's name for consecrated men and women, who, not needing to wait till the church's hands can support them, shall support themselves with their own hands, and yet minister for Christ Jesus wherever Providence may have cast their lot.

I. *The person wanted,* as described in the questions, "Whom shall I send? Who will go for us?"

The person wanted is viewed from two points. He has a character bearing two aspects. The person wanted has a divine side; "whom shall *I* send?" Then he has a human aspect; "who will go *for us*?" But the two meet together—the human and divine unite in the last words *for us.* Here is a man, nothing more than a man of human instincts, but clad through divine grace with superhuman, even with divine, authority.

Let us look, then, at this two-sided person. He is *divinely chosen*—"Whom shall *I* send?" As if in the eternal counsels this had once been a question, "Who shall be the chosen man, who shall be the object of my eternal love, and in consequence thereof shall have this grace given him that he should tell to others the unsearchable riches of Christ?" Beloved, what a mercy it is to us who are believers that *to us* this is no more a question; for sovereignty has pitched upon us and eternal mercy, not for anything good in us, but simply because God would have it so, has selected us that we may bring forth fruit unto his name. As we hear the question, let us listen to the Savior's exposition of it. "Ye have not chosen me, but I have chosen you and ordained you that ye should go and bring forth fruit, and that your fruit should remain." The workers for the living God are a people chosen by the most High. He sends whom he wills, he makes choice of this man and not another, and in every case exercises his own sovereign will.

This question indicates a person *cheerfully willing,* and this is what I meant by the human side of the messenger. "Who will *go for us*?" The man sought for is one who will go with ready mind; there would be no need to ask, "who will go?" if a mere slave, or machine without a will could be sent. Beloved, the purpose of God does not violate the free agency, or even the free will of man. Man is saved by the will of God, but man is made willing to be so saved. The fault is not in the hyper-Calvinist that he insists upon sovereignty, nor in the Arminian that he is so violent for free agency; the fault is in both of them, because they cannot see more truths than one, and do not admit that truth is not the exclusive property of either, for God is a sovereign, and, at the same time, man is a responsible free agent. Many among us are perpetually seeking to reconcile truths which probably never can be reconciled except in the divine Mind. I thank God that I believe many things which I do not even wish to understand. I am weary and sick of arguing and understanding and misunderstanding. I find it true rest and joy, like a little child, to believe what God has revealed, and to let others do the puzzling and the reasoning. If I could comprehend the whole of revelation, I could scarcely believe it to be divine; but inasmuch as many of its doctrines are too deep for me, and the whole scheme is too vast to be reduced to a system, I thank and bless God that he has deigned to display before me a revelation far exceeding my poor limited abilities. I believe that every man who has Jesus has him as a matter of his own choice; it is true it is caused by grace, but it is there—it is there. Ask any man whether he is a Christian against his will, and he will tell you certainly not, for he loves the Lord, and delights in his law after the inward man. Thy people are not led unwillingly to thee in chains, O Jesus, but thy people shall be *willing* in the day of thy power. We willingly choose Christ, because he has from of old chosen us.

In the matter of holy work, every man who becomes a worker for Jesus is so because he was chosen to work for him; but he would be a very poor worker if he himself had not chosen to work for Jesus. I can say that I believe God ordained me to preach the gospel, and that I preach it by his will, but I am sure I preach it with my own; for it is to me the most delightful work in all the world, and if I could exchange with an emperor, I would not consent to be so lowered. To preach the gospel of Jesus Christ is one of the sweetest and noblest employments, and even an angel might desire to be engaged in it. The true worker for God must be impelled by divine election, but yet he must make and will make, by divine grace, his own election of his work.

The two meet together in this—the man is sent by the Three in One, who here asks, "Who will go for us?" Every faithful Christian laborer labors for God. Brethren, when we tell others the story of the cross, we speak of *God the Father.* It is through our lips that the prodigal son must be reminded that the hired servants have bread enough and to spare. It may be through us that he will be shown his rags and his disgrace; through us he will discover more clearly the disgrace of feeding swine. The Spirit of God is the efficient agent, but it is by us that he may work. It is by us that the divine Father falls upon the neck of his prodigal child. *He* does it, but it is through the teaching of his Word in some form or other. The promises are spoken by our lips, the sweet invitations are delivered by our tongues. We, as though God did beseech them by us, are to pray them in Christ's stead to be reconciled to God. God the Father says to you who know and love him, "Will you go for me and be an ambassador for me?" Nor must we forget our tender *Redeemer.* He is not here, for he is risen. He will come again, but meanwhile he asks for someone to speak for him, someone to tell Jerusalem that her iniquity is forgiven; to tell his murderers that he prays for them, "Father, forgive them"; to assure the blood-bought that they are redeemed; to proclaim liberty to the captive, and the opening of the prison doors to them that are bound. Jesus from his throne of glory says, "Who will go for me and be a speaker for me?" Moreover, that blessed *Spirit,* under whose dispensatorial power we live at the present hour, has no voice to speak to the sons of men audibly except by his people; and though he works invisibly and mysteriously in the saints, yet he chooses loving hearts and compassionate lips and tearful eyes to be the means of benediction. The Spirit descends like the cloven tongue, but he sits *upon* disciples; there is no resting place for the Spirit of God nowadays within walls, and even the heaven of heavens contains him not, but he enthrones himself within his people. He makes us God-bearers, and he speaks through us as through a trumpet to the sons of men. So that the adorable Trinity cry to you, you blood-bought, blood-redeemed sons of God, and say, "Are you seeking to promote our glory? Are you effecting our purposes? Are you winning those purchased by our eternal sacrifice?" Turning to the church here assembled, the Lord pronounces those ancient questions, "Whom shall I send? Who will go for us?"

II. By God's help, we would say a little upon *the person offering himself.* "Here am I; send me."

The person offering himself is described in the chapter at very great length—he must be an Isaiah. Being an Isaiah, he must in the first place *have felt his own unworthiness.* My brother, my sister, if you are to be made useful by God in soul winning, you must pass through the experience which Isaiah describes in the chapter before us. You must have cried in bitterness of spirit, "Woe is me, for I am a man of unclean lips!" God will never fill you with himself until he has emptied you of your own self. Till you feel that you are weak as water, you shall not see the splendor of the divine power. May I ask then those of you who feel desirous to serve God this experimental question, "Have you been made fully conscious of your own utter unfitness to be employed in any work for God, and your own complete unworthiness of so great an honor as to become a servant of the living God? If you have not been brought to this you must begin with yourself; you cannot do any good to others: you must be born again; and one of the best evidences of your being born again will be a discovery of your own natural depravity and impurity in the sight of God.

Now, beloved, I want you to notice how it was that Isaiah was made to feel his unworthiness. It was first by *a sense of the presence of God.* "I saw the Lord sitting upon a throne, high and lifted up." Have you ever had a consciousness of the presence of God? The other day I was prostrated in soul, utterly prostrated, with this one word "I AM!" There is everything in that title, the I AM! God is the truest of all existences. With regard to all other things, they may or may not be, but I AM! It came with such power to me. I thought, "Here am I sitting in my study, whether I am, or whether that which surrounds me really is, may be a question, but, God *is*—God *is here.* And when I speak God's word in his name, though I am nothing, God is everything, and as to whether or not his word shall be fulfilled there cannot be any question, because he still is called not "I was," but "I AM," infinite, omnipotent, divine. Think of the reality of the divine presence, and the certainty of that divine presence, everywhere, close here, just now! "I AM!" O God, if *we* be not, yet *thou art*! I scarcely think that any man is fitted to become a teacher of others till he has had a full sense of the glory of God crushing him right down into the dust, a full sense of that word, "I AM." You know a man cannot pray without it, for we must believe that he is, and that he is the rewarder of them that diligently seek him; and if a man cannot pray for himself, much less can he rightly teach others. There must be the fullest conviction of the reality of God, an overwhelming sight and sense of his glory, or else you cannot benefit your fellows.

The source of Isaiah's sense of nothingness was this, that Isaiah *saw the glory of Christ.* Have you ever sat down and gazed upon the cross till, having read your own pardon there, you have seen that cross rising higher and higher till it touched the heavens and overshadowed the globe? Then you have seen and felt the glory of him who was lifted up, and have bowed before the regal splendor of divine love, incarnate in suffering humanity, and resplendent in agony and death. If you have ever beheld the vision of the crucified, and felt the glory of his wounds, you will then be fit to preach to others. I have sometimes thought that certain brethren who preach the gospel with such meager power and such lack of unction have no true knowledge of it. There is no need to talk of it with bated breath. It is sneered at as being such a very simple tale—"Believe and live"; but after all, no philosopher ever made such a disclosure; and if a senate of discoverers could sit through the ages, they could not bring to light any fact equal to this, that God was in Christ reconciling the world unto himself. Well may you open your mouth boldly when you have such a subject as this to speak upon; but if you have never perceived its glory, you are utterly incapable of fulfilling God's errand. Oh, to get the cross into one's heart, to bear it upon one's soul, and above all, to feel the glory of it in one's whole being, is the best education for a Christian missionary whether at home or abroad.

It will strike you too, dear friends, that the particular aspect in which this humiliation may come to us will probably be *a sense of the divine holiness,* and the holiness of those who see his face. "Holy, holy, holy, Lord God of hosts!" was the song which overawed the prophet. What messengers are those who serve so holy a God? From earth and all its grossness free, like flames of fire they flash at his command. Who then am I, a poor creature, cribbed, cabined, and confined within this house of clay? Who am I, a sinful worm of the dust, that I should aspire to the service of so thrice holy a God? Oh, let us serve the Lord with fear and rejoice with trembling; fearful lest we should do mischief while seeking to do good, and pollute the altar while attempting to offer sacrifice upon it.

The next preparation for Christian work is, we must possess *a sense of mercy.* Then flew one of the seraphims and took a live coal from off the altar. We explained in our reading that the altar is for sacrifice, and that the lip must be touched with a coal of that sacrifice; then, being so touched, it derives two effects therefrom. In the first place, *the lip is purged* of iniquity; and in the next place, *it feels the influence of fire,* enabling it to speak with vehemence and force. Beloved hearer, you say perhaps in zeal, "I desire to serve Christ and to tell abroad the story of his cross." Have you proved that story to be true? Were you ever washed in the fountain? How can you bid others come if you have never come yourself? Have your sins been put away? "I hope so." Do you know it? I question if you can preach with any power till you have a full assurance of your own salvation. To teach the gospel with "but" and "if" is a poor teaching. You Sunday school teachers cannot hope to do much good to others while you doubt your own acceptance in the Beloved. You must know that you are saved. O beloved, you must feel the touch of that live coal, you must feel that Christ gave himself for you. You Little Faiths may get to heaven, but you must keep in the back rank while here; we cannot put you in the front of the battle. Though God may make you of service, we cannot expect you to be eminently of service. The man who would serve God must know himself to be saved.

The effect of that live coal will be to fire the lip with heavenly flame. "Oh," says one man, "a flaming coal will burn the lip so that the man cannot speak at all." That is just how God works with us; it is by consuming the fleshly power that he inspires the heavenly might. O let the lip be burned, let the fleshly power of eloquence be destroyed, but, oh, for that live coal to make the tongue eloquent with heaven's flame—the true divine power which urged the apostles forward, and made them conquerors of the whole world.

According to the text, *the man who will be acceptable must offer himself cheerfully.* "Here am I." Though how few of us have in very deed given ourselves to Christ. It is with most professors, "Here is my half guinea; here is my annual contribution"; but how few of us have said, "Here am I." No; we sing of consecration as we sing of a great many other things which we have not realized, and when we have sung it, we do not wish to be taken at our word. It is not

"Here am I." The man whom God will use must in sincerity be a consecrated man. I have explained that he may keep still to his daily work, but he must be consecrated to God in it; he must sanctify the tools of his labor to God, and there is no reason why they should not be quite as holy as the brazen altar or the golden candlestick.

You will observe that the person who thus volunteered for sacred service gave himself *unreservedly.* He did not say, "Here am I; use me where I am," but, "send me." Where to? No condition as to place is so much as hinted at. Anywhere, anywhere, anywhere—send me. Some people are militia-Christians—they serve the King with a limitation and must not be sent out of England; but others are soldier-Christians, who give themselves wholly up to their Lord and Captain; they will go wherever he chooses to send them. Oh, come, my Master, and be absolute Lord of my soul! Reign over me, and subdue my every passion to do and be, and feel all that your will ordains. Blessed prayer! May we never be content till we get all that is to be got by way of joyful experience and holy power, nor until we yield all that is to be yielded by mortal man to the God whose sovereign right to us we claim.

Notice one more thought, that while the prophet gives himself unreservedly, he gives *obediently,* for he pauses to ask directions. It is not "Here am I; away I will go," but "Here am I; send me." I like the spirit of that prayer. Some people get into their head a notion that they must do something uncommon and extraordinary, and though it may be most unreasonable and most irrational, it is for that very reason that the scheme commends itself to their want of judgment. Because it is absurd, they think it to be divine; if earthly wisdom does not justify it, then certainly heavenly wisdom must be called in to endorse it. Now, I conceive that you will find that whenever a thing is wise in God's sight, it is really wise, and that a thing which is absurd is not more likely to be adopted by God than by man; for though the Lord does use plans which are called foolish, they are only foolish to fools, but not actually foolish; there is a real wisdom in their very foolishness, there is a wisdom of God in the things which are foolish to man. When a project is evidently absurd and ridiculous, it may be my own but it cannot be the Lord's, and I had better wait until I can yield up my whims, and subject myself to divine control, saying, "Here am I; send me."

III. In the last place, *the work which such persons will be called to undertake.*

Isaiah's history is a picture of what many and many a true Christian laborer may expect. Isaiah was sent to preach very unpleasant truth, but like a true hero he was very bold in preaching it. "Isaiah is very bold," says the apostle. Now if you are called of God either to preach or teach, or whatever it is, remember the things you have to preach or teach will not be agreeable to your hearers. Scorn on the man who ever desires to make truth palatable to unhallowed minds. If he modulates his utterances or suppresses the truth which God has given him even in the slightest possible degree to suit the tastes of men, he is a traitor and a coward: let him be drummed out of God's regiment, and driven from the army of God altogether. God's servants are to receive God's message, and whether men will hear or whether they will forbear, they are to deliver it to them in the spirit of old Micaiah, who vowed, "As the LORD my God liveth, whatsoever the LORD saith to me, that will I speak."

But this is not the hardest task; the severest labor is this: we may have to deliver unpleasant truth to people who are resolved not to receive it, to people who will derive no profit from it, but rather will turn it to their own destruction. You see in the text that ancient Israel was to hear but not to receive; they were to be preached to, and the only result was to be that their heart was to be made fat, and their ears dull of hearing. What! Is that ever to be the effect of the gospel? The Bible tells us so. Our preaching is a savor of death unto death, as well as of life unto life. "Oh," says one, "I should not like to preach at that rate." But remember, brother, that the preaching of the cross is a sweet savor of Christ either way. The highest object of all to a Christian laborer is not to win souls, that is a great object; but *the* great object is to glorify God; and many a man has been successful in this who did not succeed in the other. If Israel be not gathered, yet, if we bear our testimony for God, our work is done. No farmer thinks of paying his men in proportion to the harvest. He pays his workers for work done, and so will it be with us, by God's grace, and if I happen to be a very successful laborer here, I boast not, nor claim any large reward on that account. I believe that had I preached the gospel with earnestness and waited upon God, if he had denied me conversions, my reward would be as great at the last, in some respects, because the Master would not lay to my door a nonsuccess which could not be attributed to myself.

Now it would be a very pleasant thing for me to ask you whether you would go for God in your daily vocation and tell of Jesus to sinners who are willing to hear of him; you would all be glad to do that. If I were to ask which sister here would take a class of young women, all anxious to find Christ, why you would all hold up your hands. If I could say, "Who will take a class of boys who long to find the Savior?" you might all be glad of such an avocation; but I have to put it another way, lest you should afterward be dispirited. Who among you will try and teach truth to a drunken husband? Who among you will carry the gospel to despisers and profligates, and into places where the gospel will make you the object of rage and derision? Who among you will take a class of ragged roughs? Who among you will try and teach those who will throw your teaching back upon you with ridicule and scorn? You are not fit to serve God unless you are willing to serve him anywhere and everywhere. You must with the servant be willing to take the bitter with the sweet; you must be willing to serve God in the winter as in the summer. If you are willing to be God's servant at all, you are not to pick and choose your duty and say, "Here am I; send me where there is pleasant duty." Anybody will go then; but if you are willing to serve God, you will say today, "Through floods and flames if Jesus leads, I will by the Holy Spirit's aid be true to my following."

Now, though I have said nothing particularly with regard to foreign missions, I have preached this sermon with the view that God will stir you all up to serve his cause, and particularly with the hope that the missionary feeling being begotten may show itself in a desire also to carry the gospel into foreign parts. Pastor Harms has lately been taken to his rest, but those of you who know the story of his life must have been struck with it; how an obscure country village, on a wild heath in Germany, was made to be a fountain of living waters to South Africa. The poor people had little care for the name of Jesus till Harms went there; and, notwithstanding that I have no sympathy with his Lutheran high-churchism and exclusiveness, I may say he went there to preach Christ with such fire that the whole parish became a missionary society, sending out its own men and women to preach Christ crucified. That ship, the *Candace,* purchased by the villagers of Hermansburgh with their own money, went to and from South Africa, taking the laborers to make settlements, and to undertake Christian enterprise in that dark continent. The whole village was saturated with a desire to serve God and preach the gospel to the heathen, and Harms at the head of it acted with a simple faith worthy of apostolic times. I would that my God would give me what I should consider the greatest honor of my life, the privilege of seeing some of the brethren and sisters of this church devoted to the Lord, and going forth into foreign parts. One gave his farm for students to be educated, another gave all he had, until throughout Hermansburgh it became very much like apostolic days when they had all things in common, the grand object being that of sending the gospel to the heathen. The day may come when we who have been able to do something for this heathen country of England may do something for other heathen countries in sending out our sons and daughters.

Jonah: Sleepers Aroused

Published on Thursday, September 29, 1904; delivered on Thursday evening, July 27, 1876, at the Metropolitan Tabernacle, Newington. No. 2903.

But Jonah was gone down into the sides of the ship; and he lay, and was fast asleep.—JONAH 1:5

We are told, before this fact is mentioned, that the Lord sent out a great wind into the sea to overtake the bark in which Jonah was sailing for Tarshish. The great wheels of Providence are continually revolving in fulfillment of God's purposes concerning his own people. For them, winds blow, and tempests rise. It is a wonderful thing that the whole machinery of nature should be made subservient to the divine purpose of the salvation of his redeemed. I was in a diamond-cutting factory at Amsterdam, and I noticed that there were huge wheels revolving, and a great deal of power being developed and expended; but when I came to look at the little diamond—in some cases a very small one indeed—upon which that power was being brought to bear, it seemed very remarkable that all that power should be concentrated upon such a little yet very precious object. In a similar style, all the wheels of providence and nature, great as they are, are brought to bear, by divine skill and love, upon a thing which appears to many people to be of trifling value, but which is to Christ of priceless worth; namely, a human soul. Here is this common-looking Jew, Jonah, named, according to the general rule that names go by contraries, "a dove," for, at any rate, on this occasion he looked more like the raven that would not come back to the ark; and for this one man—this altogether unamiable prophet—the sea must be tossed in tempest, and a whole shipful of people must have their lives put in jeopardy. This truth is a very far-reaching one. You cannot well exaggerate it. The vast universe is but a platform for the display of God's grace, and all material things that now exist will be set aside when the great drama of grace is completed. The material universe is but scaffolding for the church of Christ. It is but the temporary structure upon which the wonderful mystery of redeeming love is being carried on to perfection. See then, that as the great wind was raised to follow Jonah and to lead to his return to the path of duty, so all things work together for the good of God's people, and all things that exist are being bowed and bent toward God's one solemn eternal purpose—the salvation of his own.

But note also that, while God was awake, Jonah was asleep. While storms were blowing, Jonah was slumbering. It is a strange sight, O Christian, that you should be an important item in the universe, and yet that you should not know it, or care about it; that for you all things are keeping their proper place and time, and yet that you are the only one who does not seem to perceive it; and therefore you fall into a dull, lethargic, sleepy state. Everything around you is awake for your good, yet you yourself are slumbering even as the fugitive prophet was while the storm was raging.

I am going to speak upon the case of Jonah, first, as we may regard it as a useful lesson to the people of God; and, second, as it may be considered as *an equally valuable warning to the unconverted.*

I. First, then, I shall use the case of Jonah as *a useful lesson to the people of God;* and I may very fairly do so when we remember who Jonah was.

First, *Jonah was a believer in God.* He worshiped no false god; he worshiped only the living and true God. He was a professed and avowed believer in Jehovah. He was not ashamed to say—even when his conduct had laid him open to blame, and when there was nobody to support him—"I am a Hebrew; and I fear the Lord, the God of heaven, which hath made the sea and the dry land." Yet, though he was a believer in God, he was in the sides of the ship, fast asleep. O Christian man—a real Christian man, too—if you are in a similar condition, how is it that you can be slumbering under such circumstances? Should not the privileges and the honor, which your being a believer has brought to you by divine grace, forbid that you should be a slumberer, inactive, careless, indifferent? I may be addressing dozens of Jonahs, those who are really God's people, but who are not acting as if they were, chosen of the most High; but are forgetful of their election, their redemption, their sanctification, the life they have begun to live here below and the eternal glory that awaits them hereafter.

Besides being a believer, or as a natural consequence of being a believer, *Jonah was a man of prayer.* Out of the whole company on board that ship, he was the only man who knew how to pray to the one living and true God. All the mariners "cried every man unto his god." But those were idle prayers because they were offered to idols; they could not prevail because they were presented to dumb, dead deities. But here was a man who could pray—and who could pray aright, too—yet he was asleep. Praying men and praying women—you who have the keys of the kingdom of heaven swinging at your girdle—you who can ask what you will, and it shall be done for you—you who have many a time in the past prevailed with God in wrestling prayer—you who have received countless blessings in answer to your supplications—can you be, as Jonah was, sleeping in the time of storm? Can it be possible that he, who knows the power of prayer, is restraining it; that he, to whom God has given this choice privilege, is not availing himself of it? I fear that this may be the case with some of you; and looking at Jonah, a praying man sinfully asleep, I cannot help feeling that I may be speaking to many others who are in exactly the same condition.

More than this, Jonah was not merely a believing man, and a praying man, but *he was also a prophet of the Lord*. He was one to whom God had spoken, and by whom God had spoken. He was a minister; that is to say, one of God's own sent servants, though he was not in his proper place when he was in the ship sailing toward Tarshish. But can God's ministers neglect their duty like this? If I had been asked at that time, "Where is the prophet of the Lord?"—perhaps the only prophet of his age; at any rate, a man who was the very foremost in his time—if I had been asked, "Where is he?" I should have said that he must be looked for amid the masses of the dense population of Nineveh, carrying out his Master's commission with unstaggering faith; or else that he might be looked for amid the thousands of Israel, denouncing their idol gods and their wicked ways. But who would have thought of finding Jonah asleep on board such a ship as that? He is a seer, yet he sees not, for he is sound asleep. He is a watchman, but he is not watching, for he is slumbering and sleeping. Everything is in confusion; yet this man, upon whom rests the divine anointing, and into whose mouth God has put a message to multitudes of his fellow creatures, is sleeping instead of witnessing. Come, Mr. Preacher, see to yourself while I am talking about Jonah, and I will take the message to myself while I am talking to you; for this is a matter which ought to come home to all of us upon whom such great responsibilities are laid, and to whom such high privileges are given. But all of you, who love the Lord, are witnesses for Christ in some capacity or other; and it would be a very sad thing if you, who are called to speak in the name of the Lord, though it should only be in your Sunday school class, or in a little cottage meeting, or to your own children, should be asleep when you ought to be wide awake and active. May the Lord awaken you; for you are the wrong person to be asleep! You, above all others, are bound to have both your eyes open, and to watch day and night to hear what

God the Lord will speak to you, and what he would have you say to the ungodly or to his own chosen people in his name.

It is also worthy of notice that, at the very time when Jonah was asleep in the ship, he was not only a prophet, but he was *a prophet under a special commission*. He was not on furlough; he was, on the contrary, empowered by special warrant, under the King's seal and sign manual, to go at once to a certain place, and there to deliver the King's message; and yet there he is, asleep in this ship, and going in the very opposite direction to the one given him! When prophets sleep, it should be when their errand has been done, and their message has been delivered; but Jonah had not been on his Lord's errand, nor had he delivered his Lord's message; no, he had refused to obey his Lord, and had run away from the path of duty and here he lies, fast asleep, in the sides of the ship. O dear brothers and sisters, if we could truthfully say that our own work for the Lord was done, we might be somewhat excused if we took our rest. But is our life-work done? Mine is not, that I feel certain; it seems to be scarcely begun. Is yours finished, my brother, my sister? Have you so lived that you can be perfectly content with what you have done? Would it not be a cause of grief to you if you were assured that you would have no more opportunities of glorifying God upon the earth? I think you would feel that very much. Well, then, how can you be willing to be indifferent, cold, and dead, when so much of God's work lies before you scarcely touched as yet? All that you and I have done, so far, has been like apprentice work; we have been just getting our hand in, we have not become journeymen in God's great workshop yet; certainly we cannot claim to be wise master builders yet. Few of us, if any, have attained to that degree; so let us not go to sleep. O sir, shame on you! Asleep in the early morning? A man may take his rest when he gets weary after a long day's toil; but not yet, with all that work to be done—with the King's commission pressing upon us. With the call of the myriads of Nineveh sounding in his ears, Jonah, God's appointed messenger, should not have been found asleep in the sides of the ship.

This, then, is who the man was. He was a believing man and a praying man, and a prophet, and a prophet under a special commission. But where was he? Where had he got to?

Well, he had gone down into the sides of the ship; that is to say, *he had gone where he hoped he should not be observed or disturbed*. He had gone down into the sides of the ship—not among the cargo; the mariners threw that overboard, yet the noise did not wake the sleeping prophet. He was not upon the deck, ready to take a turn at keeping watch; but he had got as much out of the way as ever he could; and I have known Christian people try, as far as they could, to get out of the way. Possibly, they are not living inconsistently, or doing, as far as others can see, anything that is glaringly sinful; but they have just retired from their Master's business. They have got into a little quiet place where nobody notices them. I wonder whether there is a Christian man who has gone to live in a country village, where he has not yet said anything for Christ, although, when he lived in London, he was a busy worker for God. He has, like Jonah, gone down into the sides of the ship, into a quiet place where nobody can see him. Around him there are very few Christian people—perhaps hardly any—and he does not want anybody to know that he is a Christian. He would like now to live in quite a private way. If he were asked about himself, he would answer, as Jonah did, "I fear God"; but he does not wish to be asked anything about himself. He does not want people to fix their eyes upon him; he is afraid of being too conspicuous. He says that he always was of a retiring disposition, like the soldier, who ran away as soon as the first shot of the battle was fired, and so was shot as a deserter. He says that he is like Nicodemus, who came to Jesus by night, or like Joseph of Arimathea, a disciple, but secretly, for fear of the Jews. He has gone down into the sides of the ship, though, at one time, he was one of the foremost workers for Christ.

He has gone, too, *where he will not lend a hand in any service that needs to be done*. He was in the Sunday school once, but he says that he has had his turn at that, and does not intend to do anything more. He used to be, perhaps, a deacon of a church, but now he does not wish for such a position as that. He says there is a great deal of trouble and toil in connection with such offices, and he intends, for the future, to avoid everything that will give him trouble, or cause him the slightest toil. Once he took delight in preaching the Word; and, in those days, if anybody had said that he would live to be silent, and not speak in Christ's name, he would have been very angry at the man who made such a statement; but it has come true now. Jonah is not up on deck helping to hold the rudder or to set a sail or to do anything, not even a hand's turn to help the poor laboring vessel. He has gone to sleep in the sides of the ship where nobody inquires about him, at least for the present, and where there is nothing for him to do.

Observe, too, that *Jonah was stopping away from the prayer meeting*. Do you ask, "What prayer meeting?" Why, every other man on board that ship was crying unto his god, but Jonah was asleep in the sides of the ship. He was not praying; he was sleeping, and perhaps dreaming, but he was certainly not praying; and it is a very bad thing when a true servant of God, a praying man, and one by whom God has spoken aforetime, begins to get into such a spiritually sleepy state that he not only does nothing to help the church, but he does not even join in prayer in the time of danger. Do you know anybody in such a state as that, my brother? "Yes," you reply, "several." Are you in that state yourself, brother? If so, let charity for people who are doing wrong begin at home; it may extend to others afterward. But if this cap fits you, wear it, and wear it till you wear it out, and have improved yourself through wearing it.

This man, asleep in the sides of the ship, *represents one who cannot even take any notice of what was going on around him*. At first, he did not wish to be himself observed; but now, he does not care to observe others. What is the condition of the millions of heathen in foreign lands? That is a subject that he avoids; he is of opinion that they will be converted in the millennium, or that, even if they are not converted, their future lot may be a happy one. At any rate, it is a subject about which he does not concern himself. Jonah is asleep in the sides of the ship, and he appears quite content to let the millions of heathen perish. Then, with regard to the church of Christ at home, sometimes he is told that everything is prospering, but from other quarters he is informed that we are all going to the bad. Well, he does not know which report is the true one, and he does not particularly care; and, as for the church of which he is a member, does he not care for that?

Well, yes, in a certain fashion; but he does not care enough for the Sunday school, for instance, to lend a hand there, or for the preaching society to lend a hand there. He never encourages the minister's heart by saying that the love of Christ constrains him to take his share of holy service. Jonah is asleep in the sides of the ship. He is not much noticed, if at all, for those around him have come to the conclusion that he is good for nothing; and he himself, as I have shown you, does not take much notice of what is going on, though all the while he is a man of God, a man of prayer, and one whom God has used in times past. I wonder whether these descriptions are at all applicable to any of my hearers. At any rate, I know that they represent, as in a mirror, the lives of many professors of religion. We trust they are sincere in heart in the sight of God; but to us their sleepiness is more apparent than their sincerity.

Now, further, what was Jonah doing at that time? *He was asleep—asleep amid all that confusion and noise*. What a hurly-burly shore was outside that vessel—storms raging, billows roaring—and Jonah was not a sailor, but a landsman, yet he was asleep. Certainly he must have been in a remarkable state to be able to sleep through such a storm as that. And what a noise there was inside the ship as well as outside! Everybody else was crying to his god; and the mariners had been throwing the cargo out of the ship, so they must have stirred the whole place up from one end to the other. There seems to have been scarcely any opportunity for anybody to rest, yet Jonah could sleep right through it all, no matter what noise the men made as they pulled the ropes or threw out their wares, or what outcries they made as they presented their prayers to their idol gods. Jonah was asleep amid all that confusion and noise; and, O Christian man, for you to be indifferent to all that is going on in such a world as this, for you to be negligent of God's work in such a time as this is just as strange. The devil alone is making noise enough to wake all the Jonahs if they only want to awake. Then there are the rampant errors of the times, the sins of the times, the confusions of the times, the controversies of the times, all these things ought to wake us. And then, beyond the times, there is eternity, with all its terrors and its glories. There is the dread conflict that is going on between Christ and Belial—between the true and the false—between Jesus and antichrist. All around us there is tumult and storm, yet some professing Christians are able, like Jonah, to go to sleep in the sides of the ship. I think, brethren and sisters, if we are spiritually awake, if we only look at the condition of religion in our own country, we shall often be obliged at night to lie awake literally, and toss to and fro, crying, "O God, have mercy upon this distracted kingdom, and let your truth triumph over the popery which many are endeavoring to bring back among us!" But, alas! the great multitude of believers have little or no care about this matter; they do not even seem to notice it, for they are sound asleep in the midst of a storm.

Notice, also, that *Jonah was asleep when other people were awake.* All around us people seem to be wide awake, whether we are asleep or not. When I see what is being done by Romanists, and observe the zeal and self-denial of many persons who have dedicated themselves to the propagation of their false faith, I am astonished that we are doing so little for the true faith. Is it really the case that God has the dullest set of servants in the whole world? It is certain that men are all alive in the service of Satan; then we should not be half alive in the service of our God. Are the worshipers of Baal crying aloud, "O Baal, hear us," and the devotees of Ashtaroth shouting, "Hear us, O mighty Ashtaroth"; and yet the prophet of Jehovah is lying asleep in the sides of the ship? Is it so? Does everything else seem to arouse all a man's energies, but does true religion paralyze them? I have really thought, when I have been reading some books written by very good men, that the best thing for sending a man to sleep was a book by an evangelical writer; but that the moment a man becomes unsound in the faith, it seems as if he woke up, and had something to say which people were bound to hear. It is a great pity that it should be so, just as it was a great pity that everybody should have been awake on that vessel with the exception of Jonah; yet I fear that it is still only too true that those who serve the living God are not half filled with the arousing fervor which ought to possess them for the honor of the Lord most High.

Jonah was asleep, next, not only in a time of great confusion, and when others were awake, but also *in a time when he was in great danger*, for the ship was likely to sink. The storm was raging furiously, yet Jonah was asleep. And, believer, when you and those about you are in danger of falling into great sin through your careless living; when your family is in danger of being brought up without the fear of God; when your servants are in danger of concluding that religion is all a farce because you act as if it were; when those who watch you in business are apt to sneer at Christian profession because they say that your profession is of very little worth to you; when all this is taking place, and there is imminent danger to your own soul, and to the souls of others, can you still sleep in unconcern?

And Jonah was asleep *when he was wanted to be awake*. He, above all other men, was the one who ought to awake, and call upon his God. If anybody goes to sleep nowadays, it certainly ought not to be the believer in the Lord Jesus Christ. All things demand that Christians should be in real earnest. I know of no argument that I could gather from time or eternity, from heaven or earth or hell, to allow a Christian man to be supine and careless, but if I am asked for reasons why Christians are wanted to be in downright earnest and full of consecrated vigor in the service of God, those arguments are so plentiful that I have no time to mention them all. The world needs you; careless souls need to be awakened; inquiring souls need to be directed; mourning souls need to be comforted; rejoicing souls need to be established; the ignorant need to be taught; the desponding need to be cheered. On all sides, for a very Christian man, there is an earnest cry; and certainly, in these days, God has made a truly godly man to be more precious than the gold of Ophir; and that man, who keeps himself back from earnest service for God in such a time as this, surely cannot expect the Lord's blessing to rest upon him. Verily, the old curse of Meroz may well be pronounced upon the man who, in this age, and under present circumstances, like Jonah, goes down into the sides of the ship, lies down, and goes to sleep.

Jonah was asleep, with all the heathens around him, upbraiding him by their actions. They were praying while he was sleeping; and, at last, it came to this—that the shipmaster sternly addressed the prophet of God, and said, "What meanest thou, O sleeper?" It is sad indeed when things have come to such a pass that a heathen captain rebukes a servant of God; and yet I am afraid that the church of God, if she does not mend her ways, will have a great many similar rebukes from heathen practices and heathen utterances. Look at the enormous sums that the heathen spend upon their idols and their idol temples and worship, and then think how little we spend upon the service of the living God. One is amazed to read of the lakhs [hundreds of thousands] of rupees that are given by Indian princes for the worship of their dead deities, and yet our missionary societies languish, and the work of God in a thousand ways is stopped, because, God's stewards are not using what he has entrusted to them as they should. Think, too, of the flaming zeal with which the votaries of false faiths compass sea and land to make one proselyte, while we do so little to bring souls to Jesus Christ. One of these days you will have Hindus and Brahmins talking to us in this fashion: "You profess that the love of Christ constrains you, but to what does it constrain you?" They even now ask us what kind of religion must ours be that forces opium upon the poor Chinese. They quote our great national sins against us, and I do not wonder that they do. I only wish that they could be told that Christians reprobate those evils, and that they are not Christians who practice them. But we must do more than even the best Christians are now doing or else we shall have the heathen saying, as the semiheathen at home do say, "If we believed in eternal punishment, we should be earnest day and night to rescue souls from it"—which is to me a strong corroboration of the truth of that doctrine.

We do not want any doctrine that can make us less zealous than we are. We certainly do not want any doctrine that can give us any excuse for want of zeal. Still there is great force in the remark I quoted just now. We are not as earnest to save men from going down to the pit as we ought to be if we do indeed believe that they are hastening to that doom. The shipmasters are again rebuking the Jonahs. Those who believe in error, those who worship false gods, turn round upon us and ask us what we mean. O Jonah, sleeping Jonah, is it not time that you were awake?

But why was Jonah asleep? I suppose that it was partly the reaction after the excitement through which his mind had passed in rebelling against God. He had wearied himself with seeking his own evil way; so now, after the disobedience to God of which he had been guilty, his spirit sinks, and he sleeps. Besides, it is according to the nature of sin to give—not physical sleep, I grant you—but to give spiritual slumber. There is no opiate like the commission of an evil deed. A man who has done wrong is so much less able to repent of the wrong, so much the less likely to do so. Jonah's conscience had become hardened by his willful rejection of his Lord's commands, and therefore he could sleep when he ought to have been aroused and alarmed.

Besides, he wished to get rid of the very thought of God. He was trying to flee from God's presence. I suppose he could not bear his own thoughts;

they must have been dreadful to him. So, being in a pet against his God, and altogether in a wrong spirit, he hunts about for a snug corner of the ship, stretches himself out and there falls asleep, and sleeps on right through the storm. O sleepy Christian, there is something wrong about you too! Conscience has been stupefied. There is some darling sin, I fear, that you are harboring. Search it out, and drive it out. Sin is the mother of this shameful indifference. God help you to get rid of it! Brother, I am speaking to you with as much directness as I possibly can, yet not with more than I use toward myself. Have I, in my preaching, been slumbering and sleeping? If you find that I am not in earnest, I charge you, my brother in Christ, tell me of it, and wake me out of my sleep if you can, as I now tell you of it, and say, by all that God has done to you in saving you by his grace, and in making you his servant, give not up your soul to slumber, but awake, awake, put on strength, and arouse yourself, by the power of the Holy Spirit, to prayer and to the service of your God.

Thus I have spoken, perhaps at too great length, to Christians.

II. Now, more briefly, I want to give *a warning to the unconverted.*

Jonah, asleep on board that ship, is a type of a great number of unconverted people who come to our various places of worship. Jonah was in imminent danger, for God had sent a great storm after him: and, my unconverted hearer, *your danger, at this present moment, is beyond description*. There is nothing but a breath between you and hell. One of our beloved elders was with us here last Sabbath day; he is now with the spirits of just men made perfect; but if it had been the lot of any unconverted person here to suffer and to expire in the same manner, alas, how sad it would have been for you, my hearer! Driven from the presence of God, you would be cast in the outer darkness where there is weeping and wailing and gnashing of teeth. The sword of divine justice is already furbished, will you yet make mirth? Can you laugh and jest when there is but a step between you and death—but a step between you and hell? An enemy to God, unforgiven, the angel of justice seeking you out as the storm sought out Jonah in that ship, "What meanest thou, O sleeper," when the peril of everlasting wrath is so near thee?

You are asleep, too, *when there are a great many things to awake you*. As I have already said, there was a great noise in the vessel where Jonah was, a great noise inside and outside the ship, yet he did not awake. I do believe that many of you, unconverted people, find it hard to remain as you are. You get hard blows sometimes from the preacher. At family prayer often your conscience is touched. When you hear a passage from the Bible read, or when you hear of a friend who has died, you get somewhat aroused. Why, the very conversion of others should surely awaken you. If nothing else had awoke Jonah, the prayers of the mariners ought to have awakened him; and the earnestness of your mother and father, the pleading of your sister, the cries of new converts, the earnest anxieties of inquirers, ought to have—and if you were not so deeply sunken in slumber, would have some influence over you to arouse you.

You are asleep, brother, *while prayer could save you*. If your prayers could not be heard, I think I should say, "Let him sleep on." If there were no possibility of your salvation, I do not see why you should be aroused from your slumbers. Despair is an excellent excuse for sloth; but you have no reason to despair. "Arise, call upon thy God," said the shipmaster to Jonah; and we say to you, "Friend, how is it that you are so indifferent, and do not pray, when it is written, 'Ask, and it shall be given you; seek, and ye shall find'; and when the facts prove the truth of the words of Jesus, 'for he that asketh receiveth, and he that, seeketh findeth'?" Heaven is within your reach, yet you will not stretch out your hand. Eternal life is so near to you that Paul writes, "If thou shalt confess with thy mouth the Lord Jesus, and shalt believe in thine heart that God hath raised him from the dead, thou shalt be saved." Assuredly, that man who has food heaped up before him, but who sits down and goes to sleep with his head in Benjamin's mess [largest share, from Genesis 43:34], and yet will not eat of it, deserves to be starved. He who can slumber when the river runs up to his very lip; he who is dying of thirst, yet will not drink, deserves to die; does he not? With such wondrous blessings set before you in the gospel—with heaven itself just yonder, and the pearly gates set wide open, yet you are so indifferent that you despise the good land, and murmur, and refuse to accept the Savior who would lead you to it—why, surely, you must be sleeping the sleep of death! You are sleeping while God's people are wondering at you, just as those mariners in the ship wondered at Jonah; and while they are weeping over you and praying for you. There are some, in this place, who are the constant subjects of prayer. Some of you, who are seated here, do not perhaps know it, but there are those who love you and who mention your name day and night before God; and yet, while they are concerned about you, you are not concerned about yourself. O God, if storms cannot awaken these sleeping Jonahs, awaken them by some other means, even though it be by one like themselves, or one even worse than themselves! Send a message that shall upbraid them. Set some blasphemer to ask them how they can attend the means of grace, and yet be undecided. I have known that to happen. I have known a coarse, vile-living man to accost a moral and excellent attendant on the means of grace, and say to him, "Why are you not either one thing or the other? If religion is all a lie, why don't you be as I am; but if it is true, why don't you become a Christian?" And verily may they put such questions as those to some of you.

O friends, I pray you, if you are out of Christ, do not pretend to be happy! Do not accept any happiness till you find it in him. To some of you, I would speak very pointedly. Are you sick? Do you feel that your life is very precarious? O my dear friend, you are like Jonah when the ship was like to be broken. Do not delay. Are there the beginnings of consumption about you? Is it supposed to be so? Do not delay. Has some relative been taken away, and does there seem some likelihood that you may have the same disease? Oh, do not sleep, but awake! Are you getting old, friend? Are the gray hairs getting thick around your brow? Oh, do not delay! For unsaved young people, it is wrong to sleep, for he that sleeps when he is young sleeps during a siege; but he that slumbers when he is old sleeps during the attack, when the enemy is actually at the breach, and storming the walls. Do any of you work in dangerous trades? Do you have to eat your bread where an accident might easily happen, as it has often happened to others? Oh, be prepared to meet your God!

But having begun this list, I might continue it almost indefinitely; but I will end it in a sentence or so. *Are you a mortal man*? *Can* you *die*? *Will* you die? May you die *now*? May you drop dead in the street? May you go to sleep and never wake up again on earth? May your very food or drink become the vehicle of death to you? May there be death in the air you breathe? May it be so? Will you one day, at any rate, have to be carried to your long home, like others, and lie asleep in the grave? Will you give account to God for the things done in the body? Will you have to stand before the great, white throne, to make one of that innumerable throng, and to be there put into the balance to be weighed for eternity? If so, sleep not, I beseech you, as do others; but bestir yourself. May God's Holy Spirit bestir you to make your calling and election sure! Lay hold on Jesus Christ with the grip of an earnest, humble faith, and surrender yourself, henceforth, to the service of him who has bought you with his precious blood. God grant to all of us the grace to awake, and arise, that Christ may give us life and light, for his dear name's sake! Amen.

Daniel: Undaunted Courage

Delivered on Sunday morning, June 14, 1868, at the Metropolitan Tabernacle, Newington. No. 815.

> *Now when Daniel knew that the writing was signed, he went into his house; and his windows being open in his chamber toward Jerusalem, he kneeled upon his knees three times a day, and prayed, and gave thanks before his God, as he did aforetime.*—DANIEL 6:10

Daniel had been exalted to very great worldly prosperity, but his soul had prospered too. Oftentimes outward advancement means inward decline. Tens of thousands have been intoxicated by success. Though they bade fair in starting in the race of life to win the prize, they were tempted to turn aside to gather the golden apples, and so they missed the crown. It was not so with Daniel—he was as perfect before God in his high estate as in his lowlier days; and this is to be accounted for by the fact that he sustained the energy of his outward profession by constant secret communion with God. He was, we are told, a man of an excellent spirit, and a man abundant in prayer; hence his head was not turned by his elevation, but the Lord fulfilled in him his promise to "make his servant's feet like hinds' feet, that they may stand upon their high places." Yet, although Daniel preserved his integrity, he did not find a position of greatness to be one of rest. As the birds peck at the ripest fruit, so his envious enemies assailed him; and as the most conspicuous warriors most attract the arrows of the foe, so the honors of Daniel brought upon him the enmities of many.

Seek not then, beloved, seek not then, with an excess of desire, or an unrest of ambition, to be great among the great ones of the earth. There are more precious things than honor and wealth. A Persian king, wishing to give two of his courtiers a token of his regard, gave to one of them a golden cup and to the other a kiss: he who had obtained the golden cup considered that he was hardly done by, and envied the courtier who received the kiss from the monarch's own mouth. And let me say, let who will receive the wealth and honors of the world, which make up her golden cup, if you receive a kiss of favor from the lip of God and feel the sweetness of it in your inmost soul, you have received more than they; you have no reason whatsoever to repine though that kiss should come to you in poverty and sickness, but rather to rejoice that God has counted you worthy, in his infinite grace, to receive the more of spirituals though you have the less of temporals.

Luther declared that all the greatness of the world was but a bone which God threw to a dog. "For," says he, "he gives more to the pope and to the Turk than to all his saints put together," and so verily it is. To be great, distinguished, and wealthy may be the lot of a Haman, who shall be hanged upon a gallows, while God's true servant may sit at the gate and bear contempt as did Mordecai. Better to pine with Lazarus than feast with Dives, for the love of God more than compensates for temporary disadvantages. Better an ounce of divine grace than a ton of worldly goods. Though the good things come not as the left-handed blessings of outward prosperity, be more than content if you win the right-handed benediction of spiritual joy.

The example of Daniel I present you for your observation today, believing that these are times when we need to be as firm and resolute as he, and that at any rate, occasions will come to every one of us before we win our crown, when we shall need to put our foot down firmly, and be steadfast and unflinching for the Lord and his truth.

I. First, let me invite your attention to *Daniel's habitual devotion:* it is worthy of our study. We might never have known of it if he had not been so sorely tried, but fire reveals the hidden gold.

Daniel's habitual devotion. We are told that aforetime, before the trial, he had been in the constant habit of prayer. He prayed much. There are some forms of spiritual life which are not absolutely essential, but prayer is of the very essence of spirituality. He that has no prayer lacks the very breath of the life of God in the soul. I will not say that every man who prays is a Christian, but I will say that every man who prays sincerely is so; for, recollect, men may pray after a fashion, and even practice private prayer too, and yet may be deceiving themselves; for as the frogs of Egypt came up into the bedchambers, so does hypocrisy intrude itself even into the private places where men pretend to worship God; but I do say that a cheerful constancy in sincere private devotion is such a mark of grace, that he who has it may fairly conclude himself to be one of the Lord's family.

Daniel always had subjects for prayer and reasons for prayer. He prayed for himself that in his eminent position he might not be uplifted with pride, might not be taken in the snares of those who envied him, might not be permitted to fall into the usual oppressions and dishonesties of Eastern rulers. He prayed for his people. He saw many of the house of Judah who were not in such prosperous circumstances as himself. He remembered those who were in bonds, as being bound with them. Those who were bone of his bone and flesh of his flesh, he brought in the arms of faith before his God. He interceded for Jerusalem. It grieved him that the city was laid waste, that still the brand of the Chaldean destroyer was upon Mount Zion, so beautiful, and once the joy of the whole earth. He pleaded for the return from the captivity, which he knew was ordained of his God. He prayed for the glory of his God, that the day might come when the idols should be utterly abolished, and when the whole earth should know that Jehovah rules in heaven, and among the sons of men. It would have been a delightful thing to have listened at the keyhole of Daniel's closet, and to have heard the mighty intercessions which went up to the Lord God of hosts.

We read next, that with all his prayers he mingled thanksgiving. Do observe it, for so many forget this, "He prayed and gave thanks to God." Surely, it is poor devotion which is always asking and never returning its gratitude! Am I to live upon the bounty of God, and never to thank him for what I receive? Surely, prayers in which there is no thanksgiving are selfish things: they rob God; and will a man rob God—rob God even in his prayers and yet expect that his prayers should be successful? Have I not often said in this place that prayer and praise resemble the process by which we live? We breathe in the atmospheric air, and then breathe it out again: prayer takes in deep drafts of the love and grace of God, and then praise breathes it out again.

Prayer and praise, with sins forgiven,
Bring down to earth the bliss of heaven.

Good Daniel had learned to praise as well as to pray, and to offer to God that sweet incense which was made of diverse spices, of earnest desires and longings mingled with thanksgivings and adorations.

It is worthy of notice, that the text says, "Daniel prayed and gave thanks before his God." This enters into the very soul of prayer—this getting before God. O brethren, do you not often catch yourselves praying to the wind, and in private uttering words as though you were only to be heard by the four walls which bound your little room? But prayer, when it is right, comes before God, in realizing the majesty of the throne of his grace, and seeing the blood of the eternal covenant sprinkled thereon; in discerning that God is gazing right through you, reading every thought and interpreting every desire; in feeling that you yourself are speaking into the ear of God, and are now, as it were,

Plunged in the Godhead's deepest sea,
And lost in his immensity.

This is praying, when we draw near to God. I shall not care if you do not use a single word, if you feel the majesty of God to be so overwhelming that words are out of place; and silence becomes far more expressive when you bow with sobs and tears and groanings that cannot be uttered. That is the prayer which wins its suit of God, and is dear to the majesty of heaven. Thus Daniel prayed and gave thanks, not before men to be seen of them, nor yet in private before himself to satisfy his conscience, but "before God," of whom he had an audience thrice each day.

That little word *his* I must not let slip, however. He prayed and gave thanks before his God. He spoke not to God merely as God who might belong to any man and every man, but unto his God, whom he had espoused by a solemn determination that he would not turn aside from his service, that determination having resulted from God's having determined to select him and to make him his own man, peculiarly set apart unto his own praise. "*His* God." Why, it seems to me to bring up that word *covenant*—his "covenant God," as though he had entered into covenant with God according to the language of the most High, "I will be their God, and they shall be my people." True son of Abraham and Isaac and Jacob was this Daniel when he looked upon God as being his own, his property, could claim him, could say as we sometimes sing in that sweet psalm, "Yea, mine own God is he!" Oh, to feel that the Lord belongs wholly to me! My God, my God, if no other man can claim him; my Father, my Shepherd, my Friend, my Lord, and my God! Yes, here lies power in prayer, when a man can talk with God as his covenant God. That man cannot miss; every arrow sticks in the center of the target when he pleads "before his God." That man must conquer the angel at Jabbok's brook who grips him with both hands by a faith which knows its heaven-wrought claims. It is not winning mercies from another's God, nor pleading outside the covenant, but the believer feels that he is asking of his own God mercies already promised and made sure to him by oaths and covenant and blood.

Some other particulars in the text are not quite so important; nevertheless, observe that he prayed *three times a day*. That does not tell you how often he prayed, but how often he was in the posture of prayer. Doubtless he prayed three hundred times a day if necessary—his heart was always having commerce with the skies; but thrice a day he prayed formally. It has been well said that we usually take three meals in the day, and that it is well to give the soul as many meals as the body. We want the morning's guidance, we need the eventide's forgiveness, do we not also require the noontide's refreshment? Might we not well say at noontide, "Tell me, O thou whom my soul loveth, where thou feedest, where thou makest thy flock to rest at noon." If you find from morn till eve too long an interval between prayer, put in another golden link at midday. There is no rule in Scripture as to how often you should pray, and there is no rule as to when you should pray; it is left to the man's own gracious spirit to suggest season. We need not come back to the bondage of the Mosaic covenant, to be under rule and rubric; we are left to that free Spirit who leads his saints aright. Yet three times a day is a commendable number.

Notice, also, *the posture.* That, also, is of little consequence, since we read in Scripture of men who prayed on the bed, with their face to the wall. We read of David sitting before the Lord. How very common and acceptable a posture was that of *standing* before God in prayer! Yet there is a peculiar appropriateness, especially in private prayer, in the posture of kneeling. It seems to say, "I cannot stand upright before thy majesty; I am a beggar, and I put myself in the position of a beggar; I pursue of thee, great God, on bended knee, in the posture of one who owns that he deserves nothing, but humbles himself before thy gracious majesty." The reason why he kneeled on the particular occasion mentioned in the text was, no doubt, because he always had kneeled, and therefore always would kneel, and he would not be driven from the posture, little as that might be, at a tyrant's word. No, if all earth and hell should be against him, if he had found it more to God's honor to kneel, then kneel still he would, even though he should be cast into the lions' den for it.

One more observation. We are told that Daniel kneeled upon his knees *with his windows open toward Jerusalem.* This was not done with any view to publicity. It may be that nobody could see him, even when his windows were open, except the servants in the court. I suppose the house to have been erected as most Eastern houses were, with an open square in the center; and though he would be looking toward Jersualem, the windows would be looking into the court, where he could only be observed by those who might be residents in the house or visitors on business. Probably his fellow counselors knew the hour which he usually set apart for devotion, and therefore called in so as to find him in the act. Besides, you must recollect that, though it would be strange here for a man to pray with his windows open, where he could be heard, it was not at all strange among the Orientals, since you will find the Pharisees and others not at all slow to perform their devotions in any place, when the hour of prayer comes, and therefore it would not be regarded at all as being of a Pharisaic nature, that he should pray with his windows open.

The windows being open toward Jerusalem may have been suggested by the prayer of Solomon, when he asked that if the Lord's people were banished at any time, when they sought the Lord with their faces toward that holy place, God would hear them. It may have helped him also to recollect that dear city toward which every Jew's heart turns with affection, even as the needle trembles toward its pole. The thought of its ruin assisted his earnestness, the recollection of its sin humbled him, and the promises concerning it comforted him. He turned toward Jerusalem. And what does this say to us? Men and brethren, it tells us that we ought to take care when we pray, to have our windows open toward Calvary. Neither turn you to the east, nor to the west, but let your spirits turn toward the cross of Christ. That is the great point toward which all the faces of the faithful must continually be turned, where Jesus died, where Jesus rose, where Jesus intercedes before the throne of mercy. There it is that the eyes of faith must look. With your windows open toward Calvary always pray; look upon the precious blood; gaze steadfastly upon the risen Lord; behold the authority of his plea, as before his Father he wins his suit for his people, and you will grow strong to wrestle until you prevail.

II. We must now turn to a second consideration, *Daniel's action under trial.*

There is nothing that kings and queens are much fonder of than meddling with religion. Though the Prussian king tried to make a number of watches all tick together, and could not do it, yet notwithstanding the experiment and its failure, there are always evil counselors who would force men's consciences to keep stroke. Folly is in the throne when monarchs patronize or oppress religion. Caesar always muddles when he meddles with the things of God. In Daniel's day there was an act of uniformity passed in some respects similar to the famous act which was thrust upon this land. Darius ordained that no man should pray for thirty days: the other Act of Uniformity commanded that no man should pray at any time in public without his book. There is not very much to prefer between the two. When this act of uniformity was passed, several courses were open to Daniel. He might, for instance, have said, "This does not answer my purpose. I have a high position in society. I am chief president over all these dominions, and though I am willing to suffer something for my religion, yet gold may be bought too dear, and therefore I shall cease to pray." He might have found many precedents and many companions. What crowds, when it has come to a question between life and truth, between honor and Christ, have made the evil choice and perished infamously? Daniel does not seem to have raised that question. Yet he might have said, "Well, well, we must be prudent; God must be worshiped certainly, but there is no particular reason for my worshiping him in the usual room, nor even in the city where I live; I can retire in the evening, or find some more secret spot in my own house, and especially there is no occasion to open the window. I can pray with the window shut, and I shall be just as acceptable before God. I think, therefore, I shall keep my conscience clear, but not obtrude my religion in these evil days."

Daniel did not so reason; he was a lionlike man, and scorned to lower his standard in the presence of the foe; for see, in his position, if he had not prayed as before, it would have been a scandal to the weak and a scorn to the wicked; for the weak would have said, "See, Daniel is cowed by the decree." Then every poor Jew throughout the realm would have found excuse for forsaking his principles; and the wicked would have said, "Note, he serves his God when all goes well, but see where he drifts when trouble comes!" He would not seek the secrecy which prudence might have suggested. Still it might have suggested to him that he could pray inwardly. Prayers without words are just as acceptable to God: could he not do this? He felt he could not, inasmuch as the decree was not inward, and the king's opposition to religion was not inward. He did not believe in opposing outward falsehood by an inward truth. He did, in the language of the hymn we were singing, "strength to strength oppose." He would give distinct outward avowal of his own convictions in opposition to the outward persecuting edict.

As Daniel did not happen to have one of those rotating, double-acting consciences, he did not try to import a new meaning into the terms of the decree or invent a compromise between it and his own convictions, but he went straightforward in the plain path. He knew what the edict meant, and therefore down on his knees he went before his God in direct defiance of it. Whether the edict might be read in a milder sense or not, did not trouble him; he knew what Darius meant by it, and what the captains and the counselors meant by it, and he knew also what he himself intended to do, and therefore he did the right thing, and before his God he dared the lions, rather than soil his conscience with aught of ill.

Observe with care what Daniel did. He made up his mind to act as he had done aforetime. Note how *quietly* he acted. He did not say to any of his enemies, "I mean to carry out my convictions." Not at all; he knew that talk was lost upon them, so he resorted to actions instead of words. He quietly went home when he found the law was passed—though grieved that such a thing was done—without a single word of repining or caviling he sought his chamber. I do not find that he was at all distracted or disturbed. The words "as he had done aforetime" seem to imply that he went upstairs as calmly as he had been accustomed to do. His servants would not have known from his behavior that any law had been made. He always had gone at that hour to pray, and they could hear him pray just as earnestly as he ever had done. He was stayed on God, therefore continued at perfect peace.

Note again, how he acted unhesitatingly—*immediately*! He did not pause; he did not ask for time to consider what he should do. In matters of perilous duty, our first thoughts are best. When there is anything to be lost by religion, follow out the first thought of conscience, namely, "Do the right." Who needs to question where duty points the way? Where God commands, there is no room for reason to raise cavils. Yet I have no doubt, if the devil could have whispered into the prophet's ear, he would have said, "Now Daniel, you had better consider a little while. You are in a position where you can materially help your friends. You are of very great authority in this court; you may be of assistance to the true religion. You do not know how many may be converted by your example. You ought not lightly to give up a position where you can do so much good." That argument I have heard hundreds of times when people have been urged to come out of false positions and do the right. But what have you and I to do with maintaining our influence and position at the expense of truth? It is never right to do a little wrong, to obtain the greatest possible good. Your duty is to do the right: consequences are with God; and after all it never can be, in the long run, a good thing either for you or for others to do wrong.

You will observe also, that Daniel did not act under excitement, but *with a full knowledge of the result*. The record expressly has it: "when Daniel knew that the writing was signed." Many people will do right in a hurry, and under strong excitement will go further than they would have done in cold blood; but Daniel, probably shut out from the council by some crafty device of the counselors, no sooner heard that the statute stood good than, without parley, his resolution was formed and his mind made up. It was not for him to delay and to hesitate; he had all the data before him, and obedience made her determination known. Count the cost, young man, before you profess to be a Christian; do not espouse, upon a sudden, an enterprise for which you will be unequal. Devote yourselves to the Lord your God by his grace, but let it be according to the command of Christ, after having first made an estimate of that which will be required of you, and seek grace from on high that you may accomplish what otherwise will be impossible.

I like that word, and must go back to it again, *"as he had done aforetime."* Here he makes no alteration; he takes not the slightest possible notice of the king's decree. At the same place, at the same hour, in the same posture, and in the same spirit, the prophet is found. This indicates to us the Christian's duty under persecution—he should act under persecution as he would have done if none had arisen. If you have worshiped God under the smile of your Christian friends, worship him under the crown of the ungodly. If you have, as a tradesman, pursued a course of honest action in more prosperous times, do not for God's sake, for Christ's sake, tamper with that honest course because the times have changed. What has been right is right, and therefore abide by it. What you have done sincerely still do, and God will give you a blessing in it. Daniel could not have performed that act of praying, when the lions' den was to be the penalty, if he had not fallen into the habit of constant prayer beforehand. It was his secret communion with God which gave him strength and vigor to push on. Because he was right, he found it easier to keep right, whatever the penalty might be. I dare say I address some young man who has come from the country from a godly family where true religion has been daily set before him, and now he is placed in a workshop where he is startled to find that Jesus is ridiculed, and religion is a byword. Now friend, so as you used to do at home, make no difference to please vain men; take care that you begin as you mean to go on. I would not say merely, "Do not give up the spirit of religion," but, "Do not even yield the form." The devil never gives up to us; do not give up to him. He takes care to fight us with all his might; let us do the same to him.

I believe hundreds of Christian men make a hard lot to themselves by little yieldings at first, for generally is it so in this world, that if a man is determined and makes up his mind, after a while the world will let him alone. In the barrack room, when the soldier kneels to pray, how often has he been the subject of a thousand ribald jests, and so has given up all thought of bowing the knee! Yet we have heard of a real convert, who, when he came into the regiment, having been converted, knelt down to pray, and as he persisted in so doing, his comrades said, "Ah! he's one of the plucky ones; he's a genuine fellow"; and they left him alone afterward; whereas, if he had once sneaked into his bed without prayer, he would never after that have dared to kneel. There is nothing like following Daniel's example, by never giving in, for thus you will win the respect of those who otherwise would have sneered at you. How soon the world will find out our real meaning! We may think we are playing our game so prettily that they cannot make us out, and that we shall be pleasing the world and pleasing God too, but it always comes to a dead failure, and then, while the world despises, we have not the comfort of our conscience to sustain us.

Oh, if our fathers, the Puritans, would but have yielded a little; if they could have made but a nick in their consciences, as some are now doing, then, instead of being cast out of house and home, and prevented from opening their mouths to preach Christ, their yielding and consenting would have kept them in ease and honor; but where, then, would have been that gospel light which gladdens the nations? Where those pure and sacred institutions which they have handed down to us? Now, at this hour, through their intrepid resolution, they remain among the blessed, and men honor them. Let us not, the sons of brave fathers, let us not be craven. Recollect the days of Cromwell, and the times when the godless Cavaliers felt the edge of the Roundheads' sword, and though we take not carnal weapons, but eschew them utterly, let us show our foemen that the manhood of England is in us still, and we are of the same mettle as our sires.

III. Let us turn to the third point, with which we conclude, *the secret support of Daniel.*

There was something in the man which gave him this backbone; there was a secret something which made him so magnanimous. What was it? It resulted from several things. It sprang from the fact that *Daniel's religion was not the offspring of passion, but of deep-seated principle.*

There are some men whose religion is like the flower which lives upon the surface—they soon dry up when the sun of persecution burns; but there are others who, like the forest trees, send down their roots into the deep soil of principle, who know what they know, have learned thoroughly what they have learned, and hold fast what they have received, and these, in the time of trial, are sustained by springs of secret grace, and their leaf is not withered. Because the Holy Ghost had worked into Daniel's' spirit the principles of faith, he was sustained in the time of trial; but I doubt not that Daniel was also supported *by what he had read of the works of God* in the olden times. He was a great searcher of books, and he had found that in olden times Jehovah was always victorious. The prophet's eye gleamed as he thought of Pharaoh and the Red Sea, as he remembered Og, king of Basham, and the brooks of Arnon, and as his mind flew on to Sennacherib and the hook put into leviathan's jaws to turn him back by the way which he came. Recollecting the works of the Lord, for which his spirit made diligent search, he felt quite certain that the living God would prove himself true to his own.

Besides, the prophet's spirit was sustained *by what he had himself seen.* He had been brought in close contact with the three holy children who were brought before Nebuchadnezzar. Where Daniel was at that time we do not precisely know, but he must have been well aware of that heroic deed. He had seen King Nebuchadnezzar defied, had beheld the Son of God walking in the furnace with the three heroes, and had seen them come forth with not so much as the smell of fire passed upon them: here was grand encouragement. Besides, *Daniel had personal* experience of his God. He stood before Nebuchadnezzar to tell him the dream, and the interpretation thereof; yes, on a yet more dread occasion, without fear and trembling, he had faced the king Belshazzar, when the thousands of his guests were shouting to their gods, and the king and his wives and concubines in gorgeous state were drinking wine out of the bowls consecrated to Jehovah. That lone man stood erect amid the ribald crew, and pointing to the mysterious letters, read the terrible sentence, "Mene, Mene, Tekel, Upharsin," a monarch's doom proclaimed in his presence by a man unarmed! Was such a one likely now to be afraid! He that trembled not before tens of thousands of fierce soldiery, shall he fear now, when nothing but lions are in his way? Not he. He had looked into the face of his God, and would not fear the face of a lion; Jehovah had overshadowed him, and the den into which he would be cast had nothing in it terrible to him. His own experience helped to strengthen him. He had this conviction, that God could deliver him, and that if God did not deliver him, yet still such was *his love to the God of Israel* that he would be content to give himself to die.

It is blessed to have such a confidence as this. You good people who are tried, and who may expect to be tried yet more, you will never stand unless you come to this: "God can deliver me; but if he does not deliver me, still I am well content to be a sacrifice for Jesus' sake." Ah! some of you would fain be Christians, but in the time of trial you give it up; like the freshwater sailor, who, seeing the ship decked with all her colors, and her fair white sails bellying to the wind, thinks it must be a fine thing to be a mariner, but he is not far out to sea before qualms have come upon him; he dreads the storm, and vows, "*If* I can but once get safe to shore, I had done with sailoring forever." Many have said, "We will follow the Lord with Daniel." Yes, and well content they are to be with Daniel at Shushan, in the king's palace, but when it comes to the lions' den, then, "Daniel, good-bye." Take heed to yourselves that you be not deceived with a fair profession which shall afterward fail you. Daniel failed not, because his love to his God rested deep in his inmost heart: it had become part and parcel of himself, and sustained by the two hands of love and faith, he was graciously upborne over the rough and thorny places.

Remember that Daniel is a type of our Lord Jesus Christ. Jesus had enemies who sought to destroy him; they could find nothing against him except "touching his God." They accused him of blasphemy, and then afterward, as they did Daniel, they brought a charge of sedition. He was cast into the den, into the grave: his soul was among the lions. They sealed his tomb with their signet, lest any should steal him by night, but he arose as Daniel did, alive and unhurt, and his enemies were destroyed. Now if Daniel is a type of Christ, and the Lord Jesus is the great representative Man for all who are in him, you, believer, must expect that there will be those who will attack you, who will assail you especially in your religion. You must expect, too, that they will prevail against you for a time, so that you may be cast into the den, that they will seek to fasten you in as though you were destroyed forever; but there will be a resurrection not only of bodies but of reputations, and you shall arise. When the trumpet shall sound, not merely the corporeal particles, which make the man, but the man's memory shall rise; his good name, which has been buried beneath the clods of slander, shall rise to life, while as to his enemies, they and their reputations shall find devouring destruction from the presence of the Lord. Oh, to be a follower of Jesus, the great Daniel! To tread in his footsteps wherever he goes! To be much with him, whether in private or public! This is a thing to be desired, and though I exhort you to it, I do not expect you to attain to it in your own strength, but I point you to the Holy Ghost, who can work this in you, and make you to be greatly beloved as was this prophet of old.

Index to Key Scriptures